LET
FURY
Have the
HOUR

For AnnaRosa Amodei D'Ambrosio.
A hero everyday.

LET FURY Have the HOUR

THE PUNK ROCK POLITICS OF JOE STRUMMER

edited with an introduction by
ANTONINO D'AMBROSIO

Nation Books / New York

LET FURY HAVE THE HOUR
THE PUNK ROCK POLITICS OF JOE STRUMMER

Published by
Nation Books
An Imprint of Avalon Publishing Group Inc.
245 West 17th St., 11th Floor
New York, NY 10011

AVALON
publishing group incorporated

Library of Congress Cataloging-in-Publication Data is available.

ISBN 10: 1-56025-625-7
ISBN 13: 978-1-56025-625-0

9 8 7 6 5 4

Book design by Paul Paddock
Printed in the United States of America
Distributed by Publishers Group West

There are those that struggle one day and they are good. There are others who struggle a year and they are better. There are some that struggle many years and they are very good. But there are others that struggle their whole lives and these are the heroic ones.

—Bertolt Brecht

CONTENTS

The REBEL WAY

The WORLD Is Worth FIGHTING FOR

his book owes much to many people. It was a process that was at once an affirmation and a discovery as any worthwhile project must be. The scores of people I corresponded and met with offered unconditional guidance and participation in support of Joe Strummer's legacy as a gifted musician and indefatigable political activist. All believed as strongly as I did in the message of the book, giving me the energy and the necessary enthusiasm to see it to completion.

Parts of this book first appeared in *Monthly Review*. I am very grateful to the respective editors and their colleagues. I am enormously indebted to Claude Misukiewicz, an associate editor at *Monthly Review*, but more importantly a trusted and loyal friend who believed in the original idea and took great care to see that it was published. The original essay, "Let Fury Have the Hour: The Passionate Punk Rock Politics of Joe Strummer" became one of the most widely-read in *Monthly Review*'s fifty-five year history. Claude made this possible and continued to offer a much-needed dose of encouragement as I went through the often pressure-filled process of expanding the essay into a book.

I would like to take this opportunity to thank all the contributors. Each, in their own way, made this book come alive. Joel Schalit provided a spark early on with his openness and excitement. Charlie Bertsch offered continual support for my work and as a result a new friendship was born. Sylvie Simmons, Ann Scanlon, Greil Marcus, Kristine McKenna, Peter Silverton, and Mikal Gilmore quickly agreed to be part of this book, for which I am deeply appreciative, as I am honored to place my writing along side their wonderful essays. Deepest gratitude to John Morthland and Theron Raines for their assistance in acquiring Lester Bangs' Clash writings for this book. Dennis Broe, who over time has become a reassuring colleague, has once again stepped forward with a moving essay that cuts to the heart of cultural resistance. It was a pleasure to work with incomparable writers including Amy Phillips, Carter Van Pelt, Luciano D'Orazio, and Dan Grunebaum.

Billy Bragg deserves special notice as he carries Strummer's banner of creative-activism. He was the very first to agree to be included in this book and I am forever grateful. And the next generation of creative-activists is represented as well and I am proud to call them friends and collaborators. Not4Prophet and Anthony Roman are gifted musicians who continue the struggle for justice with their recordings and performances. Their contributions in this book are fresh and capture Strummer's spirit.

I would be remiss if I did not mention those that provided me early on with a framework for which to challenge my thinking and societal injustice. Dr. Geffrey B. Kelly of La Salle University, who first opened my eyes to the plight of oppressed people both here and abroad. Dr. Gerard Fergerson, who became a mentor while I was a graduate student at New York University. He instilled in the me the significance of taking the power back with words and the importance of having one's voice heard over the din by reclaiming that what is the right of the people: freedom of speech and the responsibility to resist. The late Neil Postman and Noam Chomsky are two others that have at times made themselves available to me in ways that allowed me to grow when it seemed that I had encountered a wall that I could not climb.

Two people who have passed on to, I hope, a more democratic place, must be acknowledged for their contribution to this book. The first is, of course, Joe Strummer. If it were not for his music my life would have veered, I hate to think, into a decidedly different path. The second is my late father, Lorenzo D'Ambrosio. Both with his life and death he gave me the courage to continue on in the face of what often times seems insurmountable odds. The words found in this book are but a small testament to man who lived his life with dignity. To be the son of this man is perhaps my greatest achievement.

Perhaps the greatest indication of the importance of this work was my interaction with Joe Strummer's contemporaries. I found them everywhere—music, film, theater, schools, the shop floor— the list is long and diverse. I simply mentioned Strummer and this project and their eyes lit up with the conspiratorial knowledge that we shared a bond that brought us together. Strummer's music and message was that link. Chuck D, Tim Robbins, Michael Franti, Alex Cox, Dick Rude, Jim Jarmusch, Tony Kushner, and what seemed like hundreds of others were those that opened their hearts to me, infusing this book with the humanity and creativity that makes it breathe.

Special thanks to Matthew Pascarella, who worked vigorously in helping research and complete this book. His commitment suggests a future that is full of promise as he is already a talented writer and socially aware individual. It was invaluable. I would like to thank Carl Bromley, editorial director of Nation Books, for his continued support for my work with La Lutta NMC and as a writer. He continues to be a long-standing ally and friend. Sincerest love and respect to Ben Scanlon, a brilliant artist and wonderful friend. He provided artistic consultation throughout the production of this book and while his covers and layout do not appear here, they are certain to grace future books.

Thanks to Bob Gruen for use of his photos and Bill May and Virginia Lohle for helping me to find those Strummer images that most spoke to me. Thanks to Tami Peterson of www.strummer news.com, Graham Jones of www.blackmarketclash.com, and Paule Woolfe of Strummerville: The Joe Strummer Foundation for New Music (www.strummerville.com). They were a critical resource in the early stages of this book's life. Additional thanks to Ruth Baldwin, Stanislao Pugliese, Tom Robinson, Simon Frith, Mick Jones, Paul Simonon, Mikey Dread, Steven Barclay, Rachel Denigz, Peter and Mushi Jenner, Mark Perry, John Holstrom, Jay Babcock, Don Letts, Jason Kucsma, and the folks of *Clamor* magazine, Hilly Kristal of CBGBs, Claire White, Guerilla Management, Paolo Hewitt, the folks at *The Nation, The Progressive,* and all the zines, indy media outlets, music sheets, filmmakers, musicians, and countless others I tapped along the way for information on Joe Strummer.

I have had the immense fortune, over many years, of forging relationships that continue to inspire and challenge me to produce the best work possible. The list is long and I apologize if some names do not appear but know that you are ever present and I am ever thankful. Next, I would like to thank Kevin Ryan, we have worked for many years together to realize some important political and cultural changes and his counsel always remains vital. I would like to thank Rasmia Kirmani for her early thoughtful feedback as I furiously wrote to complete the book in a short time frame. To AnnaRosa D'Ambrosio who refuses to yield and never will.

I offer heartfelt thanks to the following people who showed unwavering support and encouragement: Amy Chozick, Franco D'Ambrosio, Maria Disandro, Nicola DiSandro, Kevin O'Rangers, Larry Bogad, Mark Nowak, Luke Scanlon, Pasquale D'Ambrosio, Giovanni D'Ambrosio, Anthony Campana, Danielle Disandro, Nina Siegal, Emile Stewart, Mary, Rick, and Sophia van Valkenburg, Ina

Howard, Matthew Nicolau, Junno Lee, People-Link, Karim Lopez, Andrew Gefell, Chris Perez, Piccolo Coli in Philadelphia, RICANSTRUCTION, the 512 Collective, and the entire La Lutta NMC group, board, and partners. I am humbled and privileged to know you all.

—Antonino D'Ambrosio, New York City

STRANGE BEDFELLOWS—HOW THE CLASH INSPIRED PUBLIC ENEMY

By Chuck D

Originally Published in Interview *magazine, December/January 2004*

The first time I heard the Clash was in 1981. I was in college at Adelphi University on Long Island, and one night I went down to this show in Manhattan—one of Kurtis Blow's hip-hop package shows. The crowd was rough. People from different camps were there—the hip-hop people and the punk rock people. They even started throwing tomatoes at Kurtis, so that's the type of wild kids who were there. But the Clash completely broke it that night. It was an awakening for a New York cat like myself.

As I delved more into the music scene, I started learning about how the kids across the water in England were rebelling against the Queen and the aristocracy. Around the same time, Bill Stepheny, a friend of mine from Adelphi and one of the original members of Public Enemy, started playing the Clash's records on his hip-hop radio show, which opened up a lot of people's minds. He would reach into the Clash's catalogue, as well as the Sex Pistols', and make those kinds of songs work in the context of a hip-hop show. He was instrumental in exposing a lot of hip-hop cats to what the Clash were doing. I had great respect for Joe Strummer. How he used his music—incorporating a lot of black music like hip-hop and reggae—was very different from the guys who invented rock 'n' roll: He always paid homage to those who came before him. I admired him for his humility as an artist and for the fact that he dug musical cats, no matter what type of music they played. He was constantly pushing the boundaries of the Clash's sound and of what music could do on a greater level. And Joe was still rebellious: he was speaking about things he saw in his life—the things right in front of his face that no one wanted to talk about—and taking his message around the world.

Public Enemy is an American group but we address the same issues—political, social, musical—on an international level: we take our conversation worldwide. I learned the importance of that from Joe Strummer. Right now there's a hunger out there for a musician like that. As a musician, it's not an easy way to go, but there are people who are doing it in hip-hop right now—politically outspoken groups like Dead Prez and the Coup, who are totally fearless and noncapitulating in their work. That's Joe Strummer's legacy—the idea that you need to stand by your word every step of the way.

INTRODUCTION:
THE FUTURE IS UNWRITTEN

By Antonino D'Ambrosio

I think people ought to know that we're antifascist, we're antiviolence, we're antiracist and we're pro-creative. We're against ignorance.

—Joe Strummer, 1976

We're all going to have to learn to live together and develop a greater tolerance and get rid of whatever our fathers gave us in the way of hatred between nations.

—Joe Strummer, 2000

n the day Joe Strummer died, December 22, 2002, United States forces began dropping leaflets and making radio broadcasts over Iraq urging Iraqis to rise up against Saddam Hussein. The Bush administration stated that the war to overthrow Saddam's regime would start with U.S. bombing followed by a popular Iraqi insurgent uprising that would gain control of the streets. President George W. Bush declared that this was going to be a battle between good and evil. It was a strange, jarring day. As the U.S. seemed poised to embark on the latest "war on terror," the Clash antiwar song "The Call Up" came to mind: "It's up to you not to heed the call-up/I don't wanna die!/It's up to you not to hear the call-up/I don't wanna kill!" As Strummer remarked when the song was first recorded, "The song is a statement against the build up to war and the potential it creates for bringing catastrophe." Nearly two years after Strummer's death, over one year into the "liberation of Iraq," and twenty years after Strummer wrote this song, these words certainly are prophetic.

Let Fury Have the Hour has been over twenty years in the making. It began for me in 1983 when, for the first time, I heard the Clash blaring at me from those huge 1970s-style speakers in my cousin's house on Lawndale Street in northeast Philadelphia. Of course, I had heard the Clash before then. It was impossible not to. They were the biggest band in the world at the time. They had a huge worldwide hit with "Rock the Casbah" and a video in heavy rotation on the fledgling video network, MTV. But we did not have MTV and even though I secretly loved "Rock the Casbah," it seemed to be a radio-friendly pop song. When I heard, really heard the Clash's music for the first time, it came by way of the song "Clampdown." I related to it as it seemed written for me. It became more than a song: "Clampdown" was my own personal anthem. The Clash promised rebellion. And I was certain that they could deliver it and liberate me from a sense of hopelessness and a life of "wearing blue and brown."

When punk first became a social and cultural phenomenon in 1976–77, I was five years old and too young to be part of the scene or understand the music that would become an important part of my life only a few years later. Even so, music was already a central part of my life. My parents, immigrants from Italy, possessed a deep love for music. My mother was drawn to rock 'n' roll—the Beatles and Elvis. She liked John not Paul; he was the one who always had something important to say. Lennon was her working-class hero and I would find mine in Joe Strummer. My father loved country music, especially Willie Nelson. Also not a bad choice as music rebels go. All the same, they always returned to the traditional music of their homeland spending hours listening to La Banda di Duronia and the beautifully melodic tarantellas of Molise.

Watching my mother dance and sing along to the music she loved taught me that melodies possess something more powerful than film or painting, or any other art form I had encountered up to that point. It grabs a hold of you in a place you never knew existed, shakes you to your core and shatters everything you hold as true. It is transcendent. Illuminating. Empowering. Emancipating. I'm not talking about bubblegum pop and sticky sweet love songs that are a safe standard of mainstream radio. What we all need to help us cope with a world that is anything but comfortable, is the kind of music that intoxicates you with crushing hooks that open the mind wide with lyrics that make you think. "Clampdown" did that for me. The Clash did that. Joe Strummer did that.

Strummer forged a pact with his audience, guaranteed for a lifetime. You could be part of something positive. Change can happen if you are willing to change yourself. I think I was fortunate to discover this music when I did. I looked at the Clash not as a band or as music of the moment, but as a harbinger of the future. I rejected the affected nihilism of the Sex Pistols, considered THE definitive punk band. They were about negating; the Clash was about producing positive action. Other groups were fun to listen to and some like the compelling Crass even had important things to say, but only the Clash made me believe.[1] Each song became an anthem delivering me from anguish, teaching me not to waste a moment of my life. The world is not ending. It is just beginning. This is a truth I learn every time I hear Strummer launch into "London's Burning" and begin that thrilling ride all over again.

Strummer gave me the strength to have faith that the people's movements that had scored some big democratic victories in the

1960s could happen again. The Lettrists. The Situationists. May '68. Grosvenor Square. Allende's Chile. The hot summer of Italy. It was happening again, you could hear it in his voice and in the music. Forget about waiting on the side of the road for someone to come along and pick you up. It was all about DIY. Do it yourself not for yourself but for each other. Bonded together in what matters, forsaking intolerance, embracing justice. And this is one of the unique gifts Strummer possessed: he made everyone feel like a member of the team, not a consumer of anything trivial. One way to do this is through music.

Politics and art do mix and if done right can change your life. Reggae. Skanking. Dub. Rap. R&B. Soul. Honky-Tonk. Samba. Cumbia. It didn't matter what the music was or where it came from—only that it brought you to your feet, made you listen with your heart, and opened up your mind. I applied this to my life and discovered the music of Steel Pulse, Lee "Scratch" Perry, Junior Murvin, Mikey Dread, the Skatalites, the Equals, Public Enemy, and countless more. Strummer opened my ears so I would be able to hear when the music called, promising me salvation and a better day.

Seeming fit and vibrant just a few weeks before he died, Strummer had performed a blistering set at a benefit show for the Acton Fire Brigade at Acton Town Hall where Mick Jones briefly joined him on stage.[2] His passing at the age of fifty on December 22, 2002, of a rare heart condition was sudden and shocking. He leaves behind an extraordinary career that will affect generations. Still, this does not lessen the sting of his loss for an important voice has been silenced, one that used his music as a platform to cut a path for something better, at least for a moment. He now sits in the pantheon of artists like Bob Marley, Kristy MacColl, Robert Johnson, Buddy Holly, and Victor Jara who left this world in their prime and before their time.

Yet, unlike these musicians, some believed that Strummer was past his prime with his best years behind him. Characteristic of Strummer's "rebel way" he fooled all who dismissed him. While everyone was waiting for the Clash to get back together, Strummer quietly attained a level of creativity and originality with his albums *Rock Art and the X-ray Style, Global A Go-Go,* and *Streetcore.* The newness of his music was a revelation. The growth and breadth of his worldview was inspirational and timely. The potential of the work to come, we are left to imagine, was boundless. As Strummer himself said, "The best moments of any career are those that are unexpected."

Strummer's moment, for many, had come and gone in the late 1970s after the release of *London Calling*[3] and the departure of Mick Jones from the band. Things would never be the same. Strummer, Jones, Simonon, and Headon had raised the bar and then were expected to go higher. Instead, they wanted to go deeper. As a member of the Clash, Strummer cut a cool, brash pop cultural figure with his guttural Cockney-accented voice, electric guitar leg, and upturned upper lip. The group, with Strummer out in front, personified rebellion rock and took Bobby Fuller Fours "I Fought the Law" and made it into an enduring protest anthem all their own.[4] Strummer embodied the soul of punk rock and the potential it possessed as both a social movement and political vehicle. It went beyond a pop cultural moment or reactionary pose and became a principle that guided his life until the end.

In the final decade of his life, Strummer dedicated himself to important political causes by opposing globalization, advocating climate control with his work for Future Forests, and spreading a message of unity by embracing multiculturalism.[5] Before there was even a category for world music in record stores, Strummer was infusing his music with global sounds. In the 1990s, he had a radio show on the BBC World Service called "Joe Strummer's

London Calling" and had filmed the pilot for a television show called *Global Boom Box* that focused on world music.[6]

For Strummer, music and politics went hand-in-hand and this book is a reflection of his ongoing influence upon them. The essay that opens the book, "Let Fury Have the Hour," was written for an audience that never heard of the Clash or punk rock. For this reason, I placed it as an introductory piece to frame the book. The essays that follow in the first section capture the exciting moments of a major musician at the start of his career.

The second section—The Rebel Way—explores the period in which Strummer described himself as going from "hero to zero" following his departure from the Clash. During this period he acted in films from Alex Cox's *Straight to Hell* to Jim Jarmusch's *Mystery Train,* and composed soundtracks, most notably for Cox's *Walker.* As Charlie Bertsch writes, "Even at his most combative, he was more interested in building up a community of rebels than in tearing down those who failed to make the grade."

In the third section—You Can't Have a Revolution Without Songs—I place Strummer in the canon of great political folk musicians and discuss his recent work in relation to the astounding music of Caetano Veloso, Silvio Rodriguez, Victor Jara, and Mercedes Sosa. Strummer always referred to himself as a folk musician at heart. He mentioned that he loved Woody Guthrie's "Buffalo Skinner," a song where the workingman gets the better of his corrupt employer. Strummer had more than a bit of the "Buffalo Skinner" in him and after years of battling Epic Records, he was free to make the music he wanted, how he wanted.

As Michael Franti of Spearhead tells me in the first essay in the fourth section—The World Is Worth Fighting For—"The underlying message that you get from Strummer's music is the world can be a terrible, scary place but it is worth fighting for." Strummer continued the fight even when his music was no longer played on the radio. This section gives Strummer's contemporaries —Tim Robbins, Chuck D, Anthony Roman, Not4Prophet—an opportunity to discuss the indelible mark he left on their lives as artists, activists, and human beings.

A final note on the contributors and contributions that make this book come alive. When approached to put this book together, I decided to include a mix of essays from the past (Lester Bangs, Greil Marcus, Sylvie Simmons, Pete Silverton) as well as new pieces (Amy Phillips, Dennis Broe, Charlie Bertsch). Even more, it was important to speak with a wide range of musicians, directors, actors, writers, and everyone in between whom Strummer influenced spiritually, creatively, and politically. In some cases, these individuals contributed their own work to the book. Such as Billy Bragg, who continues to be an important musical and political voice, and was the very first to contribute with "The Joe I Knew," a passionate eulogy.

Perhaps the greatest testament to Strummer was the generosity and support of everyone I spoke with. Many, including Kristine McKenna, Billy Bragg, and Carter Van Pelt donated their work in tribute to Strummer to be part of this important project. Michael Franti and Chuck D took time out of their hectic touring schedules to speak with me. Then there are those who could not contribute material to the book but offered wonderful support like Pulitzer Prize–winning playwright Tony Kushner who told me he "loved, loved, loved Joe Strummer" as his work served as a model for him throughout his life and continues to do so.

Let Fury Have the Hour is not only a testament to a profound creative-activist but also serves as a historical record to motivate, encourage, and inspire others to take the difficult yet rewarding path of thinking for others instead of merely for themselves. Strummer was always most interested in getting his new music out to as many people as possible who would truly listen. A tougher task than one would think for someone like Strummer. He remained undaunted in light of the fact that his new music was not selling well and that sometimes people even said, "Joe who? You used to be in what band?"

The excitement he displayed at sharing his new music or his love of new artists like Manu Chao was as infectious as when he first plugged in his old Telecaster guitar and cranked out "London's Burning," that wondrous blur of a night long ago in 1976. By the end of his life, Strummer was making music for "people who are beyond the parameters of the demographic fascists who decides what sells and what gets advertised and what gets on play lists."[7]

Finally, this book was written during a period I consider one of the darkest and most distressing in our history. In the months that led up to the book, the American occupying force in Iraq massacred civilians in Fallajuah and were exposed for participating in torture and sexual abuse, at the Abu Ghraib detention facility. America's credibility abroad has been badly damaged, while domestically unemployment has skyrocketed alongside tax cuts for the wealthy. Money that should be going into health care, public education, and the environment is being siphoned off to further fund the military. As Strummer asked over a quarter of a century ago, "Are you going backwards?/Or are you going forward?"

As I wrote the essays and edited the work for *Let Fury Have the Hour*, the process became a wholly invigorating and necessary one. It became a labor of hope sustained by the belief that I was putting something out to the world that could, in some way, "move us forward." One of the last things Strummer told me in our April 2002 meeting in Brooklyn was that the goal all along was to keep things hopeful and remain optimistic. "We must be positive and know that truth is on our side," he said. "Music can turn people on to the beauty of a life still to be lived . . . we choose to not take anymore and not be miserable." He leaves this world achieving much more than he realized, a person who changed countless lives by becoming the unofficial leader of a people's movement. Echoing a favorite statement of his, the future is indeed unwritten how we write it and what we do offers us all a grand hope and a compelling opportunity.

—Antonino D'Ambrosio,
New York City, May 2004

LET Fury HAVE the Hour

THE PUNK ROCK POLITICS OF JOE STRUMMER

By Antonino D'Ambrosio

Originally appeared in Monthly Review, *June 2003*

J oe Strummer, the pioneering punk rock musician, former front man of the Clash, and political activist, died of a rare heart condition at his home in Broomfield, Somerset, England at the age of fifty on Sunday, December 22, 2002. Barely a quarter of a century after the Clash burst loudly onto the London music scene, they became one of the greatest rebel rock bands of all time, fusing a mélange of musical styles with riotous live performances and left-wing political activism that continues to inspire many to this day.

In the mid-1970s, England's postwar prosperity began quickly melting away into rising unemployment, shrinking social service programs, and increasing poverty. The wracked economy helped spark an incendiary social situation where racism, xenophobia, and police brutality became the order of the day.

Trying to make sense of this mess were England's young people whose mounting anger, frustration, and a sense of isolation left them feeling hopeless. Along came punk rock. More than just hard-driving rock 'n' roll, punk rock was heralded by many as a counterculture movement, a philosophy, and a way of life. It stood in direct opposition to the reigning rock establishment dominated by a sound and style called "glam" and it attacked conventional society. Glam was pretentious, over-produced, slick, and bourgeois—and so was modern society.

Punk rock, on the other hand, was angry, loud, aggressive, and rooted in working/lower-class alienation. With its four chords, simple catchy melodies, fast tempo, and ironic and witty lyrics, it was irresistible. Unfortunately, many punk rock bands distorted and twisted politics into simplistic empty slogans, and disappointingly, much of the music devolved into neofascism.

Spurred to action by groups like Detroit's MC5, a cultural organ of the White Panthers, Strummer told me, "We wanted to be more like them, using our music as a loud voice of protest . . . punk rock, at the heart of it, should be protest music." While most bands spiraled downward into ridiculous caricatures of themselves, the Clash, under Strummer's influence, became the definitive punk rock band. They drew a line in the sand and dared all to cross it and join them. While the Sex Pistols spent their time being all tawdry and snide, the Clash were thoughtful and serious.

Throughout his twenty-five years in music, Strummer touched millions. Billy Bragg, a fellow English musician and activist inspired by Strummer's socially conscious music, said it best by describing Strummer as unwavering in "his commitment to making political pop culture." Living true to his words, Strummer held onto his political ideals throughout his life in spite of intense media rancor and the highly demanding expectations of fans as they clung to every song as if it were scripture. The pressure would have crushed a lesser person.

Like many people growing up during the Reagan era, discovering the Clash transformed my worldview. It was nothing like I had ever heard before or since. The music's energy, spirit, and searing lyrics gave voice to feelings of alienation and hopelessness, as well as anger and defiance that I had not yet articulated.

Through his songwriting Strummer consistently critiqued capitalism, advocated racial justice, and opposed imperialism, just to name a few topics. He showed young people there are alternatives to the complacency, opportunism, and political ambivalence that dominate music. Strummer's musical output remains an enduring legacy of radicalism, defiance, and resistance.

CREATIVE RESISTANCE

In April 2002, I had the good fortune to speak with him several times discussing a wide range of issues. One thing was clear as I spoke with Strummer: the importance of using the past to better understand the present and to shape the future was fundamental to his creative activism. May '68 in Paris, the student and labor movements of Italy, and the election of Allende in Chile are just some of the key events that deeply politicized Strummer. Punk rock and Strummer in particular would borrow heavily from these movements—not just ideologically but aesthetically as well. "Punk rock for me was a social movement," he stated. "We tried to do the things politically we thought were important to our generation and hopefully would inspire another generation to go even further."

As a musician Strummer had redefined music and reaffirmed the principals of committed and intelligent opposition. He seemed to be involved in so many different movements and supported so many causes long before they were fashionable. They were at the forefront of the Rock against Racism movement (RAR) founded in the seventies to combat the rise of the National Front. Never afraid of controversy, Strummer pushed the Clash to publicly support causes like the H-Block protests in Northern Ireland, which started in 1976 when the British took away the political status of IRA "prisoners."

In an ironic twist, on November 15, 2002 he would perform (with Mick Jones) for the last time ever at a benefit for striking fireman in London. For someone who used his music to galvanize and urge progressive action, this final performance is most fitting.

Strummer's unique partnership with Mick Jones brought a revolutionary sense of excitement to modern music. Strummer and Jones quickly recognized the power of rap music that was just emerging from New York City's underground in the late seventies. "When we came to the U.S., Mick stumbled upon a music shop in Brooklyn that carried the music of Grandmaster Flash and the Furious Five, the Sugar Hill Gang . . . these groups were radically changing music and they changed everything for us."

In classic Clash inventiveness, they became one of the first white groups to experiment with and incorporate rap into their music. As a tribute to the Sugar Hill Gang, they recorded "The Magnificent Seven," one of their best known and most important singles. In another example that marked the Clash's commitment to challenging the status quo, they enlisted various New York City rap groups as support acts on their huge Clash on Broadway tour. At the time this was extremely controversial since it was thought that the two disparate groups from different backgrounds and genres would cause racial mayhem and chaos performing together.

Reflecting on the group's influence, I suggested to Strummer that hip-hop has replaced punk rock as the dominant political pop cultural force in spirit, vitality, and creativity. "No doubt about it, particularly in respect to addressing the ills of capitalism and providing a smart class analysis . . . underground hip-hop, not the pop-culture stuff, picked up where punk left off and ran full steam ahead."

Strummer's originality is a trait characterizing both the man and the musician. With his most recent and final music project, the Mescaleros, Strummer was reborn. Remarkably, his new music displays a steadfast work ethic both creatively and politically. Irrespective of what he had accomplished up to this point in his career, I had a sense that he was restless and that his best work would lie ahead.

THE GREATEST REBEL ROCK BAND OF ALL-TIME

On New Year's Eve 1976, the Clash played a show in support of headliner's the Sex Pistols. Impressed, the Sex Pistols asked the Clash to join them on the infamous 1977 Anarchy in the UK tour, which due to the wild and foolish antics by the bands, intense media scrutiny, and police harassment, identified punk rock as public enemy number one. While parents, police, and politicians sounded the alarm, young people were hooked.

Strummer, a former street musician and squatter, characterized the early days as filled with hope and frustration. "Many in the punk scene were confused, mixing various political ideologies." The effect was that punk rock musicians were easy targets for ridicule and attack by the monarchy, media, Parliament, and the police. According to Strummer, the objective was to present a clearer, unified stance with a more thoughtful and relevant political message. It was also obvious to Strummer early on that punk rock was vulnerable to co-optation by the music industry with great assistance from opportunistic musicians so in typical Strummer fashion he condemned them for this in the song "White Man in Hammersmith Palais":

Punk rockers in the UK
They won't notice anyway
They're all too busy fighting
For a good place under the lighting

The new groups are not concerned
With what there is to be learned
They got Burton suits, ha you think it's funny
Turning rebellion into money

All over people changing their votes
Along with their overcoats
If Adolf Hitler flew in today
They'd send a limousine anyway

As a result, blame must be shared by many of the bands of the time for allowing punk rock to degenerate into a "shameful product hawked by the record companies" and "used to promote right-wing ideals." In no way did Strummer want to be part of the creative and social diluting of the punk rock philosophy. The Clash's self-titled first studio album clearly marked where they stood on things.

The album addressed social issues including classism, racism, and police and state-sanctioned brutality. By bringing together a broad range of musical influences, which had previously been segregated by the music industries' marketing strategies, it significantly changed modern music. There were brilliant covers of old rock classics, infusions of R&B, fractured pop, well-balanced mix of ska, dub, and reggae, and of course, what became the signature sound of the Clash: thought-provoking lyrics sung in Strummer's unique Cockney, a blistering and angry style layered over aggressive compositions.

The Clash's music coupled with its explosive live performances let people know that they were not only a creative bunch but that they also had something important to say on the state of things. The record companies took note. Although produced for next to nothing, the Clash's first album became the largest selling American import in music history. America loved the Clash's music and its message.

"The same issues we were struggling against then are even more important now like British and U.S. imperialism," Strummer continued. "When we wrote 'I'm So Bored With the U.S.A.,' it touched a nerve for young people on both sides of the Atlantic." The lyrics are sharp and compelling:

> *Yankee dollar talk*
> *To the dictators of the world*
> *In fact it's giving orders*
> *An' they can't afford to miss a word*

Other songs addressed the growing disaffection young people felt as they faced the harsh realities of the job market in 1976. "Career Opportunities" became a classic protest song for many:

> *They offered me the office, offered me the shop*
> *They said I'd better take anything they'd got*
> *Do you wanna make tea at the BBC?*
> *Do you wanna be, do you really wanna be a cop?*

Career opportunities are the ones that never knock
Every job they offer you is to keep you out the dock
Career opportunity, the ones that never knock

"Industrial society offered nothing really, and as we moved to this more fragmented society with more emphasis on technology, the state was looking for us to work according to our class . . . it all seemed about controlling class, particularly the lower classes."

CLASHING WITH AMERICA

In 1979, the Clash headed to America. In between this tour and their first album, the Clash had conquered the UK and Europe. They released another album *Give 'Em Enough Rope* and were in the process of putting together the Clash's "masterpiece," *London Calling.* "Two devastating things happened at this time," Strummer recalled. "Margaret Thatcher became prime minister of England and Ronald Reagan became president of the U.S. . . . it was hard to tell who would be worse but we knew that a tremendous struggle was ahead . . . their tendencies leaned to the far right if not fascism."

The Clash always drew inspiration from, and paid homage to, other rebel musicians, especially black musicians from the U.S. and the Caribbean. Still, it was when they collaborated with these musicians they ran head-on into the racism of the music industry, and some of their fans. While touring the U.S. the Clash had selected the pioneering American rock 'n' roll artist Bo Diddley as their opening act. Diddley was a hero to Strummer. The Clash was excited that the tour would help them connect with its American audience but they were frightened by the intense racism the tour encountered in the South because of Diddley's presence. "The record label was unsupportive from the word go because *Give 'Em* did not sell like our first album, they hated our choice of Bo Diddley and we refused to pick a different support act and resisted their attempt to repackage us as *new wave.*"

The lack of record support was just the start. The bad press that greeted the Clash here in the U.S. because "they were evil punk rockers" looking to "spread communism to American youth" as many headlines declared, was disappointing to Strummer.

The short eight-date tour further politicized Strummer. It opened his eyes to the "commodification of music" and "exposed the terrible resistance and hatred of anything that attempts to grow outside the dominant economic and social structure." On the other hand, there were a few shows like the legendary performance at New York's Palladium that taught Strummer many important lessons. "We must use negative situations," Strummer said, "to refocus and redirect anger and frustration, and fashion music that is powerful to all who listen, always upsetting the status quo."

LONDON CALLS AND SO DO THE SANDINISTAS

Upon the completion of their American tour, the Clash began their next album, *London Calling*. It showed maturity and growth in many areas. Musically it incorporated roots music, folk, New Orleans R& B, reggae, pop, lounge jazz, ska, hard rock, and punk. Recorded in Wessex Studio, London, the landmark album still is influential. I discussed this with Strummer and related my own experience of hearing the album for the first time. The themes, music, and attitude sharply mirrored my own reality as a kid in an immigrant family growing up in an industrial park in the mid-1980s.

One song in particular, "Clampdown," affected me deeply. The song is a pointed and stark account of work in a Darwinian capitalist society. At its core, the song presents the contradictions that force us to believe that if only we work hard, don't complain, and don't rock the boat, we can get ahead. Step on whomever you wish, it doesn't matter, just look out for number one.

The song expressed the anxieties of working-class youth who were wanted only for menial jobs, to be part of the state's repressive apparatus, or to join racist right-wing movements:

> *You grow up and you calm down*
> *You're working for the clampdown*
> *You start wearing the blue and brown*
> *You're working for the clampdown*
> *So you got someone to boss around*
> *It makes you feel big now*
> *You drift until you brutalize*
> *You made your first kill now*

The same song also expresses an alternative and a common Strummer theme of the need for working-class rebellion:

> *The judge said five to ten—but I say double that again*
> *I'm not working for the clampdown*
> *No man born with a living soul*
> *Can be working for the clampdown*
> *Kick over the wall 'cause government's to fall*
> *How can you refuse it?*
> *Let fury have the hour, anger can be power*
> *D'you know that you can use it?*

"Yeah," Strummer began, "this song and our overall message was to wake up, pay attention to what really is going on around you, politically, socially all of it . . . before you know it you have become what you despise." The album catapulted the Clash into the international spotlight. They played and the world listened.

Being the biggest rock band on the planet at the time brought increased attention and the inevitable harsh criticism, particularly in regards to Strummer's and the group's political stances.

The red-baiting and right-wing attacks increased tenfold when the Clash publicly supported the Sandinista Revolution.

"Our support of the Sandinistas was the worst thing in the world we could do according to our record label," Strummer recalled. "The label heads said our music would not sell—too political—especially in America where the Reagan administration was conspiring to destroy the Sandinistas." Strummer wrote "Washington Bullets" criticizing the U.S.'s involvement in Central and South America, while noting Jimmy Carter's brief withdrawal of aid to the Somoza regime:

> As every cell in Chile will tell
> The cries of the tortured men
> Remember Allende, and the days before,
> Before the army came
> Please remember Victor Jara,
> In the Santiago Stadium,
> Es verdad—those Washington Bullets again
>
> For the very first time ever,
> When they had a revolution in Nicaragua,
> There was no interference from America
> Human rights in America
>
> Well the people fought the leader,
> And up he flew . . .
> With no Washington bullets what else could he do?

In 1980 the Clash released their triple album *Sandinista!*, which added gospel, dub, and rap to their growing list of musical influences. The long simmering disputes with their label CBS soon became a pitched battle when the band demanded the album be priced affordably, which meant selling it for the cost of one album. CBS finally relented but only after the Clash agreed to cover the difference out of their pockets. "Political decisions never balance out well with business unless of course they're capitalist-based political decisions . . . if we did an album in support of the Contras it would have been different," Strummer joked.

A BIG HIT AND THEN A CRASH

The sales of the last Clash album notwithstanding, their following was bigger than ever. *Combat Rock,* released in 1982, again highlighted the social consciousness and leftist politics that forever distinguish the band and Strummer. With the release of "Rock the Casbah," the Clash had a huge hit on their hands. In a bizarre twist, imperialists have appropriated the song, which is a cry for speech and expression. "You know the U.S. military played this song in the first Gulf War to the troops and now are using it again as they prepare for war," Strummer shared. "This is just typical and despicable."

The king called up his jet fighters
He said you better earn your pay
Drop your bombs between the minarets
Down the Casbah way

As soon as the shareef was
Chauffeured outta there
The jet pilots tuned to
The cockpit radio blare

As soon as the shareef was
Outta their hair
The jet pilots wailed

CHORUS
The shareef don't like it
Rockin' the Casbah
Rock the Casbah
The shareef don't like it
Rockin' the Casbah
Rock the Casbah

At Shea Stadium in Queens, New York, in 1982, the Clash played a series of sold-out shows opening up for the Who. The group's manager and Strummer would eventually force Mick Jones out of the band. Strummer confided, "although Mick was impossible to be around or work with it was still one of the most difficult things I ever had to do. After releasing a disappointing album in 1985—*Cut the Crap*—featuring a new lineup, the Clash broke up for good.

"I'M GONNA KEEP FIGHTIN' FOR WHAT I BELIEVE IS RIGHT"

Strummer and the Mescaleros recorded two highly innovative studio albums, 1999's *Rock Art and the X-Ray Style* and 2001's *Global A Go-Go*. The music Strummer recorded with the Mescaleros is as diverse a sound as I've heard. There are the familiar influences of rockabilly, traditional rock 'n' roll and R&B, but added to the mix are new sounds. Strummer brought together music from Africa, Latin America, and the West Indies as well as heavy doses of hip-hop style beats.

These albums showcase a renewed and vibrant Joe Strummer

producing music that is remarkably different from his previous work. I mentioned that I watched a taped interview in which he cautioned young people about buying his new music. I asked him to elaborate. "Simple," he said. "New bands are going around saying we love the Clash but they have no sense or understanding of history both culturally and politically." He added that they "pick up the new stuff and expect to hear songs like 'Rock the Casbah,' which is not at all what I am doing now and furthermore 'Casbah' is an easy song everyone knows from the Clash."

Like his work with the Clash, the music is original and political, but more insightful and mature. With the musical growth there is a deepening of political consciousness reflected in stunning compositions and poetic, freely associative lyrics concerning a host of global subjects. Both albums focus on many social issues but most poignantly *Global A Go-Go* captures Strummer's take on how war, poverty, and intolerance are ripping the world apart. Songs like "Johnny Appleseed" chart the impact of globalization, "Bhindi Bhagee" discusses need for ethnic tolerance, and "Shaktar Donetsk" highlights the struggles of refugees who suffocated in a truck en route to England. The music is intelligent Woody Guthrie (one of Strummer's earliest influences) like meditations but with a multinationalist slant that serves as a defense against global capitalism. In "Shaktar Donetsk" Strummer laments:

> *Welcome to Britain in the third Millenium*
> *This is the diary of Macedonian*
> *He went to Britain in the back of lorry*
> *"Don't worry, don't worry, don't hurry."*
> *Said the man with a plan*
> *He said, If you really wanna go—you'll get there in the end."*
> *If you really wanna go—alive or dead my friend*
> *Well, you can levitate you know—long as the money's good you're in*

Speaking on the day of Strummer's death, Bragg found the right words once again: "Joe was always breaking new ground musically and politically . . . he is one of the last artists who was not afraid to be on the left politically, a thorn in the side of capitalism."

Strummer left much unfinished. With Bono of U2 and Dave Stewart formerly of the Eurhythmics, Strummer was in the process of recording a song in tribute to Nelson Mandela entitled "46664," after Mandela's prison number. They were going to perform together at the end of the Mandela "SOS AIDS" benefit concert for Africa on Robben Island on February 2. The Clash had planned a one-night-only reunion at March 2003's Rock and Roll Hall of Fame induction ceremony.

At the end of each show, Strummer and the Mescaleros performed a cover of the classic resistance song "The Harder They Come, The Harder They Fall" by reggae great Jimmy Cliff. As with all he did, Strummer put his indelible mark and unique spin on the song. Playing the same Telecaster guitar he started out with over twenty-five years ago and using his cutting, brash voice with uncompromising bluster to, he let us know:

> *And I keep on fighting for the things I want,*
> *Though I know that when you're dead you gone*
> *But I'd rather be a free man in my grave*
> *Than living as a puppet or a slave . . .*

T he year punk broke in England has been immortalized as "year zero." Everything that came before 1976 never existed; punk was a promise for something completely new and more importantly, better. It was a movement away from bloated rock stars and overproduced music. Mixed along the hordes of youth who found themselves transfixed and transformed by the new punk scene was bank clerk Mark Perry. Perry found himself in the middle of "something big" and he wanted to be a part of it. His contribution would take the form of the first comprehensive punk zine. Yet *Sniffin' Glue and Other Rock 'N' Roll Habits* was more than just a fanzine. It was a magnificent music sheet that translated punk's DIY ethic, compelling visceral style, and strident social power into an accessible document for all to read. Perry named the zine after the Ramones' "Now I Wanna Sniff Some Glue" because, as he described in *Sniffin' Glue: The Essential Punk Accessory,* "I thought that if anything summed up the basic approach to the new music, it was the lowest form of drug taking."

The Rock On record stall in Chinatown's Newport Court was the first to sell *Sniffin' Glue*. The first issue, which appropriately featured the Ramones, sold very quickly. In that issue, Perry described the Ramones as giving him "power and freedom and that's what I want." Just as punk music was straightforward-all-systems-go, there was a hunger for the type of music journalism that told the reader directly what was happening in the new music scene that seemed poised to take over England. With a no glitz or glam approach, Perry did this and more by filling the gap between the music and the audience with witty, well-informed, and timely writings that served as a sharp contrast to the lackluster media attention, which was mostly negative or derisive, enveloping punk at the time. Even more, *Sniffin' Glue* served as a counterpoint to the slickly produced magazines that were still stuck reporting on the arena rock stars and glam bands that dominated the early part of the 1970s.

The articles went right from the typewriter to the Xerox machines. Titles were handwritten. No fancy graphic design and layout here. Simple drawings were sometimes interspersed and it wasn't until the third issue that pictures found their way into *Sniffin' Glue* when Brian James of the Damned graced the cover. Albeit never mentioned by name, the first time Strummer would find his music discussed on the pages of *Sniffin' Glue* was not as a member of the Clash but with his prior band, the 101ers. In the first issue, Perry reviewed the 101ers' single "Keys to Your Heart," describing it as "a really great song by a really great band." In issue 3 1/2, the Clash would make the first of a number of appearances in the magazine with Perry branding the group as the "most powerful band on scene," in his review of the 100 Club Punk Festival

It is no surprise then that *Sniffin' Glue* would provide the first good interview and glimpse into the world of the Clash, "The Very Angry Clash," written by Steve Walsh. Perry and Walsh had managed to arrange an interview with the Clash at their rehearsal studios near the Roundhouse in Chalk Farm (Camden, London). According to Perry, meeting the Clash was like going to "a secret training camp for urban guerrillas." Perry added that the time with the Clash "proved the band were totally committed to their music and they understood that the best way to avoid being misrepresented in the press was to put on a united front." He concluded by describing the Clash "as the most important band to emerge" up to that point and "if anyone was going to win the revolution I felt it was going to be the Clash."

As Strummer points out in the documentary *Westway to the World* (2000), *Sniffin' Glue* offered the first true punk rock criticism and analysis. The magazine would be instrumental in getting the music and message of punk out to many who otherwise may not have been exposed to the scene. Perry boldly achieved one of the promises of punk: if you do it yourself, you will find yourself. By finding his voice, *Sniffin' Glue* became a vital part of the punk rock moment. In all, Perry and all the contributors to the magazine covered the punk scene for just one year, producing twelve issues. Nearly three decades after banging out the first issue of *Sniffin' Glue,* it now serves as an important historical document of a music scene that quickly faded away.

THE VERY ANGRY CLASH

By Steve Walsh

Originally appeared in Sniffin' Glue and Other
Rock 'N' Roll Habits, *September 1976*

CLASH

All the power's in the hands,
Of people rich enough to buy it,
While we walk the streets
Too chicken to even try it.
And everybody does what they're told to,
And everybody eats supermarket soul-food,
White riot!

—"White Riot" by the Clash

T he Clash rehearsal studios are situated somewhere between Dingwalls and the Roundhouse. Inside it has been decorated—pink and black color scheme—by the band. The downstairs studio, where the band rehearses, is equipped with a jukebox, pink drapes hang from the ceiling—very tasteful. I talked to three of the band (Mick Jones—guitar, Paul Simonon—bass and Joe Strummer—guitar) in the upstairs office.

Mick tells me, he and Paul have been together for about six months and with Joe since the 101ers broke up. They told me boredom inspires their songs—"It's just that I can't stand not doing anything," Joe explained.

Steve Walsh: What's the name about, why call yourselves Clash?

Paul Simonon: Well, it's a clash against things that are going on . . . the music scene, and all that we're hoping to change quite a lot.

Steve Walsh: Does this mean you're political?

Mick Jones: Yes, we're definitely political!

Joe Strummer: We wanna be the apathy party of Great Britain, so that all the people who don't vote go out and don't vote for us!

Mick Jones: We're really into encouraging creativity. . . . We ain't a bunch of raving fascists!

Steve Walsh: Are you a bunch of raving anarchists?

Joe Strummer: I don't believe in all that anarchy bollocks!

Mick Jones: Yeah, anarchists believe in lawlessness. . . . Look, the important thing is to encourage people to do things for themselves, think for themselves and stand up for what their rights are.

Steve Walsh: You hate apathy?

Mick Jones: Oh, I fuckin' hate apathy but I hate ignorance more than anything.

Steve Walsh: Do you try to put this over in your songs?

Mick Jones: All our songs are about being honest, right? The situation as we see it, right?

Steve Walsh: Right! So the songs relate directly to you and your environment?

Mick Jones: Right, otherwise we'd be writing bullshit!

Steve Walsh: So, what do you want to happen today?

Joe Strummer: What I'm most aware of at the moment, is that most people in London are going out every night to see groups or something and they're making do with rubbish and because everything else around is rubbish, it's not immediately apparent that it's rubbish. People are prepared to accept rubbish, anything that's going. I mean, every single LP anybody plays me in any flat I go to and they say, "this is good" . . . it's rubbish and they have got nuthin' else to play . . . the thing is they've got to think it's good, otherwise they go insane. . . .

Mick Jones: . . . And it's all shit!

Steve Walsh: What's shit?

Mick Jones: All them records, right . . . you know, you can't go out and buy a record 'cause you know it's just, like, fuckin' bollocks . . . just a load of shit!

Joe Strummer: The only good one is that Ramones one.

Mick Jones: Yer, the Ramones record is good. (Doorbell rings—in strolls Mark P. to spoil my fun.)

HERITAGE

Joe Strummer: It's our heritage. . . . What are we livin' for, two-room apartment on the second floor. That's English, not what's goin' on now.

Mick Jones: They're the most important English band. Like Mott the Hoople's Ian Hunter always spoke to the kids straight and even when they went to the States and they were getting a bit flash and a bit dopey he still used to sing about the dole and he had to translate for the Americans and say, "Look, this is really the welfare." They don't know what the fuckin' dole is, where as we're all down the dole anyway, coppin' our money off Rod Stewart's taxes!

> *In 1977 I hope I go to heaven,*
> *'Cos I been too long on the dole,*
> *And I can't work at all.*
> *Danger, stranger! You better paint your face,*
> *No Elvis, Beatles or Rolling Stones, in 1977!*
> —"1977" by the Clash

Steve Walsh: What do you think is wrong with people today?

Mick Jones: They're apathetic . . . boring . . . boring music bores me! Boring 'cause it's not new, boring 'cause it's not . . .

Joe Strummer: It's a lie . . .

Mick Jones: . . . They ain't pushin' themselves nowhere, they ain't being creative.

Joe Strummer: Where's that picture of the George Hatcher Band?

Paul Simonon: Oh yeah, that's a real joke, that is . . .

Joe Strummer: We found this to be . . .

Mick Jones: Hilarious, have you seen it? (They hold up an advertisement for the George Hatcher Band showing two members in typical stage pose.)

Joe Strummer: I mean, the whole thing is a lie, it means nothing.

Mick Jones: Except that they're on tour with Dr. Feelgood.

Joe Strummer: All this crap like, oh yeah, they've got long hair and he's got his arm up here and look at his cowboy shirt and the trousers.

Steve Walsh: What have clothes got to do with it?

Mick Jones: Well, this is what rock 'n' roll's supposed to look like . . .

Joe Strummer: It's a state of mind.

Mick Jones: What's the difference between this ad and the cover of last week's *NME*, it's the same pose ain't it? I think that's the same pair of trousers, from "Jean Machine." (Mick was referring to the previous week's cover pic of the Rod's Dave Higgs.)

Mark P. But they're a pair of trousers!

Joe Strummer: No, you can't say that's clothes and this is music, it's a state of mind, a complete thing. If anything was going on in that bloke's head he would do something about it.

Mick Jones: To show he was a person, he would've done something to himself. Now, he's just showing that he's one of the many—a consumer, i.e., I eat shit all the time!

Steve Walsh: Everyone's a consumer, I mean, if you go down to "Sex" and buy a pair of leather trousers you're still a consumer. That's the odd thing about the '70s, in order to change society you must first consume it. (You can tell he's been to art school—Ed.)

Mick Jones: Yeah, but if it comes out of creativity. Some people change and some people stay as they are, bozos, and they don't try to change themselves in any way.

Joe Strummer: We deal in junk, you know, I just realized that the other day. We deal in junk. We deal in, like, the rubbish bin. What we've got is what other people have put in the rubbish bin. Like Mick's shirt was gonna be put in the bin until he paid 10p for it. I mean, you ain't gonna go down to "Sex" with yer ten quid stuffed in yer pocket and buy some stupid . . . er . . . I dunno, I've never even been down there.

Mick Jones: I think it's a bit easy to go down there and look great, I mean, their stuff's pretty good. Looks good to me, but I think the way we do it is much more accessible to kids 'cos anyone, at very little price and it encourages 'em to do something for themselves. It's to do with personal freedom . . . I don't think it's just the trousers though, I mean, the trousers reflect the mind.

Joe Strummer: Like trousers, like brain!

WHITE RIOT, I WANNA RIOT!
WHITE RIOT, A RIOT OF MY OWN!

Steve Walsh: Would you say your image is violent or suggestive of violence?

Mick Jones: It reflects our "no nonsense" attitude, an attitude of not takin' too much shit. I don't like violence though.

Steve Walsh: What do you think of the aura of violence that surrounds the Pistols, I mean, it can easily get out of hand.

Joe Strummer: I think it's a healthy sign that people aren't going to sleep in the back row.

Mick Jones: I think people have got to find out where their direction lies and channel their violence, into music or something creative.

Steve Walsh: Thing is, you talk about being creative but say the thing got so popular that we had all those fuckin' footballs and discos and all that lot coming down to see Pistols gigs. They'd take the violence at face value and go fuckin' crazy!

Mick Jones: So you think it can get out of hand?

Steve Walsh: You bet it can . . .

Mick Jones: It got out of hand on Tuesday (100 Club fest glass-throwing incident).

Steve Walsh: I reckon it could get worse.

Mick Jones: I definitely think it could escalate but the alternative is for people to vent their frustrations through music, or be a painter or a poet or whatever you wanna be. Vent your frustrations, otherwise it's just like clocking in and clocking out . . . clock in at the 100 Club, every one comes in, everyone clocks out, it ain't no different.

Steve Walsh: How much change do you want, d'you want a revolution?

Joe Strummer: Well . . . yeah!

Steve Walsh: A bloodless one or do you want just total chaos?

Joe Strummer: No, I'm just not into chaos, and I don't believe it when people say they are 'cause you've got to be a special type . . .

Steve Walsh: Of maniac?

Joe Strummer: Well, a Frenchman about 100 years ago could be into chaos 'cause it was possible then, but nowadays, this is like sleepytown. So, when someone tells me they're into chaos I don't believe it. What I would like to see happen is, very much . . . I realize a lot of people are quite happy, you know, at that market down the road from here. All them people, they're as 'appy as sandboys and I'd just like to make loads of people realize what's goin' on. Like, all those secrets in the government and all that money changing hands and every now and then it comes to light and someone gets sacked and someone else comes in the back-door, know what I mean? I'd like to get all that out in the open and just see what's goin' on. I just feel like no one's telling me anything, even if I read every paper, watch TV, and listen to the radio!

RADIO

Steve Walsh: What was that with the radio at the 100 Club gig?

Joe Strummer: Well, all that was . . . I'd been lucky and bought a cheap transistor in a junkshop for ten bob and it worked quite well. I'd been goin' around with it on my ear for a few days just to see what it was like. When someone broke a string I got it out and it just happened to be something about Northern Ireland.

Mick Jones: A state of emergency . . .

Steve Walsh: Yeah, bombs . . . I thought it was interesting; I thought maybe it was part of the way you approach your audience.

Mick Jones: That was part of it, but we've tried other things since then, like at the Roundhouse . . . er . . . we "talked" to the audience . . .

Joe Strummer: But they were half asleep . . .

Mick Jones: The ones who were awake were pretty clever.

Joe Strummer: I didn't think so, I mean *you* could hear them, I couldn't. How can I answer smartass jibes when I can't hear 'em? All I could hear was some girl sayin', "nyah, nyah, nyah!" and then everyone goes, "aha, ha, ha" (bursts out laughing. If you can't hear what they're saying, then you can't really get out your great wit!

Mick Jones: Well, I'm sure they were funny 'cause everyone was laughing at 'em but when Joe said something like, you know, "Fuck off, fatso!" there was just complete silence! (more laughter)

Steve Walsh: So, what do you wanna do to your audience?

Joe Strummer: Well, there's two ways, there's that confronting thing, right! No . . . three ways. Make 'em feel a bit . . . threaten 'em, startle 'em and second—I know it's hard when you see rock 'n' roll bands, to hear what the lyrics are but we're workin' on getting the words out and makin' 'em mean something and the third thing is rhythm. Rhythm is the thing 'cause if it ain't got rhythm then you can just sling it in the dustbin!

> *He's in love with rock 'n' roll, wooaghhh!*
> *He's in love with getting stoned, woooagh!*
> *He's in love with Janie Jones, wooagggh!*
> *But he don't like his boring job, no—oo!*
> —"Janie Jones" by the Clash

ANY INFLUENCE?

Joe Strummer: That's a tricky question . . . Paul's are the Ethiopians, and what's that other band?

Paul Simonon: The Rulers.

Joe Strummer: I've never heard of 'em!

32

Mick Jones: Up until now, I thought everything was the cat's knickers and every group was great. I used to go to all the concerts all the time and that's all I did. Until, somehow, I stopped believing in it all, I just couldn't face it. I s'pose the main influences are Mott the Hoople, the Kings, the Stones, but I just stopped believing. Now, what's out there (points out the window) —that's my influence!

Steve Walsh: What changed your way of looking at things?

Mick Jones: I just found out it weren't true, I stopped reading all the music papers 'cause I used to believe every word. If they told me to go out and buy this record and that, then, I'd just go out and do it. You know, save up me paper round and go out and buy shit and now I'm in a position where I'm selling the records 'cause I don't have much money and they're showing me how much shit's worth! 'Cause I paid two quid for them albums and they give me ten pence down at the record shop, that's how much they think you're worth!

MICK

Mick Jones—I've played with so many arse 'oles and my whole career has been one long audition. Like, I was the last kid on my block to pick up a guitar 'cause all the others were repressing me and saying—"No, you don't want to do that, you're too ugly, too spotty, you stink!" . . . and I believed 'em. I was probably very gullible and then I realized that they weren't doing too well and I said, ah fuck, I can do just as well!

London's Burning With Boredom,
London's Burning, Dial 999!

Steve Walsh: What do you think of the scene so far?

Mick Jones: Well, it's coming from us, the Pistols, Subway Sect, and maybe the Buzzcocks, that's it, there are *no* other bands!

Mark P. What do you think of bands that just go out and enjoy themselves?

Mick Jones: You know what I think, I think they're a bunch of ostriches; they're sticking their heads in the fuckin' sand! They're enjoying themselves at the audience's expense. They're takin' their audience for a ride, feeding the audience shit!

Mark P. What if the audience say they're enjoying themselves?

Joe Strummer: Look, the situation is far too serious for enjoyment, man. Maybe when we're fifty-five we can play tubas in the sun, that's alright then to enjoy yourselves, but now!

Mick Jones: I think if you wanna fuckin' enjoy yourselves you sit in an armchair and watch TV, but if you wanna get actively involved, 'cause rock 'n' roll's about rebellion. Look, I had this out with Bryan James of the Damned and we were screamin' at each other for about three hours 'cause he stands for enjoying himself and I stand for change and creativity.

Joe Strummer: I'd rather play to an audience and them not enjoy it, if we were doin' what we thought was honest. Rather than us go up and sing, "Get outta Denver, baby," and do what we didn't think was honest.

Mick Jones: If they enjoy us then they come with us. If you ask me what I think of groups like the Hot Rods, I think they're a load of bozos and they're not telling the audience to do anything other than stay as they are. They're playing old stuff and I don't think much of their originals. The situation is where the Hod Rod's audience are bozos and it's easy to identify with a bozo. I mean, obviously they're goin' down. . . . like, people queuing outside the Marquee, they've got a great thing goin' for themselves, but it's not to do with change, it's just keeping people as they are!

Steve Walsh: What do you think the scene needs now?

Mick Jones: Ten more honest bands!

Joe Strummer: More venues . . .

Mick Jones: More events!

Joe Strummer: . . . Just more people who care; if we could get our hands on the money and get something together . . . immediately. None of the promoters running any of the venues in London care. Ron Watts, the 100 Club bloke, has done something but no one else really cares. They don't give a shit about the music, not one shit!

GREATNESS FROM GARAGELAND

By Peter Silverton

Originally appeared in Trouser Press, *February 1978*

U nannounced, to say the least, a kid in boots, suspenders, and short-cropped hair clambers through the photographers' pit and up onto the stage of London's Rainbow Theatre. Benignly ignored by band, stage crew and security alike, he wanders around the stage a little drunkenly, uncertain quite what to do now that he's made it up onto the hallowed, sacrosanct boards and is not making quite the impression he thought. Decision flickers across his face, lit by the giant spots, and he grabs hold of the singer's mike and prepares to join in on the harmonies. When the singer wants his mike back, the kid's frozen to the stand in fear-drenched exhilaration so the singer has to shout the lines over the kid's shoulder while the kid pumps in the response lines on perfect cue.

The encore over, the band leaves the stage and the kid's stuck there in front of two and a half thousand people and unsure what to do next. With the merest jerk of his head the bass player motions the kid to join the band backstage and everyone goes home happy.

Sounds like some fantasy of what rock 'n' roll should be about or at least a case of a cunning audience plant, doesn't it? It wasn't. It was the Clash. And it happened just that way at the first of their three nights at the Rainbow in December.

That's the thing about the Clash; they can break rules you hadn't realised existed till they trashed 'em. That's why, in a year, without any kind of Springsteen-like hype—except from zealot journalists like myself—they've gone from empty college and club halls to three nights at a major London venue. Like the Pistols, they're so special that they've created not only their own style but also their own rule structure. Only the most carping would say that the Clash are like anybody or anything else.

Because of events like the one just described, the Clash command an awesome respect, even adulatory deification from their fans. Some of them really do expect the Clash to slip 'em the meaning life in a three minute rock 'n' roll song. Mind you, full-grown rock writers have been known to make the same mistake. And to think, all that achieved with only two national tours of Britain and but one album and three singles (in total seventeen songs, nineteen tracks) in general circulation.

And I still don't think the Clash realize themselves what kind of position they're in. It's as if they're (very understandably) scared of facing up to the fact of that worship and its implications.

Here's another little scene which might help explain what I'm getting at. A few days before I sat down to tap this through my crappy little Smith-Corona portable I found myself at a gig, competing with Clash meistersinger Joe Strummer for the bartender's attention. (Incidentally, I won.)

Having known Strummer for almost two years, I wasn't too surprised when, after exchanging the usual pleasantries, he turned on me a little drunkenly and demanded know who my favourite English band was. More than a little embarrassed, I told him:

"Your lot."

"Nah, come on," he replied, "Tell me who you really think's the best."

"The Clash," my voice getting louder. "Honest!"

Joe didn't believe. "I bet you'll tell the Hot Rods the same thing tomorrow."

So, here in cold type, let's set the matter straight with an open letter.

Dear Joe,

The Clash are not only the best band in Britain. They're the best band in the world. (I think that for a magnitude of reasons I'll explain in good time.) For me, you're the latest in a straight three-act lineage: Chuck Berry, the Stones, the Clash. No one else comes near. The Beatles may have written better songs but. . . . The Pistols may have been a bigger force of change but . . . Fercrissakes, if I didn't believe all this stuff, you don't think you'd catch me spieling out all these cascades of yeeugh-making praise, do you now? There's a whole lot more becoming things for an adult to do, you know.

Yours,
Pete

> P.S. But I still don't believe that you're the saint, let alone godhead that some of your more impressionable fans crack you up to be. I know you're just as big a head-case as the rest of us.

Good. That out of the way, I can move on to telling you good and patient—you must be if you've got this far—readers just how and why the Clash have come to occupy such a prominent place in my—and a lot of other people's—affections.

The Clash at core are three people. Mick Jones on lead guitar, vocals and Keef lookalike. He was in the London SS, about whom the myths outweigh the facts at least tenfold. Paul Simonon plays bass, smiles a lot, lopes around like a grossly underfed gorilla on a vitamin B-and-methedrine cure for malnutrition and catches the fancy of more women than the rest of the band put together— Patti Smith, for example. Joe Strummer sings in a manner that some find so unmusical as to be repulsive (you find those kind of philistines everywhere) and others reckon is compulsive and entrancing. Joe was the leading light in the "world-famed" 101ers and still plays the same tortured, demonic rhythm guitar that was the highlight of that band.

And then there's the fourth man, Nicky "Topper" Headon, the drummer. He gets left out of the central three because he's the last in a long line of skin-beaters with the Clash—Terry Chimes (a.k.a. Tory Crimes) plays on the album—and, although Nicky's occupied the stool longer and deservedly so than anyone else, he's still relatively unimportant in the overall image of the band. But who knows, a year from now, he might be as important as Ringo was to the Fabs.

How did they come together? Well, not to put too fine a point on it, the line they usually hand out to gullible journalists is a heap of shit. They claim that Paul and Mick were trotting down Portobello Road one balmy Saturday, already intent on forming their own band, when they chanced upon Joe Strummer and, knowing him from the still-in-existence-at-this-point 101ers, asked him to be their lead singer. After a couple of days to think it over, he junked the 101ers and threw in his lot with Mick and Paul. That's the fantasy. The reality, as usual, is both more complex and much less romantic.

To explain for the benefit of future historians of the social mores of the seventies, I must backtrack to the first time I encountered Mr. Strummer.

I'd been writing for this rag for a bit and I'd decided I wanted to do a short piece on what it was really like for a struggling band in London, supposed Mecca of rock 'n' roll. On the recommendation of a friend who'd known Joe since schooldays, I went down to a truly scummy college benefit to check out the 101ers.

At this point (two years ago) I was just emerging from a five-year period where I was so disgusted by the rock 'n' roll scene that I spent all day in bed listening to Chuck Berry and reading Trotsky. I'd come to like quite a few of the current pub rock bands but however much I enjoyed them, I knew in my heart of hearts, there was something lacking. And, although, if pressed, I'd say it had something to do with lack of stage presence, it wasn't till I saw Joe that night that I realised just what was lacking—full-blooded desperation to become a star and communicate with your audience and the sense to realise that not only is that a far from easy task but that, if you don't find your own way of doing it, you might as well junk the idea right there and then.

The 101ers were an immensely loveable but generally pretty ramshackle bunch who'd rip through Chuck Berry and R&B numbers with not a trace of genuflection at the altar of the greats. What they—or rather what Joe took—was theirs/his.

I became so enamoured with the 101ers that what had started out as a short article ended up as a veritable thesis which *Trouser Press* has on file (and I hope they don't dig it out, even if it is the definitive work on the subject). The day I mailed the piece, the band broke up. The rest of the 101ers dropped into the limbo of obscurity but Joe, with much flourish, hair cutting and clothes altering, hooked up with Paul and Mick.

That something of the kind had been the offing I'd suspected since I'd been with Joe watching the Pistols (who were at this time supporting the 101ers). As someone else put it, he saw the light and the Sex Pistols simultaneously.

Meanwhile Mick Jones, Brian James (later of the Damned), and Tony James (now in Generation X) had been sorting out their chops in a basement under the name of the London SS and the tutelage of future Clash manager Bernard Rhodes, a close pal of Sex Pistols' manager Malcolm McLaren. The London SS, unable to locate a suitable drummer, never actually played a gig but, according to the few who've heard them, their tapes were very impressive.

When Brian James walked off/was pushed off to form the Damned, the rest of London SS faced up to facts, chucked in the towel and went their separate ways.

This is when Mick joined forces with Paul—who'd never even touched a bass before ("I used to be an art designer till I discovered the Clash")—and Keith Levine, who only stayed long enough to do a few early gigs and cop a co-credit for "What's My Name" on the album. He was a great guitarist but . . . well, just check out "Deny."

Masterminded by their hustler-manager with tertiary verbal diarrhea, Bernard Rhodes, the three of them persuaded Strummer over a period of time that he was exactly the vocalist they needed. When Joe was finally convinced, the four of them moved into an enormous (but very cheap) rehearsal studio of their own and began to audition drummers. Getting the name was easy enough. After an initial flirtation with Weak Heart Drops (after a Big Youth song), they plumped for the challenge of the Clash. But getting a drummer wasn't so easy.

They searched with an unusual but understandable and probably correct attitude toward drummers. To wit, drummers can't drum because they all suffer from a Billy Cobham complex and want to play as much as an egocentric lead guitarist. Therefore drummers have to be taught to drum. And drummers, being by and large nutters, don't take too kindly to such condescension. Also, at this time, while the rest of the band were outwardly convinced they'd be an unqualified success, under the surface they were stone scared that they couldn't live up to even their own belief in themselves. The tensions in the Clash camp (late summer '76) were running so high that just sitting around the rehearsal studio could be an exceedingly uncomfortable experience.

But, after rejecting various drummers who were more in tune with the band's commitment but couldn't really hack out the relentless trip-trap bottom line, they settled on Terry Chimes, who didn't give a flying one about the politics (in the widest sense) of the Clash but made up for it by being one of the best drummers this side of Jerry Nolan.

Anyway, that's how they'd shaped up to the point of their early gigs, so that's enough of this hagiography. That's not nearly as important as why the Clash are the CLASH.

SCENE ONE:

Bernie Rhodes holds Clash preview for the press in the studio, subtly paralleling Paris schmutter previews. Giovanni Dadomo of *Sounds* is suitably impressed and reports that the Clash are the first band to come along that look like they could really scare the Pistols.

SCENE TWO:

The reaction sets in. When the Clash support the Pistols at a London cinema gig, Charles Shaar Murray says that they're a garage band who ought to get back in the garage and leave the car motor running. (This prompts them to write "Garageland.")

SCENE THREE:

The sides settled, every Clash gig becomes an event. When Patti Smith comes over, she sees the Clash at the Institute of Contemporary Arts and is so knocked out with them that she jumps up and "jams." And some kid in the audience does a mock up of biting off someone's ear (with the aid of a tomato ketchup capsule) and the picture gets in the weekly music press. By the time they play the Royal College of Art (Arty lot, aren't they? Still, what do you expect? They all went to art college and wear some of the flashiest clothes imaginable), emotions are running way too high. They play a set under the rubric "A Night of Treason." (It was November 5th, the night that honours the burning of Guy Fawkes, the bloke who tried to blow up the Houses of Parliament.) Some of the audience, when not lobbing fireworks around, take an extreme dislike to the Clash and start bunging bottles at the stage. The rest of the audience is split between Clash fans who already think their band can do no wrong and the uncommitted whose prevailing attitude is "Well, they are playing violent music and if you play violent, well you know what they say about what you sow . . ."

The band are certain how they feel about playing in a rain of bottles. Strummer lurches off stage and tries to sort out those responsible . . . personally.

The Clash style has been set. It's a straight case of being ruthlessly certain about how you feel and what you want to do and making sure that no one gets in your way. Like the man said, "We ain't looking for trouble but if someone starts it, it ain't gonna be us that's gonna be on the losing side."

Remember this is back in '76 when punk was still seen overwhelmingly as being POLITICAL. More than anyone else it was the Clash that everyone held responsible for putting down a party line. Now they're all pretty much retreated from that position (except the Clash, they just smile Highway 61 smiles) and say aw, we're really only into having fun, maaan. But then, you've no idea what a relief it was to have songs about something else other than falling in love with some acne-infested adolescent or what a drag it is to be slogging our guts out "on the road" and staying in all these faceless hotels (when most kids in England have never even stayed in a hotel) or pathetic dirges about let's have a little more rock 'n' roll.

I know rock 'n' roll is *supposed* to be about the banalities of the pubescent dream but it had pretty much got to the stage where the average rock 'n' roll song was indistinguishable from moon/June bilge. If the Clash have done nothing else, they've given a big help to kicking out all that garbage (of course, many others have been working to the same end).

Strummer certainly didn't come from any poverty-stricken background (on the other hand, he never really pretended to) but his songs were like a well-aimed boot plonked straight into the guts of an overfed and complacent music business.

And Mick Jones was no slouch either.

"Career Opportunities" for example:

> *They offered me the office*
> *They offered me the shop*
> *They said I'd better take anything they'd got*
> *Do you wanna make tea at the BBC*
> *Do you, do you really wanna be a cop?*
> *Career opportunities*

> *The ones that never knock*
> *Every job they offer you's to keep you out the dock*
> *Career opportunities*
> *The ones that never knock.*

Okay, so it ain't gonna cop him a poetry prize (who wants 'em?) but it displays both a savage understanding of the demands for immediacy in a rock 'n' roll song and a large helping of witty comment on what it's like to be given the choice of one shitty job or another shitty job. Of course, the Clash never thought they could really change things. They're only (only!) a rock 'n' roll band, not a political party. But, if you're gonna sing about something, you might as well sing about something that doesn't usually make it onto pop singles. Unfortunately, while they handled it, lesser talents came along and decided that they'd have to write "political" songs and, as a matter of course, mostly came up with insulting simplicities like Chelsea's "Right To Work."

And then, even more important, there was the music. Even early on (and especially after Small Faces addict Glen Matlock got the boot) the Pistols were very fond of heavy metal drones. I don't think the Clash even listened to HM. Joe only cared for '50s rockers (especially bluesman Clarence "Gatemouth" Brown, believe it or not) and reggae. Jones was deeply into Mott, which shows in the Clash's attitude toward their fans both in their songs and their stage demeanour. And Paul Simonon was into football (listen to the chant on "Janie Jones") and painting (look at the clothes, stage backdrops and all their visual presentation).

By the time they'd done the Anarchy Tour with the Pistols, the Clash were in an unrivalled second position. They began to get the kind of press eulogies and fan worship that'd turn anybody's head. How could anybody fail to react to them?

Onstage, Strummer is so obviously a natural star, forcing his body and Telecaster to ever greater heights of pain/pleasure, grabbing the mike and screaming lines like he really does care.

Mick Jones bopping around like a younger Keef (yeah, that comparison again) doing a military two-step and sending out shards of steely guitar licks.

And Paul lumbering around looking looser and more relaxed but thumping his bass while indulging in perverse, arcane calisthenics.

And the clothes. Obviously paramilitary in origin—zips and slogans featured very heavily—but whoever heard of an army splashing paint all over their tunics?

All this combines to make sure the Clash, even at their worst, are never mere music. I am absolutely convinced that it's not only me that feels that they're the '70s answer to the Stones. If asked, Clash fans will say they love 'em so much because "They're good to dance to" or "I fancy Mick Jones" or "I just like 'em, that's all." If that is all, why do they shout out for "White Riot" all the time at gigs? It's not one of the Clash's best songs, but it is the one that most represents where they're coming from, what they stand for and, by extension, what particular fantasy they're enacting for their audience. If the kids just wanted to dance or screw, they could go to a disco/home to bed. They want and get more but their lack of articulacy prevents them explaining what. Where success and even the music are subordinate to the stance—they're saying not we play rock 'n' roll but we are rock 'n' roll. If Chuck Berry represents for me an idealised adolescence I never had, and the Stones were an adolescence that I lived through once removed because, like so many kids, I was too busy studying, the Clash are as good an excuse as any for me to live out a perfect adolescence ten years late. Hell, why else be a rock 'n' roll writer—there's more to it than freebie albums, you know.

Which is also why—just like the Stones—while the Clash will

fire imaginations, they'll never become a grandiosely successful band. Some reckon they won't make it in the States at all. I don't agree with that. Judging by the recent Rainbow shows, they've got enough classic big stage rock 'n' roll choreography worked out to handle any auditorium. And their newer songs, like "City of the Dead" and the as yet unissued "White Man in Hammersmith Palais" are played at a pace that even ears used to the Eagles can handle. Also, by slowing matters down a trifle, they seem to have upped the energy level—too much speed becomes nothing but a fast train blur. They learned their lesson on the first English tour. The set started out at 45 minutes. By the end of the tour it was down to 29 minutes and that included all the album plus "1977," "Capital Radio" (only available on a limited edition giveaway— which is a pity because it's one of their best songs), their truly awful version of Toots and the Maytals' sublime "Pressure Drop," and "London's Burning" twice. It gave their roadies something to boast about but if you wanted to keep up with it, you had to snort at least two grams of amphetamine.

This drop in speed/rise in intensity is obviously partly a result of their smoking a lot more dope and listening to a lot of very spliffed-out rasta roots reggae. They realised you ain't gotta run at full throttle to give out the necessary power.

Nonetheless, the Clash have come in for a lot of criticism. Ignoring the early jeers about unmusicality, the most hurtful has been that they're a kind of punk Bay City Rollers, programmed to do just what their manager tells them to do. Quite simply, that's like saying that the Stones were only Oldham's puppets. Of course, Bernie being some kind of weird conceptual artist lams in a fair share of the ideas but, at the last resort, it's Mick, Paul, Joe, and Topper that cut the cake on stage and record.

Anyway, I reckon that carping like that is just more proof of the Clash's importance. Nobody gets into the same kind of polarisations about say Slaughter and the Dogs or 999. People only get into heavy-duty arguments about bands that really matter.

Look. If you already like the Clash, you'll like 'em even more live (if they play a good show—which admittedly, they don't do as often as they should). If you hate the Clash, you'll either learn the error of your ways when you realize what great little pop songs they write or continue to hate 'em. The choice is yours.

All I can say is that any band that can bring a relatively cynical scribbler like myself to gush like a besotted fan, has got to be one of the most special things to have ever happened.

THE CLASH: ANGER ON THE LEFT
PUNK LEADERS SET SIGHTS ON AMERICA

By Mikal Gilmore

Originally appeared in Rolling Stone, *March 8, 1979*

Never mind that shit," says Joe Strummer, the thuggish-looking lead singer of the Clash, addressing the exultant kids yelling, "Happy New Year" at him from the teeming floor of the Lyceum. "You've got your future at stake. Face front! Take it!"

In sleepy London town, during a murky Christmas week, rock 'n' roll is being presented as a war of class and aesthetics. At the crux of that battle is a volcanic series of four Clash concerts—including a benefit for Sid Vicious—coming swift on the heels of the group's second album, *Give 'Em Enough Rope,* which entered the British charts at Number Two. Together with the Sex Pistols, the Clash helped spearhead the punk movement in Britain, along the way earning the designation as the most intellectual and political new wave band. When the Pistols disbanded early last year, the rock press and punks alike looked to the Clash as the movement's central symbol and hope.

Yet, beyond the hyperbole and wrangle that helped create their radical myth, the Clash brandish a hearty reputation as a rock 'n' roll band that, like the Rolling Stones and Bruce Springsteen, must be seen to be believed. Certainly no other band communicates kinetic, imperative anger as potently as the Clash. When Nicky "Topper" Headon's single-shot snare report opens "Safe European Home" (a song about Strummer and lead guitarist Mick

Jones' ill-fated attempt to rub elbows with Rastafarians in the Jamaicans' backyard), all hell breaks loose, both on the Lyceum stage and floor.

Like the Sex Pistols, the Clash's live sound hinges on a massive, orchestral drum framework that buttresses the blustery guitar work of Jones, who with his tireless two-step knee kicks looks just like a Rockettes' version of Keith Richards. Shards of Mott the Hoople and the Who cut through the tumult, while Strummer's rhythm guitar and Paul Simonon's bass gnash at the beat underneath. And Strummer's vocals sound as dangerous as he looks. Screwing his face up into a broken-tooth yowl, he gleefully bludgeons words, then caresses them with a touching, R&B-inflected passion.

Maybe it's the gestalt of the event, or maybe it's just the sweaty leather-bound mass throbbing around me, but I think it's the most persuasive rock 'n' roll show I've seen since I watched Graham Parker rip the roof off a San Francisco night club almost two and a half years ago.

I try to say as much to a reticent Joe Strummer after the show as we stand in a dingy backstage dressing room, which is brimming with a sweltering mix of fans, press, and roadies. Strummer, wearing smoky sunglasses and a nut-brown porkpie hat, resembles a roughhewn version of Michael Corleone. Measuring me with his wary, testy eyes, he mumbles an inaudible reply.

Across the room, Mick Jones and Paul Simonon have taken refuge in a corner, sharing a spliff. "You a Yank?" Jones asks me in a surprisingly delicate, lilting voice. "From 'ollywood? Evil place, innit? All laid back." According to the myth encasing this band, Jones who writes nearly all of the Clash's music, is the band's real focal nerve, even though the austere Strummer writes the bulk of the lyrics. In the best Keith Richard's tradition, fans see Mick as a sensitive and vulnerable street waif, prone to dissipation as much as to idealism. Indeed, he looks as bemusedly wasted as anyone I've ever met. He's also among the gentler, more considerate people I've ever spent time with.

But the same evening, sitting in the same spot, Mick declines to be interviewed. "Lately, interviews make me feel 'orrible. It seems all I do is spend my time answering everyone's charges—charges that shouldn't have to be answered."

The Clash have been hit recently with a wide volley of charges, ranging from an English rock-press backlash aimed at what the critics see as reckless politics, to very real criminal charges against Headon and Simonon (for shooting valuable racing pigeons) and Jones (for alleged cocaine possession). But probably the most damaging salvo has come from their former manager, Bernard Rhodes, who, after he was fired, accused the band of betraying its punk ideals and slapped them with a potentially crippling lawsuit. Jones, in a recent interview, railed back. "We're still the only ones true to the original aims of punk," he said. "Those other bands should be destroyed."

The Clash formed as a result of Joe Strummer's frustration and Mick Jones's rock ideals. Both had been abandoned at early ages by their parents, and while Strummer (the son of a British diplomat) took to singing Chuck Berry songs in London's subways for spare change during his late teens, Jones retreated into reading and playing Mott the Hoople, Dylan, Kinks, and Who records. In 1975, he left the art school he was attending and formed London SS, a band that, in its attempt to meld a raving blend of the New York Dolls, the Stooges, and Mott, became a legendary forerunner of the English punk scene.

Then, in early 1976, shortly after the Sex Pistols assailed London, Mick Jones ran into Strummer, who had been singing in a pub-circuit R&B band called the 101ers. "I don't like your band," Jones said, "but I like the way you sing." Strummer, anxious to join the punk brigade, cut his hair, quit the 101ers and joined Jones, Simonon (also a member of London SS), guitarist Keith Levine (now a member of Public Image Ltd), and drummer Terry Chimes to form the Clash in June of 1976. Eight months later, under the tutelage of Bernard Rhodes, the Clash signed with CBS Records for a reported $200,000.

Their first album, *The Clash* (unreleased in America; Epic, the group's label stateside, deems it "too crude"), was archetypal, resplendent punk. While the Sex Pistols proffered a nihilistic image, the Clash took a militant stance that, in an eloquent, guttural way, vindicated punk's negativism. Harrowed rhythms and coarse vocals propelled a foray of songs aimed at the bleak political realities and social ennui of English life, making social realism— and unbridled disgust—key elements in punk aesthetics.

But even before the first album was released, the punk scene had dealt the Clash some unforeseen blows. The punks, egged on by a hysterical English press, began turning on each other, and drummer Chimes, weary of ducking bottles, spit, and the band's politics, quit. Months passed before the group settled on Nicky Headon (also a member of Mick Jones's London SS) as a replacement and returned to performing. By that time, their reputation had swelled to near-messianic proportions.

When it was time for a new album, CBS asked Blue Oyster Cult producer Sandy Pearlman to check out the Clash's shows. "By a miracle of God," says Pearlman, "they looked like they believed in what they were doing. They were playing for the thrill of affecting their audience's consciousness, both musically and politically. Rock 'n' roll shouldn't be cute and adorable; it should be violent and anarchic. Based on that, I think they're the greatest rock 'n' roll group around." Mick Jones balked at first at the idea of Pearlman as their producer, but Strummer's interest prevailed. It took six months to complete *Give 'Em Enough Rope*, and it was a stormy period for all concerned. ("We knew we had to watch Pearlman," says Nicky Headon. "He gets too good a sound.")

But nowhere near as stormy as the album. *Give 'Em Enough Rope* is rock 'n' roll's *Stage of Seige*—with a dash of *Duck Soup* for comic relief. Instead of reworking the tried themes of bored youth and repressive society, Strummer and Jones tapped some of the deadliest currents around, from creeping fascism at home to Palestinian terrorism. The album surges with visions of civil strife, gunplay, back-biting, and lyrics that might've been spirited from the streets of Italy and Iran: "A system built by the sweat of the many/Creates assassins to kill off the few/Take any place and call it a courthouse/This is a place where no judge can stand." And the music—a whirl of typhonic guitars and drums—frames those conflicts grandly.

The day after the Clash's last Lyceum show, I meet Joe Strummer and Paul Simonon at the Tate Gallery, an art museum. Simonon leads us on a knowledgeable tour of the gallery's treasures until we settle in a dim corner of the downstairs café for an interview.

We start by talking about the band's apparent position as de facto leaders of punk. Strummer stares into his muddy tea, uninterested in the idea of conversation, and lets Simonon take the questions. Probably the roughest looking member of the group, with his skeletal face and disheveled hair, Simonon is disarmingly guileless and amiable. "Just because I'm up onstage," he says in rubbery English, "doesn't mean that I'm entitled to a different lifestyle than anyone else. I used to think so. I'd stay up all night, get pissed, party all the time. But you get cut off from the workaday people that way. I like to get up early, paint me flat, practice me bass. I see these geezers going off to work and I feel more like one of them."

But, I note, most of those same people wouldn't accept him. They're incensed and frightened by bands like the Clash.

Strummer stops stirring his tea and glowers around. "Good," he grunts. "I'm pleased."

This seems a fair time to raise the question of the band's recent bout with the British rock press. After *Give 'Em Enough Rope,* some of the band's staunchest defenders shifted gears, saying that the Clash's militancy is little more than a fashionable stance, and that their attitude toward terrorist violence is dangerously ambiguous. "One is never sure just which side [the Clash] is supposed to be taking," wrote Nick Kent in *New Musical Express.* "The Clash use incidents . . . as fodder for songs without caring."

Strummer squints at me for a moment, his thoughtful mouth hemming his craggy teeth. "We're against fascism and racism," he says. "I figure that goes without saying. I'd like to think that we're subtle; that's what greatness is, innit? I can't stand all these people preaching, like Tom Robinson. He's just too direct."

But that ambiguity can be construed as encouraging violence.

"Our music's violent," says Strummer. "We're not. If anything, songs like "Guns on the Roof" and "Last Gang in Town" are supposed to take the piss out of violence. It's just that sometimes you have to put yourself in the place of the guy with the machine gun. I couldn't go to his extreme, but at the same time, it's no good ignoring what he's doing. We sing about the world that affects us. We're not just another wank rock group like Boston or Aerosmith. What fucking shit."

Yet, I ask, is having a record contract with one of the world's biggest companies compatible with radicalism?

"We've got loads of contradictions for you," says Strummer, shaking off his doldrums with a smirk. "We're trying to do something new; we're trying to be the greatest group in the world, and that also means the biggest. At the same time, we're trying to be radical—I mean, we never want to be really respectable—and maybe the two can't coexist, but we'll try. You know what helps us? We're totally suspicious of anyone who comes in contact with us. Totally. We aim to keep punk alive."

The conversation turns to the Clash's impending tour of America. "England's becoming too claustrophobic for us," says Strummer. "Everything we do is scrutinized. I think touring America could be a new lease on life."

But the American rock scene—and especially radio—seems far removed from the world in flames that the Clash sing about. (While the Clash may top the English charts, they have yet to dent Billboard's Top 200. "We admit we aren't likely to get a hit single this time around," says Bruce Harris of Epic's A&R department. "But *Give 'Em Enough Rope* has sold 40,000 copies and that's better than sixty percent of most new acts.") I ask if a failure to win Yankee hearts would set them back.

"Nah," says Strummer. "We've always got here. We haven't been to Europe much, and we haven't been to Japan or Australia, and we want to go behind the Iron Curtain." He pauses and shrugs his face in a taut grin. "There are a lot of other places where we could lose our lives."

Those may seem like boastful words, but I doubt that's how Strummer means them. Few bands have fought more battles on more fronts than the Clash, and maybe none with better instincts. Of course, it's doubtful that the American and British underclass—or the teenage middle class for that matter—are any more willing than the music industry to be shaken up as much as the Clash would like.

As producer Sandy Pearlman says: "No one's really very scared of punk, especially the record companies. They've sublimated tendencies this art is based on. The Clash see the merit in reaching a wider audience, but they also like the idea of grand suicidal gestures. We need more bands like this as models for tomorrow's parties."

THE CLASH IN AMERICA

By Sylvie Simmons

Originally appeared in Sounds, *February 17, 1979*

So you think we lost the battle—then go home and weep about it. Sometimes you've got to wake up in the morning and think, "Fuck it you're going to win the battle."

—Joe Strummer

T here were no riots, no outraged citizens, no glaring headlines when Pearl Harbour '79 came to an old elegant building in downtown Vancouver last week. The only report in the newspaper's music section was that the local symphony orchestra had gone on strike. The Clash's first American tour is being felt by the press as the stimulating aftershock of the Pistols' U.S. invasion a year ago or not at all.

The Pearl Harbour '79 tour posters depict the Statue of Liberty bundled up in rope. A more illuminating picture, I think, could have been taken outside the Berkeley Community Theatre in San Francisco a few days and a long bus ride later. An hour before the doors were due to open a line of people stretched quietly from the front steps in a perfect shape of a walking stick, where two young security guards shone torches on the few rebels who wanted to hang out rather than wait in the queue for their numbered seat. There was something numbing about that picture. U.S. rock on Quaaludes.

Maybe, these were the Bo Diddley fans. The middle-aged usher who showed me to my seat felt the need to tell me who he was. He stood up there with his square guitar and growled "This feels like 1965 all over again," and almost everyone cheered and gave him standing ovations.

The difference between a living legend and a living band I thought to myself when Diddley left the stage, and the hired DJ brought over for the tour playing Buzzcocks and Sid's "My Way" is between standing up and shouting because you feel you ought to—and standing up and shouting because you simply had to. There's simply nowhere else for all that passion to go. The best rock music someone once said is like a good whore, it's both aggressive and relieving. I didn't get any of that from Bo Diddley's macho strutting. The Clash supplied an overdose.

The audience was divided into factions: the delirious converts who made the most of the Clash's rule that the bouncers weren't to force people into their seats, flooded the front section and pogo'd madly.

Towards the back the typical U.S. rock fans observed the action at a distance through binoculars (imagine the only place you'd ever seen your favourite band play is half a mile from the stage in a place like Earls Court—out here it's as inevitable in rock as death and taxes are in life) and an even more staid bunch sat in the balcony. I suspect they were the ones queuing quietly outside to guarantee a safe spot for their voyeurism.

There were a number of old style bondage and safety pin punks—remember nothing has happened on this scale since the Pistols' gig at Winterland at the end of '77. Now the Pistols are dead, Sid's dead, Winterland's dead and San Francisco is still the Grateful Dead. The Clash have got a lot of reviving to do.

There were a lot more Ramones lookalikes, storm troopers in sneakers with elaborate punk badges, a couple of miniature *Sun* front page headlines "I want justice for my Sid" and a large crowd of U.S. music press analyzing the action like it was the interval of a Bernard Shaw play complaining that they couldn't make out the words when Joe Stummer called from the stage, "If you can't understand the words, don't worry, you're not alone."

We were thanked for bothering to come tonight. Bothering? It was magnificent. Though I could see little more than the flag used a backdrop and Jones' and Simonon's electrocuted leaps about head level, all other rock 'n' roll senses were gratified. Contact with hot pogoing bodies, smell of overheated energy (something you forget is sanitized for your protection in sports arena rock gigs) and the sound; a brain battering "Tommy Gun," an exhilarating "Stay Free," a scorching "Guns On The Roof," "I Fought The Law," "Cell Block No. 9," and the hardest, fastest, most powerful encore in rock with "White Riot."

As for the audience reaction, some seemed to feel uncomfortable but more felt salvation. I can't remember having seen a performance so shot with adrenalin, outdone though it would be by the next night's show.

Backstage there wasn't much talking. In the five days the band spent in San Francisco they must have talked to just about everyone who wanted to listen. A press conference on Monday with a barrage of dumb questions led the band to turn it into their own personal comedy show; record store appearances, radio interviews, and private viewing with anything from *Time* magazine to *Cashbox*.

In the dressing room someone asked Mick if he liked the jam (to a suitably non-committal answer) and someone else warily suggested that Clash had some sort of pact going with Elvis Costello (whose tour bus was parked in Japan town near the next night's gig) who was going to have old rocker Carl Perkins on his tour (Perkins in fact backed out a while ago), only to be told politely that if anyone was doing the copying it was Elvis, who doesn't seem that popular with Clash. Mick and I swapped notes on what a strange place this is.

Tomorrow night's gig hasn't exactly left their record company brimming with philanthropic joy. It's a benefit concert for New Youth, a fledging organization aiming to keep ticket prices down, get larger percentages for the bands, and a place for new wave acts to play.

Besides not being part of the official tour and bound to upset the promoters (the slyest get round any legal points by advertising "White Riot in the Fillmore with the best band ever direct from England." No names mentioned), the tickets are half the price of the Berkeley gig, the venue seatless and flooded with atmosphere. Of the eight dates on this mini-tour (the band intends to return in

June and fill in the gaps) only one failed to sell out—the Berkeley one. A good sign considering the size of the venue (the only time the Pistols played to anything in the few-thousand seat mark over here was at Winterland).

The following afternoon I head for the Villa Roma bar to find Ace, the tour manager, locked in a verbal battle with the red-faced vein-popping motel manager. A misunderstanding over a phone bill that would have evoked polite discussion at the most with the average guest. "The man's an arsehole," Mick told me by way of explanation. The manager had parked his little Pinto station wagon (one of the smallest American cars) in front of the tour bus to stop it leaving, and was threatening to call the police.

Ace was trying valiantly to keep his temper—not easy when a middle-aged man screams "You bums are freaks" to your face. The band left and the manager swaggered over to the bar, loosened his collar and had the barmaid get him a double, boasting how he "wasn't going to be taken for a ride by the like of those freaks" and how "I blocked the bus with my little Pinto wagon—it couldn't move." A hero for a day.

The benefit concert was at a moth-eaten synagogue in San Francisco next door to Jim Jones' People's Temple, tacky but majestic, and a great venue. The punters were generally shit-stoned, dribbling in, falling over, dancing with strangers, and having fun. There was a strong wired sexual sort of atmosphere here, an intangible kind of craziness. The thing that attracted you to rock 'n' roll in the first place.

There was some trouble in the line, a few bottles broken, but that's all, mostly brought on by the slowness with which they were let in. This was New Youth's first gig and they hadn't quite got it together. They only opened one cash register until Clash's manager threatened to open the doors and let everyone in free and tills appeared like magic.

The Clash were electrifying. Like a bloody great headline, commanding attention and belief. They opened with "I'm So Bored with the U.S.A." and the punters went as wild as I've ever seen them go. No time to take notes—there were more important things to do. For the first time in the U.S. I could see the relevance of pogoing. When there's no seats and everyone's crushing your ribs to powder down the front and you want to dance, there's nowhere to go but up. It's also a pretty efficient way of meeting people when you fall on top of them. One girl danced from someone's head onto the stage and dived off headfirst into the solid mass of people. That must be just about the ultimate rock fan experience.

America was getting off on the Clash and New Youth was getting a good down payment for their organization. Some hope yet. But the battle's not won. Johnnie Walker the DJ was there. He's just been fired by a San Francisco radio station for playing punk records.

On the bus after the show, Jones, Strummer, and Simonon are conducting a private post mortem on the tour in the back. Verdict: Vancouver pretty good, Berkeley OK, the benefit in 'Frisco, the best so far. Topper and a friend and the rest of us are down the front watching *Heaven Can Wait* on the video machine while fans mill around outside.

Just before the gig started, Topper was sitting on the bus watching *Star Wars* when a guy came inside and struck up a conversation and took a lot of persuading to leave. He came back a few minutes later with a bottle of champagne, shook the drummer's hand and left. The champagne was consumed on the 400-mile trip to LA. Everyone is half-dead by the time the bus reaches Santa Monica.

While Ace is sorting out a beachfront hotel, an old man wanders up and asks if he can look around the bus. He thinks we're a troop of wandering Bohemians until the driver tells him it's a rock band that's playing the Civic tonight. Undeterred, the seventy-year-old announces that he and his wife go disco dancing every fourth night. The bus breaks out in smiles. "All you've got to do is get in there and do your own thing, feel the beat," he tells this knackered-looking bunch of youngsters. No one offers him tickets for tonight's gig.

Los Angeles is less Bohemian than San Francisco. LA is big streets, big cars, big billboards, and big money. In LA anything that doesn't make a big profit is considered neither art nor desirable. Little bands are pretty much banging heads against the brick wall. The so-called "new wave" scene is barely holding its own. That the Clash sold out the 3,000 capacity Santa Monica Civic is a good sign, even if the numbers were padded out by press and poseurs and probably members of every quasi-punk band in town.

It was a good show, but not a great one. Though that's not to say that this wasn't one of the best evenings I've spent in this venue. As always here the sound was flat, but the spirit and strength of the music and the wildly vibrating floor from the frantic pogoing as good as compensated. The crowd was pretty manic tonight.

Kamikaze punks made exultant swallow dives into the audience from the stage and the editor of *Slash* fanzine leapt up to join Strummer in an unofficial duet before being dragged off and according to him, roughed up by the bouncers who seemed for the most part very easygoing for the States.

As Mick said: "We do as we can, we try to say to the guys, let them stand up, don't bash them, and if we're the headliners they've got to take some notice of us." So they've brought quite a big crew with them but they don't know all the security guards,

Joe said, and was pretty pissed off when the guy from *Slash* kept on whining about his battle scars.

"We never said it was a utopia. Rock 'n' roll is played on enemy ground. We never promised you when you were a baby that it was going to be roses all the way. But we stopped more than you can imagine. You can go on about getting the shit kicked out of you and you can go on about that guy being murdered by bouncers in London, you can go on as much as you like and I'll just sit here and listen and I'll be thinking of the times I've stopped the blood when I had the chance to."

There was a press conference at midnight after the show, rather a depressed concert as Mick described it. The band were in a lousy mood. No explanation. Mick told me it has just been a "strange day." They seemed pissed off with the way the record company was handling them, especially with the Statue of Liberty posters.

"If they're going to have ads and buy big space and show how flashy we are," said Joe, "we're going to pack information into it such as the lyrics." As in the epic "Don't know what to do with us, they're fucking us up." So what should they do? "Leave us alone for a start."

And they're understandably worn out after the ten-hour bus ride from San Francisco. In seven hours' time they'll be back on the bus again heading for Cleveland, Ohio. Some people at the record company were privately expressing anxiety about letting the band drive halfway cross-country. They might decide not to arrive at the right place at the right time.

But they spent twenty minutes slouched over a table backstage (except when Topper got up to let in the members of the Germs, an LA band who were pummeling on the windows outside). Opposite ten rows of assorted scribes giving half-hearted answers to questions: will they fill in the gap left by the Sex Pistols?

Joe: "I don't know. I haven't seen the gap yet." Will they ever release their first album here? (The record company thought the material and presentation too crude for U.S. radio's present AM or FM progammes, and with no hope of a bit on their hands, didn't bother to put it out.)

Joe: "We might release it sometime as a historical document, a greatest hits album."

Do they have problems being famous? Paul: "We can walk down the street in London, people recognize us and come up to us. It's like having loads of friends. That's the way we live, we don't even think about it."

We learn that they came here as soon as they could, that touring the odd places at home was getting tedious, that they found what they consider a healthy new wave scene everywhere they've been so far, that they intend to come back and finish off the job here in the summer, however much flogging it takes them to make it, and that their ambitions are to do away with Boston, Kansas, Foreigner, and Kiss as quickly as possible and become "the best rock 'n' roll band in the world."

If Pearl Harbour '79 continues its electrifying attack, they're going to succeed on both fronts. When it comes down to it, the battle is not tying the Statue of Liberty with rope, nor about the right to wear your safety pins, Fiorucci jeans, and prawn silk shirts without protest from your Mum.

It's about defeating apathy in rock, changing its direction, and taking over its future. And if that's too much to hope for, all who have seen this tour must agree that they're halting senility for a while.

THE CLASH

By Lester Bangs

Originally appeared in Psychotic Reactions
and Carburetor Dung, *1987*

PART ONE

The Empire may be terminally stagnant, but every time I come to England it feels like massive changes are underway.

First time was 1972 for Slade, who had the punters hooting; but your music scene in general was in such miserable shape that most of the hits on the radio were resurrected oldies. Second time was for David Essex (haw haw haw) and Mott (sigh) almost exactly two years ago; I didn't even bother listening to the radio, and though I had a good time the closest thing to a musical highlight of my trip was attending an Edgar Froese (entropy incarnate) press party. I never gave much of a damn about pub rock, which was about the only thing you guys had going at the time, and I had just about written you off for dead when punk rock came along.

So here I am back again through the corporate graces of CBS International to see the Clash, to hear new wave bands on the radio (a treat for American ears), and find the Empire jumping again at last.

About time, too. I don't know about you, but as far as I was concerned things started going downhill for rock around 1968; I'd date it from the ascendance of Cream, who were the first fake superstar band, the first sign of strain in what had crested in 1967. Ever since then things have just gotten worse, through Grand Funk and James Taylor and wonderful years like 1974, when the only thing interesting going on was Roxy Music, finally culminating last year in the ascendance of things like disco and jazz-rock, which are dead enough to suggest the end of popular music as anything more than room spray.

I was thinking of giving up writing about music altogether last year when all of a sudden I started getting phone calls from all these slick magazine journalists who wanted to know about this new phenomenon called "punk rock." I was a little bit confused at first, because as far as I was concerned punk rock was something which had first raised its grimy snout around 1966 in groups like the Seeds and Count Five and was dead and buried after the Stooges broke up and the Dictators' first LP bombed.

I mean, it's easy to forget that just a little over a year ago there was *only one thing*: the first Ramones album.

But who could have predicted that that record would have such an impact—all it took was that and the ferocious *edge* of the Sex Pistols' "Anarchy in the U.K.," and suddenly it was as if someone had unleashed the floodgates as ten million little groups all over the world came storming in, mashing up the residents with their guitars, and yammering discontented non sequiturs about how bored and fed up they were with everything.

I was too, and so were you—that's why we went out and bought all those shitty singles last spring and summer by the likes of the Users and the Cortinas and Slaughter and the Dogs, because better Slaughter and the Dogs at what price wretchedness than *one more* mewly mouthed simper-whimper from Linda Ronstadt. Buying records became fun again, and one reason it did was that all these groups embodied the who-gives-a-damn-let's-just-slam-it-at-'em spirit of great rock 'n' roll. Unfortunately many of these wonderful slices of vinyl didn't possess any of the other components of same, with the result that (for me, round about *Live at the Roxy*) many people simply got FED UP. Meaning that it's just too goddam easy to slap on a dog collar and black leather jacket and start puking all over the room about how you're gonna sniff some glue and stab some backs.

Punk had repeated the very attitudes it copped (BOREDOM and INDIFFERENCE), and we were all waiting for a group to come along who at least went through the motions of GIVING A DAMN and SOMETHING.

Ergo, the Clash.

You see, dear reader, so much of what's (doled) out as punk merely amounts to saying I suck, you suck, the world sucks, and who gives a damn—which is, er, ah, somehow *insufficient*.

Don't ask *me* why; I'm just an observer, really. But any observer could tell that, to put it in terms of Us vs. Them, saying the above is exactly what They want you to do, because it amounts to capitulation. It *is* unutterably boring and disheartening to try to find some fun or meaning while shoveling through all the shit we've been handed the last few years, but merely puking on yourself is not gonna change anything. (I know, 'cause I tried it.) I guess what it all boils down to is:

(a) You can't like people who don't like themselves; and
(b) You gotta like people who stand up for what they believe in, as long as what they believe in is
(c) Righteous.

A precious and elusive quantity, this righteousness. Needless to say, most punk rock is not exactly OD'ing on it. In fact, most punk rockers probably think it's the purview of hippies, unless you happen to be black and Rastafarian, in which case righteousness shall cover the land, presumably when punks have attained No Future.

It's kinda hard to put into mere mortal words, but I guess I should say that being righteous means you're more or less on the side of the angels, waging Armageddon for the ultimate victory of the forces of Good over the Kingdom of Death (see how perilously we skirt hippiedom here?), working to enlighten others as to their own possibilities rather than merely sprawling in the muck yodeling about what a drag everything is.

The righteous minstrel may be rife with lamentations and criticisms of the existing order, but even if he doesn't have a coherent program for social change he is informed of hope. The MC5 were righteous where the Stooges were not. The third and fourth Velvet Underground albums were righteous, the first and second weren't. (Needless to say, Lou Reed is not righteous.) Patti Smith has been righteous. The Stones have flirted with righteousness (e.g., "Salt of the Earth"), but when they were good the Beatles were all-righteous. The Sex Pistols are not righteous, but, perhaps more than any other new wave band, the Clash are.

The reason they are is that beneath their wired harsh soundscape lurks a persistent humanism. It's hard to put your finger on in the actual lyrics, which are mostly pretty despairing, but it's in the kind of thing that could make somebody like Mark P. write that their debut album was his life. To appreciate it in the Clash's music you might have to be the sort of person who could see Joe Strummer crying out for a riot of his own as someone making a positive statement. You perceive that as much as this music seethes with rage and pain, it also champs at the bit of the present system of things, lunging after some glimpse of a new and better world.

I know it's easy to be cynical about all this; in fact, one of the most uncool things you can do these days is to be committed about anything. The Clash are so committed they're downright militant. Because of that, they speak to dole-queue British youth today of their immediate concerns with an authority that nobody else has quite mustered. Because they do, I doubt if they will make much sense to most American listeners.

But more about that later. Right now, while we're on the subject of politics, I would like to make a couple of things perfectly clear:

1. I do not know shit about the English class system.
2. I do not care shit about the English class system.

I've *heard* about it, understand. I've heard it has something to do with why Rod Stewart now makes music for housewives, and why Pete Townshend is so screwed up. I guess it also has something to do with another *NME* writer sneering to me, "Joe Strummer has a fucking middle-class education, man!" I surmise further that this is supposed to indicate that he isn't worth a shit, and that his songs are all fake street graffiti. Which is fine by me: Joe Strummer is a fake. That only puts him in there with Dylan and Jagger and Townshend and most of the other great rock songwriters, because almost all of them in one way or another were fakes. Townshend had a middle-class education. Lou Reed went to Syracuse University before matriculating to the sidewalks of New York. Dylan faked his whole career; the only difference was that he used to be good at it and now he sucks.

The point is that, like Richard Hell says, rock 'n' roll is an arena in which you recreate yourself, and all this blathering about authenticity is just a bunch of crap. The Clash are authentic because their music carries such brutal conviction, not because they're Noble Savages.

Here's a note to CBS International: you can relax because I liked the Clash as people better than any other band I have ever met with the possible exception of the Talking Heads, and their music it goes without saying is great. (I mean *you* think so, don't you? Good, then release their album in the U.S. So what if it gets zero radio play; *Clive* knew how to subsidize the arts.)

Here's a superlative for ads: "Best band in the UK!"—Lester Bangs. Here's another one: "Thanks for the wonderful vacation!"— Lester Bangs. (You know I love you, Ellie.) Okay, now that all that's out of the way, here we go . . .

I was sitting in the British Airways terminal in New York City on the eve of my departure, reading *The War Against the Jews, 1933–1945* when I looked up just in time to see a crippled woman in a wheelchair a few feet away from me. My eyes snapped back down to my book in that shameful nervous reflex we know so well, but a moment later she had wheeled over to a couple of feet from where I was sitting, and when I could fight off the awareness of my embarrassment of her presence no longer I looked up again and we said hello to each other.

She was a very small person about thirty years old with a pretty face, blond hair, and blazing blue eyes. She said that she had been on vacation in the States for three months and was now, ever so reluctantly, returning to England.

"I like the people in America so much better," she said. "Christ, it's so nice to be someplace where people recognize that you *exist*. In England, if you're handicapped no one will look at or speak to you except old people. And they just pat you on the head."

It is four days later, and I've driven from London to Derby with Ellie Smith from CBS and Clash manager Bernard Rhodes for the first of my projected three nights and two days with the band. I am not in the best of shape, since I've still got jet lag, have been averaging two or three hours' sleep a night since I got here, and the previous night was stranded in Aylesbury by the Stiff's Greatest Hits tour, hitching a ride back to London with a roadie in the course of which we were stopped by provincial police in search of dope and forced to empty all our pockets, something which had not happened to me since the hippie heydaze of 1967.

This morning when I went by Mick Farren's flat to pick up my bags he had told me, "You look like *Night of the Living Dead*."

Nevertheless, I make sure after checking into the Derby Post House to hit the first night's gig, whatever my condition, in my most thoughtful camouflage. You see, the kind of reports we get over in the States about your punk rock scene had led me to expect seething audiences of rabid little miscreants out for blood at all costs, and naturally I figured the chances of getting a great story were better if I happened to get cannibalized. So I took off my black leather jacket and dressed as straight as I possibly could, the coup de grace (I thought) being a blue promotional sweater that said "Capitol Records" on the chest, by which I fantasized picking up some residual EMI-hostility from battle-feral Pistols fans. I should mention that I also decided not to get a haircut which I desperately needed before leaving the States, on the not-so-off chance of being mistaken for a hippie. When I came out of my room and Ellie and photographer Pennie Smith saw me, they laughed.

When I got to the gig I pushed my way down through the pogoing masses, right into the belly of the beast, and stood there through openers to the Lous' and Richard Hell and the Voidoids' sets, waiting for the dog soldiers of anarch-apocalypse to slam my skull into my ankles under a new wave riptide.

Need I mention that nothing of the kind transpired?

Listen: if I were you I would take up arms and march on the media centers of Merrie Olde, *NME* included, and trash them beyond recognition. Because what I experienced, this first night and all subsequent on this tour, was so far from what we Americans have read in the papers and seen on TV that it amounts to a mass defamation of character, if not cultural genocide. Nobody gave a damn about my long hair, or could have cared less about some stupid sweater. Sure there was gob and beer cups flung at the bands, and the mob was pushing sideways first right and then left, but I hate to disappoint anybody who hasn't been there but this scene is neither *Clockwork Orange* nor *Lord of the Flies*. When I got tired of the back-and-forth group shove I simply stuck my elbows out and a space formed around me.

What I am saying is that I have been at outdoor rock festivals in the hippie era in America where the vibes and violence were ten times worse than at any of the gigs I saw on this Clash tour, and the bands said later that this Derby engagement was the worst they had seen. What I am saying is that contrary to almost all reports published everywhere, I found British punks everywhere I went to be basically if not manifestly *gentle* people. *They are a bunch of nice boys and girls and don't let anybody (them included) tell you different.*

Yeah, they like to pogo. On the subject of this odd tribal rug-cut, of course the first thing I saw when I entered the hall was a couple of hundred little heads near the lip of the stage all bobbing up and down like anthropomorphized pistons in some Max Fleischer cartoon on the Industrial Revolution.

When I'd heard about pogoing before I though it was the stupidest thing anybody'd ever told me about, but as soon as I saw it in living *sproing* it made perfect sense. I mean, it's obviously no more stupid than the Seconal idiot-dance popularized five years ago by Grand Funk audiences. In fact, it's sheer logic (if not poetry) in motion: when you're packed into a standing sweatshop with ten thousand other little bodies all mashed together, it stand to reason you can't dance in the traditional manner (i.e., sideways sway).

No, obviously if you wanna do the boogaloo to what the new breed say, you gotta by dint of sheer population explosion shake your booty and your body in a *vertical* trajectory. Which won't be strictly rigid anyway; because this necessarily involves losing your footing every two seconds, the next step is falling earthward slightly sideways and becoming entangled with your neighbors, which is as good a way as any of making new friends if not copping a graze of tit.

There is, however, one other aspect of audience appreciation which ain't nearly so cut: gobbing. For some reason this qualifies as news to everybody, so I'm gonna serve notice right here and now: LISTEN YA LITTLE PINHEADS, IT'S NAUSEATING AND MORONIC, AND I DON'T MEAN GOOD MORONOIC, I MEAN JERKED OFF, THE BANDS ALL HATE IT (the ones I talked to, anyway) AND WOULD ALL PLAY BETTER AND BE MUCH HAPPIER IF YOU FIGURED OUT SOME MORE ORIGINAL WAY OF SHOWING YOUR APPRECIATION.

(After the second night I asked Mick Jones about it and he looked like he was going to puke.

"But doesn't it add to the general atmosphere of chaos and anarchy?" I wondered.

"No," he said. "It's fucking disgusting.")

End of moral lecture. The Clash were a bit of a disappointment the first night. They played well, everything was in the right place, but the show seemed to lack energy somehow. A colleague who saw them a year ago had come back to the States telling me that they were the only group he'd ever seen onstage who were truly *wired*. It was this I was looking for and what I got in its place was mere professionalism, and hell, I could go let the Rolling Stones put me to sleep again if that was all I cared about.

Back in the dressing room I cracked, "Duff gig, eh fellas?" and they laughed, but you could tell they didn't think it was funny. Later I found out that Joe Strummer had an abscessed tooth which had turned into a glandular fever, and since the rest of the band draw their energy off him they were all suffering. By rights he should have taken a week off and headed straight for the nearest hospital, but he refused to cancel any gigs, no mere gesture of integrity.

A process of escalating admiration for this band had begun for me which was to continue until it broached something like awe. See, because it's easy to *sing* about your righteous politics, but as we all know actions speak louder than works, and the Clash are one of the very few examples I've seen where they would rather set an example by their personal conduct than *talk* about it all day.

Case in point. When we got back to their hotel I had a couple of interesting lessons to learn. First thing was they went up to their rooms while Ellie, Pennie, a bunch of fans and I sat in the lobby. I began to make with the grouch squawks because if there's one thing I have learned to detest over the years it's sitting around some goddamn hotel lobby like a soggy douchebag parasite waiting for some lousy high-and-mighty rock 'n' roll band to *maybe deign* to put in an imperial appearance.

But then a few minutes later the Clash came down and joined us and I realized that unlike most of the bands I'd ever met they weren't stuck up, weren't on a star trip, were in fact genuinely interesting in meeting and getting acquainted with their fans on a one-to-one, noncondescending level.

Mick Jones was especially sociable, so I moved in on him and commenced my second misinformed balls-up of the evening. A day or two earlier I'd asked a friend what sort of questions he thought might be appropriate for the Clash, and he'd said, "Oh, you might do what you did with Richard Hell and ask 'em just exactly what their political *program* is, what they intend to *do* once they get past all the bullshit rhetoric. Mind you, it's liable to get you thrown off the tour."

So, vainglorious as ever, I zeroed in on Mick and started drunkenly needling him with what I thought were devastating barbs. He just laughed at me and parried every one with a joke, while the fans chortled at the spectacle of this oafish American with all his dumbass sallies. Finally he looked me right in the eye and said, "Hey Lester, why are you asking *me* all these fucking questions?"

In a flash I realized that he was right. Here was I, a grown man, traveling all the way across the Atlantic Ocean and motoring up into the provinces of England, just to ask a goddamn rock 'n' roll band for the meaning of life! Some people never learn. I certainly didn't, because I immediately started in on him with my standard cultural-genocide rap: "Blah blah blah deporsonalization blab blab blab solipsism blah blah yip yap etc. . . . ."

"What in the fuck are you talking about?"

"Blah blab no one wants to have any emotions anymore blab blip human heart an endangered species blah blare cultural fascism blab blurb etc. etc. etc. . . . ."

"Well," says Mick, "don't look at *me*. If it bothers you so much why don't *you* do something about it."

"Yeah," says one of the fans, a young black punk girl sweet as could be, "You're depressing us *all*!"

Seventeen punk fan spike heads nod in agreement. Mick just keeps laughing at me.

Having bummed out almost the entire population of one room, I took my show into another: the bar, where I sat down at a table with Ellie and Paul Simonon and started in on them. Paul gets up and walks out. Ellie says, "Lester, you look a little tired. Are you sure you want another lager?"

Later I am out in the lobby with the rest of them again, in a state not far from a walking coma, when Mick gestured at a teenage fan sitting there and said, "Lester, my room is full tonight; can Adrian stay with you?"

I finally freaked. Here I was, stuck in the middle of a dying nation with all these funny looking *children* who didn't even realize the world was coming to an end, and now on top of everything else they expected me to turn my room into a hippie crash pad! I surmised through all my confusion that some monstrous joke was being played on me, so I got testy about it, Mick repeated the request and finally I said that Adrian could *maybe* stay but he would have to go to the house phone, call my hotel and see if there was room. So the poor humiliated kid did just that while an embarrassed if not downright creepy silence fell over the room and Mick stared at me in shock, as if he had never seen this particular species of so-called human before.

Poor Adrian came back saying there was indeed room, so I grudgingly assented, and back to the hotel we went. The next morning when I was in a more sober if still jet-lagged frame of mind, he showed me a copy of his Clash fanzine, *48 Thrills*, which I bought for 20p, and in the course of breakfast conversation I learned that the Clash make a regular practice of inviting their fans back from the gigs with them, and then go so far as to let them sleep on the floors of their rooms.

Now, dear reader, I don't know how much time you may have actually spent around big time rock 'n' roll bands—you may not think so, but the less you are the luckier in most cases—but let me assure you that the way the Clash treat their fans falls so far outside the normal run of these things as to be outright revolutionary. I'm going to say it and I'm going to say it slow: most rock stars are goddamn pigs who have the usual burly corps of hired thugs to keep the fans away from them at all costs, excepting the usual select contingent of lucky (?) nubiles who they'll maybe deign to allow up to their rooms for the privilege of sucking on their coveted wangers, after which often as not they get pitched out into the streets to find their way home without even cab fare. The whole thing is sick to the marrow, and I simply could not believe that any band, especially one as *musically* brutal as the Clash, could depart so far from this fetid norm.

I mentioned it to Mick in the van that day en route to Cardiff, also by way of making some kind of amends for my own behavior: "Listen, man, I've just got to say that I really *respect* you . . . I mean, I had not idea that any group could be as good to its fans as this . . . "

He just laughed. "Oh, so is that gonna be the hook for your story, then?"

And that for me is the essence of the Clash's greatness, over and beyond their music, why I fell in love with them, why it wasn't necessary to do any boring interviews with them about politics or the class system or any of that: Because here at last is a band which not only preaches something good but practices it as well, that instead of talking about changes in social behavior puts the model of a truly egalitarian society into practice for their own conduct.

The fact that Mick would make a joke out of it only shows how far they're going towards the realization of all the hopes we ever had about rock 'n' roll as utopian dream—because if rock 'n' roll *is* truly the democratic art form, then the democracy has got to begin at home; that is, the everlasting and totally disgusting walls between artists and audience must come down, elitism must perish, the "stars" have got to be humanized, demythologized, and the audience has got to be treated with more respect. Otherwise it's all a shuck, a rip-off, and the music is as dead as the Stones' and Led Zep's has become.

It's no news by now that the reason most of rocks' establishment have dried up creatively is that they've cut themselves off from the real world of everyday experience as exemplified by their fans. The ultimate question is how long a group like the Clash can continue to practice total egalitarianism in the face of mushrooming popularity. *Must* the walls go up inevitably, eventually, and if so when?

Groups like the Grateful Dead have practiced this free-access principle at least in the past, but the Dead never had glamour which, whether they like it or not (and I'd bet money they do) the Clash are saddled with—I mean, not for nothing does Mick Jones resemble a young and already slightly dissipated Keith Richards— beside which the Dead aren't really a rock 'n' roll band and the Clash are nothing else but. And just like Mick said to me the first night, don't ask me why I obsessively look to rock 'n' roll bands for some kind of model for a better society . . . I guess it's just that I glimpsed something beautiful in a flashbulb moment once, and perhaps mistaking it for a prophecy have been seeking its fulfillment ever since. And perhaps that nothing else in the world ever seem to hold even this much promise.

It may look like I make too much of all this. We could leave all significance at the picture of Mick Jones just as a hot guitarist in a white jumpsuit and a rock 'n' roll kid on the road obviously having the time of his life and all political pretensions be damned, but still there is a mood around the Clash, call it whatever you want, that is positive in a way I've never sensed around almost any other band, and I've been around most of them. Something unpretentiously moral, and something both self-affirming and life-affirming—as opposed, say, to the simple ruthless hedonism and avarice of so many superstars, or the grim taut-lipped monomaniacal ambition of most of the pretenders to their thrones.

But enough of all that. The highlight of the first day's bus ride occurred when I casually mentioned that I had a tape of the new Ramones album. The whole band practically leaped at my throat: "Why didn't you say so before? Shit, put it on *right now!*" So I did and in a moment they were bouncing all over the van to the strains of "Cretin Hop." *Rocket to Russia* thereafter became the soundtrack to the rest of my leg of the tour.

I am also glad to be able to tell everybody that the Clash are solid Muppets fans. (They even asked me if I had connections to get them on the show.) Their fave rave is Kermit, a pretty conventional choice if y'ask me—I'm a Fozzie Bear man myself. That night as we were walking into the hall for the gig in Cardiff, Paul said, "Hey, Lester, I just figured out why you like Fozzie Bear—the two of you look a lot alike!" And then he slaps me on the back.

All right, at this point I would like to say a few words about this Simonon fellow. Namely that HE LOOKS LIKE A MUPPET. I'm not sure which one, some kinda composite, but don't let that brooding visage in the photos fool you—this guy is a real clown. (Takes one to know one, after all.) He smokes a lot, and when he gets really out there on it makes with cartoon non sequiturs that nobody else can fathom (often having to do with manager Bernie), but stoned or not when he's talking to you and you're looking in that face you're staring right into a red-spiked big-eyed beaming cartoon, of whom it would probably not be amiss to say he lives for pranks. Onstage he's different; bouncing in and out of crouch, rarely smiling but in fact brooding over his fretboard ever in ominous motion, he takes on a distinctly simian aspect: the missing link, Cro-Magnon, Piltdown man, Cardiff giant.

It is undoubtedly this combination of mischievous boychild and Paleolithic primate which has sent swoonblips quavering through feminine hearts as disparate as Patti Smith and Caroline Coon—no doubt about it, Paul is the ladies' man of the group without half trying, and I doubt if there are very many gigs where he doesn't end up pogoing his pronger in some sweet honey's hive. Watch out, though, Paul—remember, clap does not a Muppet befit.

The gig in Cardiff presents quite a contrast to Derby. It's at a college, and anybody who has ever served time in one of those dreary institutions of lower pedantry will know what manner of douse that portends. Once again the band delivers maybe 60 percent of what I know they're capable of, but with an audience like this there's no blaming them. I'm not saying that all college students are subhuman—I'm just saying that if you aim to spend a few years mastering the art of pomposity, these are places where you can be taught by undisputed experts.

Here at Cardiff about five people are pogoing, all male, while the rest of the student bodies stand around looking at them with practiced expressions of aloof bemusement plastered on their mugs. After it's all over some cat goes back to interview Mick, and the most intelligent question he can think of is "What do you think of David Bowie?"

Meanwhile I got acquainted with the lead singer of the Lous, a good all-woman band from Paris. She says that she resents being thought of as a "woman musician," instead of a musician pure and simple, echoing a sentiment previously voiced to me by Talking Heads' Tina Weymouth. "It's a lot of bullshit," she says. I agree; what I don't say is that I am developing a definite carnal interest which I will be too shy to broach. I invite her back to our hotel; she says yes, then disappears.

When we get there it's the usual scene in the lobby, except that this time the management has thoughtfully set out sandwiches and beer. The beer goes down our gullets, and I'm just about to start putting the sandwiches to the same purpose when I discover somebody has other ideas; a clot of bread and egg salad goes whizzing to *splat* right in the back of my head! I look around and confront a solid wall of innocent faces. So I take a bite and *wham!* another one.

In a minute sandwiches are flying everywhere, everybody's getting pelted, I'm wearing a slice of cabbage on my head and have just about accepted this level of chaos when I smell something burning.

"Hey, Lester," somebody says, "You shouldn't smoke so much!" I reach around to pat the back of my head and—some joker has set my hair on fire! I pivot in my seat and Paul is looking at me, giggling. "Simonon you fuckhead—" I begin, only to smell more smoke, look under my chair where there's a piece of eight-by-ten paper curling up in flames. Cursing at the top of my lungs, I leap up and get a chair on the other side of the table where my back's to no one and I can keep an eye on the red-domed Muppet. Only trouble is that I'll find out a day or so hence that it wasn't him who set the fires at all: it was Bernie, the group's manager. Eventually the beer runs out, and Mick says he's hungry. Bernie refuses to let him take the van out hunting for open eateries, which we probably wouldn't be able to find at 4 A.M. in Cardiff anyway, and we all go to bed wearing egg salad.

Next morning sees us driving to Bristol, a large industrial city where we put up in a Holiday Inn, much to everyone's delight. By this time the mood around the band has combined with my tenacious jet-lag and liberal amounts of alcohol to put me into a kind of ecstasy state the like of which I have never known on the road before.

Past all the glory and the gigs themselves, touring in any form is a pretty drab and tiresome business, but with the Clash I feel that I have re-apprehended that aforementioned glimpse of some Better World of infinite possibilities, and so, inspired and a little delirious, I forgo my usual nap between van trip and showtime by which I'd hoped to eventually whip the jet-lag, spending the afternoon drinking cognac and writing.

By now I'm ready to go with the flow, with anything, as it has begun to seem to me, delusory or not, that there is some state of grace overlaying this whole project, something right in the soul that makes all the headache-inducing day-to-day pain-in-the-ass practical logistics run as smoothly as the tempers of the people involved, the whole enterprise sailing along in perfect harmony and in such dazzling contrast to the brutal logistics of Led Zep–type tours albeit on a much smaller level . . . somehow, whether it really is so or just a simple basic healthiness on the part of all involved heightened by my mental state, I have begun to see this trip as a somehow symbolic pilgrimage to that Promised Land that rock 'n' roll has cynically sneered at since the collapse of the sixties.

At this point, in my hotel room in Bristol, if six white horses and a chariot of gold had materialized in the hallway, I would have been no more surprised than at room service, would've just climbed right in and settled back for that long-promised ascent to endless astral weeks in the heavenly land.

What I got instead around 6 P.M. was a call from Joe Strummer saying meet him in the lobby in five minutes if I wanted to go to the sound check. So I floated down the elevators and when I got there I saw a sheepish group of little not-quite punks all huddled around one couch. They were dressed in half-committed punk regalia, a safety pin here and there, a couple of little slogans chalked on their school blazers, their hair greased and twisted up into a cosmetic weekend approximation of spikes. "Hey," I said, "You guys Clash fans?"

"Well," they mumbled, "Sorta . . ."

"Well, whattaya mean? You're punks, aren't ya?"

"Well, we'd like to be . . . but we're *scared* . . ."

When Joe came down I took him aside and, indicating the poor little things, told him what they'd said, also asking if he wanted to get them into the gig with us and thus offer a little encouragement for them to take that next, crucial step out into full-fledged punk pariahdom and thus sorely needed self-respect.

"Forget it," he said. "If they haven't got the courage to do it on their own, I'm bloody well not gonna lead 'em on by the hand."

On the way to the sound check I mentioned that I thought the band hadn't been as good as I knew they could be the previous two nights, adding that I hadn't wanted to say anything about it.

"Why not?" he said.

I realized that I didn't have an answer. I tell this story to point out something about the Clash, and Joe Strummer in particular, that both impressed and showed me up for the sometimes hypocritical "diplomat" I can be. I mean their simple, straightforward honesty, their undogmatic insistence on the truth and why worry about stepping on people's toes because if we're not straight with each other we're never going to get anything accomplished anyway.

It seems like such a simple thing, and I suppose it is, but it runs contrary to almost everything the music business runs on: the hype, the grease, the glad-handing. And it goes a long way towards creating that aforementioned mood of positive clarity and unpreachy morality. Strummer himself, at once the "leader" of the group (though he'd deny it) and the least voluble (though his sickness might have had a lot to do with it), conveys an immediate physical and personal impact of ground-level directness and honesty, a no-bullshit concern with cutting straight to the heart of the matter in a way that is not brusque or impatient but concise and distinctly non-frivolous.

Serious without being solemn, quiet without being remote or haughty, Strummer offers a distinct contrast to Mick's voluble wit and twinkle of eye and Paul's loony tune playfulness. He is almost certainly the group's soul, and I wish I could say I had gotten to know him better.

From the instant we hit the hall for the sound check we all sense that tonight's gig is going to be a hot one. The place itself looks like an abandoned meatpacking room—large and empty with cold stone floors and stark white walls. It's plain dire, and in one of the most common of rock 'n' roll ironies the atmosphere is perfect and the acoustics great.

While the Clash are warming up at their sound check, they play something very funky which I later discover is a Booker T. number, thus implanting an idea in my mind which later grows into a conviction that in spite of the brilliance manifested in things like "White Riot," they actually play better and certainly more interestingly when they *slow down* and get, well, funky. You can hear it in the live if not studio version of "Police and Thieves," as well as in "White Man in Hammersmith Palais," probably the best thing they've written.

Somewhere in their assimilation of reggae is the closest thing yet to the lost chord, the missing link between black music and white noise, rock capable of making a bow to black forms without smearing on the blackface. It's there in Mick's intro to "Police and Thieves" and unstatedly in the band's whole onstage attitude. I understand why all these groups thought they had to play 120 miles per hour these last couple of years—to get us out of the bog created by everything that preceded them this decade—but the point has been made, and I for one could use a little funk, especially from somebody as good at is as the Clash. Why should any great rock 'n' roll band do what's *expected* of 'em anyhow? The Clash are a certain idea in many people's minds, which is only all the more reason why they should *break* that idea and broach something else. Just one critic's opinion y'understand but that's what god put us here for.

In any case, tonight is the payload. The band is taut terror from the instant they hit the stage, everything they're supposed to be and more. I reflect for the first time that I have never seen a band that *moved* like this: with most of 'em you can see the rock 'n' roll steps choreographed five minutes in advance, but the Clash hop around each other in all configurations totally non-self-consciously, galvanized by their music alone, Jones and Simonon changing places at the whims of the whams coming out of their guitars, springs in the soles of their tennis shoes.

Strummer, obviously driven to make up to this audience the loss of energy suffered by the last two nights' crowds, is an angry live wire whipping around the middle of the front stage, divesting himself of guitar to fall on one knee in no Elvis parody but pure outside-of-self frenzy, snarling through his shattered dental bombsite with face screwed up in all the rage you'd need to convince you of the Clash's authenticity, a desperation uncontrived, unstaged, a fury unleashed on the stage and writhing in upon itself in real pain that connects with the nerves of the audience like summer thunderbolts, and at this time pogoing reveals itself as such a pitifully insufficient response to a man by all appearances trapped and screaming, and it's not your class system, it's not Britain-on-the-wane, it's not even glandular fever, it's the cage of life itself and all the anguish to break through which sometimes translates as flash or something equally petty but in any case is rock 'n' roll's burning marrow.

It was one of those performances for which all the serviceable critical terms like "electrifying" are so pathetically inadequate, and after it was over I realized the futility of hitting Strummer for that interview I kept putting off on the "politics" of the situation. The politics of rock 'n' roll, in England or America or anywhere else, is that a whole lot of kids want to be fried out of their skins by the most scalding propulsion they can find, for a night they can pretend is the rest of their lives, and whether the next day they go back to work in shops or to boredom on the dole or American TV doldrums in Mom 'n' Daddy's living room, nothing can cancel the reality of that night in the revivifying flames when for once if only then in your life, you were blasted outside of yourself and the monotony which defines most life anywhere at any time, when you supped on lightning and nothing else in the realms of the living or dead mattered at all.

PART TWO

Back at the hotel everybody decides to reconvene in the Holiday Inn's bar to celebrate this back-in-form gig. I stop off by my room and while sitting on the john start reading an article in *Newsweek* called "Is America Turning Right?" (Ans: yes.) It's so strange to be out here in the middle of a foreign land, reading about your own country and realizing how at home you feel where you have come, how much your homeland is the foreign, alien realm.

This feeling weighed on me more and more heavily the longer

I stayed in England—on previous visits I'd always been anxious to get back to the States, and New York homesickness ash become a congenital disease whenever I travel. But I have felt for so long that there is something dead, rotten, and cold in American culture, not just in the music but in the society at every level down to for-mularized stasis and entropy, and the supreme irony is that all I ever read in *NME* is how fucked-up life is for you guys, when to me your desperation seems like health and my country's pabulum complacency seems like death.

I mean, at least you got some stakes to play for. *Our* National Front has already won, insidiously invisible as a wall socket. The difference is that for you No Future means being thrown on the slagheap of economic refuse, for me it means an infinity of televi-sion mirrors that tell the most hideous lies lapped up by my nation of technocratic Trilbys. A little taste of death in every mass inoculation against the bacteria of doubt.

But then I peeked behind the shower curtain: Marisa Berenson was there. "I've got films of you shitting," I said.

"So what?" she said. " I just sold the negatives to WPLJ for their next TV ad. They're gonna have it in neon laserium. I'll be *immortal*."

I mean, would you wanna be a ball bearing? That's how all the television families feel and that's how I feel when I go to discos, places where people *cultivate* their ball bearingness. In America, that is. So what did I go down into now but the Bristol ('member Bristol?) Holiday Inn's idea of a real swinging disco where vaca-tioning Americanskis could feel at home. I felt like climbing right up the walls, but there were girls there, and the band seemed amused and unafraid of venturing within the witches' cauldron of disco ionization which is genocide in my book, buddy, but then us Americans do have a tendency to take things a bit far.

• • •

This club reminded me of everything I was hosannah-glad to escape when I left New York: flashing dance floors, machine music at ball-peen volumes, lights aflash that it's all whole bulb or gone bollixed FUN FUN FUN hostility: grinding of teeth, hissing of breath, balling and banging of fists off fake Naugahyde. Fat lot of good it'll do ya, kid. Discotheques are concentration camps, like Pleasure Island in Walt Disney's *Pinocchio*. You play that goddam Baccara record one more time, Dad, or your nose is gonna grow and we're gonna saw it off into toothpicks.

I'm seething in barely suppressed rage when Glen Malock, a puckish pup with more than a hint of wry in his eye, leans across the Lucite teentall flashlight pina colada table and says, "Hey, wanna hear an advance tape of the Rich Kids album?"

"Sure!" You can see immediately why Glen got kicked out of the Pistols: I wouldn't trust one of these clean pop whiz kids with a hot lead pole. But I would tell 'em to say hello. I don't give a shit for the Raspberries and Glen looks an awful lot like Eric Carmen—except I can't help but gotta say its not such a *sissy*— and it's all Paul McCartney's fault anyway, and I mean McCartney *ca.* Beatles wonderwaxings we all waned and wuvved so well, but in spite of all gurgling bloody messes we're just gonna have to keep on dealing with these emissaries from the land of Bide-a-Wee and His Imperial Pop the Magic Dragon, besides which I'd just danced to James Brown and needed some Coppertone oil and Band-Aids.

Let's see, how else can I insult this guy, shamepug rippin' off the galvanic force of our PUNK flotilla with his courtly gestures in the lateral of melody, harmonies, Hollies, all those lies? So he puts it on his tape deck and it's the old Neil Diamond–penned Monkees 'tune, "I'm a Believer."

"Hey!" I said. "That's fuckin' *good*! That's *great*! You gotta hel-luva band there! Better than the original!"

Ol' Puck he just keeps sitting back sipping his drink, laughing at me through lighthouse teeth. Has this tad heard "Muskrat Love"?

"Whattaya *laughin'* at?" I quack. "I'm *serious*. Glen, anybody that can cut the Monkees at their own riffs is okay in my book!"

Then the next song comes on. It's also a Monkees tune. "Hey, what is this—you gonna make your first album *The Monkees' Greatest Hits?*"

Well, I know I'm not the world's fastest human . . . from the time it was released until about six months ago I thought Brian Wilson was singing "She's giving me *citations*" (instead of the factual "excitations") in "Good Vibrations"; I thought the song was about a policewoman he fell in love with or something. So far as I'm concerned the Rich Kids SHOULD make their first album (call it this too, beats *Never Mind the Bollocks* by miles) *The Monkees' Greatest Hits*. I'd buy it. *Everybody*'d buy it. Not only that, you could count on all the rock critics in *NME* to write lengthy analyses of the conceptual quagmire behind this whole helpful heaping scamful—I mean, let's see Malcolm top that one. Come to think of it, the coolest thing the Pistols could have done when they finally got around to releasing their album would be to've called it *Eric Clapton*. Who cares how much it helps sales, think of the *important* part: the *insult*. Plus a nice surprise for subscribers to *Guitar Player* magazine, would-be closet hearth-side Holm-strummed Djangos, etc. *They* don't want a baby that looks like that, even if its last name is Gibson. Les Paul, where are you? Gone skateboarding, I guess.

With Dick Dale.

Oh yeah, the Clash. Well, closing time came along as it always has a habit of doing at obscenely pubescent hours in England—I mean, what is this eleven o'clock shit anyway? Anarchy for me means the bars stay open twenty-four hours a day. Hmmm, guess that makes Vegas the model of the Anarchic Society. Okay, Malcolm, Bernie, and whoever else manages all those snorkers and droners all over the place, it's uproots lock, stock, and barrel time, drop the whole mess right in the middle of Caesar's Palace, and since Johnny Rotten is obviously a hell of a lot smarter than Hunter S. Thompson, we got ourselves a whole new American Dream here. No, guess it wouldn't work, bands on the dole can't afford anything past the slot machines, cancel that one. We go up to Mick's room for beer and talk instead.

He's elated and funny though somewhat subdued. I remark that I haven't seen any groupies on this tour and ask him if he ever hies any of the local honeys up to bed and if so why not tonite?

Mick looks more tired, more wasted than he actually is (contrary to his git-pikkin' hero, he eschews most all forms of drugs most all of the time) (whole damn healthy bunch, this—not a bent-spoon man or parlous freaksche in the lot). "We don't get into all of that much. You saw those girls out there—most of 'em are too young." (Quite true, more later.) "But groupies . . . I dunno, just never see that many I guess. I've got a girlfriend I get to see about once a month, but other than that . . ." he shrugs. "When you're plain' this much, you don't need it so much. Sometimes I feel like I'm losin' interest in sex entirely.

"Don't get me wrong. We're a band of regular blokes. It's just that a lot of that stuff you're talking about doesn't seem to . . . apply."

See, didn't I tell you it was the Heavenly Land? The Clash are not only not sexist, they are so healthy they don't even have to *tell* you how unsexist they are; no sanctimony, no phonies, just ponies and miles and miles of green Welsh grass with balls bouncing . . .

Now I will repeat myself from part one that THIS is exactly and precisely what I mean by Clash = model for New Society: a society of *normal* people, by which I mean that we are surrounded by queers, and I am not talking about gay people. I'm talking about . . . well, when lambs draw breath in Albion with Sesame Street Crayolas, we won't see no lovers runnin' each other's bodies down, get me. I mean fuck this and fuck that, but make love when the tides are right and I *do* want a baby that looks like that. And so, secretly smiling across the rain, does William Blake.

Next day was a long drive southwest. Actually this being Sunday and my three days' assignment up I'm s'posed to go back to London, but previous eventide when I'd told Mick this he'd asked me to stick around and damned if I didn't—a first for me. Usually you just wanna get home, get the story out and head beerward.

But as y'all can see my feelings about the Clash had long ago gotten way beyond all the professional malarkey: we liked hanging out together. Besides which I still kept a spyglass out for that Promised Land's colors so sure to come a-blowin' around every fresh hillock curve, hey there moocow say hello to James Joyce for me, gnarly carcasses of trees the day before had set to mind the voices Under Milk Wood . . . land rife with ghosts who don't come croonin' around no Post Houses way past midnite with Automatic Slim and Razor-Totin' Jim, no, the reality is you could be touring Atlantis and it'd still look like motorway::carpark::gasstop::pissbreak::souvenir shop::et deadening cetera . . .

Joe kills the dull van hours with Nazitrocity thrillers by Sven Hassel, Mick is just about to start reading Kerouac's *The Subterraneans* but borrows my copy of Charles Bukowski's new book *Love Is a Dog from Hell* instead, which flips him out so the next two day he keeps passing it around the van trying to get the other guys to read certain poems like the one about the poet who came onstage to read and vomited in the grand piano instead (and woulda done it again too) but they seem unimpressed, Joe wrapped up in his storm troopers and Paul spliffing in big-eyed-space monkey glee playing the new Ramones over and over and every time Joey shouts "LOBOTOMAAY!!" at the top of side two he pops a top out of somebody's head, the pogo beginning to make like spirogyra, sprintillatin' all over the place, tho' it's true there's no stoppin' the cretins from hoppin' once they start they're like *germs* that jump. Meanwhile poor little Nicky Headon the drummer who I won't get to know really well this trip is bundling his jacket tighter in the front seat and swigging cough mixture in an unsuccessful attempt to ward off miserable bronchoid. At one point Mickey, the driver, a big thick-necked lug with a skinhead haircut, lets Nicky take the wheel and we go skittering all over the road.

Golly gee, you must get bored reading such stuff. Did you know that this toot is costing IPC (who for all I know put out not just *NME* but also a you're-still-alive monthly newsletter for retired rear admirals of the Guianan Fleet) seven and a half cents a word? An equitable deal, you might assert, until you consider that in this scheme of things, such diverse organisms as "salicyla-ceous" and "uh" receive equal recompense, talk about your class systems or lack of same. NOW you know why 99 percent of all publicly printed writers are hacks, because clichés pay as good as pearls, although there is a certain unalloyed ineluctable Ramonesque-like logic to the way these endless reams of copy just plow on thru and thru all these crappy music papers like one thick plug pencil's line pile driving from here on out to Heaven.

I mean look, face it, both reader and writer know that almost all of what's gonna pass from the latter to the former is justa bunchah jizjaz anyway, so why not just give up the ghost of pretense to form and subject and just make these rags ramble fit to the trolley you prob'ly read 'em on . . . you may say that I take liberties, and you are right, but I will have done my good deed for the day if I can make you see that the whole point is YOU SHOULD BE TAKING LIBERTIES TOO. Nothing is inscribed so deep in the earth a little eyewash won't uproot it, that's the whole point of the so-called "new wave"—to REINVENT YOURSELF AND EVERYTHING AROUND YOU CONSTANTLY—especially since all of it is already the other thing anyway, the Clash a broadside a pamphlet an urgent handbill in a taut and moving fist, *NME* staff having advertised themselves a rock 'n' roll band for so many years nobody can deny 'em now, as you are writing history that I read, as you are he as I am we as weasels all together, Jesus am I turning into Steve Hillage or David Allen, over the falls in any case but at least we melted the walls leaving home plate clear for baseball in the snow.

Are you an imbecile? If so, apply today for free gardening stamp books at the tube stop of your choice. Think of the promising career that may be passing you by *at this very moment* like a Greyhound. Nobody loves a poorhouse Nazi. Dogs are more alert than most clerks.

Plan 9: In America there is such a crying need for computer operators they actually put ads on commercial TV begging people to sign up. British youth are massively unemployed. Relocate the entire under-twenty-five population of Britain to training centers in New Jersey and Massachusetts. Teach them all to tap out codes. Give them lots of speed and let them play with their computers night and day. Then put them on TV smiling with pinball eyes: "Hi! I used to be a lazy sod! But then I discovered COMPUTRO-CIDE DYNAMICS, INC., and it's changed my life completely! I'm happy! I'm useful! I walk, talk, dress, and act normal! I'm an up and coming go-getter in a happening industry! Good Christ, Mabel, I've got a *job*." He begins to bawl maudlinly, drooling and dribbling sentimental mucus out his nose. "And to think . . . that only two months ago I was stuck back in *England* . . . unemployed, unemployable, no prospects, no respect, a worthless hunk of human shit! Thank you, Uncle Sam!"

So don't go tellin' me you're bored with the USA, buddy. I've heard all that shit one too many pinko punko times. We'll just drink us these two more beers and then go find a bar where you know everybody is drinkin' beer they bought with money they earned by the sweat of their brows, from *workin'*; get me, buddy? Cause I got a right to work. Niggers got a right to work, too. Same as white men. When your nose is pushin' up grindstone you got no time to worry about the size of the other guy's snout. Because you know, like I know, like both the Vienna Boys Choir and the guy who sells hot watches at Sixth Avenue and Fourteenth Street know, that we were born for one purpose and one purpose only: TO WORK. *Haul* that slag! Hog that slod! Whelp that mute and look at us: at our uncontestable NOBILITY; at our national biological PRIDE; at our stolid steroid HOPE.

Who says it's a big old complicated world? I'll tell ya what it comes down to, buddy: one word: JOB. You got one, you're okay, scot-free, a prince in fact in your own hard-won domain! You don't got one, you're a miserable slug and a drag on this great nation's economically rusting drainpipes. You might just as well go drown yourself in mud. We need the water to conserve for honest upright workin' folks! Folks with the godsod sense to treat that job like GOLD. 'Cause that's just what it stands for and WHY ELSE DO YOU THINK I KEEP TELLING YOU IT'S THE MOST IMPORTANT THING IN THE UNIVERSE? Your ticket to human citizenship.

One man, one job. One dog, one stool.

The hotel has a lobby and coffee shop which look out upon a body of water. No one can figure out whether it's the English Channel or not. Even the waitresses don't know. I'm feeling good, having slept in the afternoon, and there's a sense in the air that everybody's up for the gig. Last night consolidated energies; tonight should be the payload.

We wind through narrow streets to a small club that reminds me much of the slightly sleazy little joints where bands like the Iron Butterfly and Strawberry Alarm Clock, uh, got their *chops* together, or, uh, paid whatever *dues* were expected of them when they were coming up and I was in school. This type of place you can write the script before you get off the bus; manager a fat middle-aged brute who glowers over waitresses and rock bands equally, hates the music, hates the kids but figures there's money to be made. The décor inside is ersatz-tropicana, suggesting that this place has not so long ago been put to uses far removed from punk rock. Enrico Cadillac vibes.

I walk in the dressing room which actually is not a dressing room but a miniscule space partitioned off where three bands are supposed to set up, almost literally on top of one another. The Voidoids' Bob Quine walks in, takes a look, and lays his guitar case on the floor: "Guess this is it."

Neither of the opening acts has been getting the audience response they deserve on this tour. These are Clash audiences, people who know all their songs by heart, have never heard of the Lous and maybe are vaguely familiar with Richard Hell. Richard is depressed because his band isn't getting the support he hoped for from their record company on this trek. The *Blank Generation* album hasn't been released yet—the Voidoids think it's because Sire wants to flog a few more import copies, although I hear later in the week that strikes have shut down all the record pressing plants in Britain. The result is that the kids in the audience don't know most of the songs, the lyrics, nothing but the

Ork/Stiff EP to go on, so they settle for gobbing on the band, screaming for the Clash.

I tell Hell and Quine that I have never heard the band so tight, which is true—there's just no way that night-after-night playing, in no matter how degraded circumstances, can't put more gristle and fire in your music. Interestingly enough, Ivan Julian and Marc Bell, Hell's second guitarist and drummer, are both in good spirits—they've toured before, know what to expect.

Someday Quine will be recognized for the pivotal figure that he is on his instrument—he is the first guitarist to take the breakthroughs of early Lou Reed and Maes Williamson and work through them to a new, individual vocabulary, driven into odd places by obsessive attention to *On the Corner*–era Miles Davis. Of course I'm prejudiced, because he played on my records as well, but he is one of the few guitarists I know who can handle the super technology that is threatening to swallow players and instruments whole—"You gotta hear this new box I got," is how he'll usually preface his latest discovery, "it creates the most *offensive noise* . . ."—without losing contact with his musical emotions in the process. Onstage he projects the cool remote stance learned from his jazz mentors—shades, beard, expressionless face, bald head, old sportscoat—but his solos always burn, the more so because there is always something constricted in them, pent up, waiting to be released.

Tonight's crowd is good—they respond instinctively to the Voidoids though they're unfamiliar with them, and it doesn't seem at all odd to see kids pogoing to Quine's Miles Davis riffs. (He steals from *Agharta!* And makes it *work!*) Hell and the Voidoids get the only encore on my leg of the tour, and they make good use of it, bringing Glen Matlock out to play bass. The Clash's set is brisk, hot, clean—consensus among us fellow travelers is that it's solid but lacks the cutting vengeance of last night.

Even on a small stage—and this one is tiny—the group are in constant motion, snapping in and out of one another's territory with electrified springs and lunges that have their own grace, nobody knocking knees or bumping shoulders, even as the Voidoids in certain states which they hate and I think among their best, reel and spin in hair's-breadth near-collisions with each other that are totally graceless but supremely driven. You can really see why Tom Verlaine wanted Hell out of Television—he flings himself all over the stage as if battering furiously at the gates of some bolted haven, and if Ivan and Bob know when to dodge you can also see plainly why Hell would have been in a group called the Heartbreakers—because that sumbitch is hard as oak, and he's just looking for the proper axe because something inside seethes poisonously to be let out.

In the dressing room I met some fans. There was Martin, who was fourteen and had a band of his own called Crissus. I thought Martin was a girl until I heard his name (no offense, Martin), but look at it this way: here, on some remote southern shore of the old Isle, this kid who is just entering puberty, this *child,* has been so inspired by the new wave that he is already starting to make his move. I asked him whether Crissus had recorded yet, and he laughed: "Are you kidding?"

"Why not? Everbody else is." (Not said cynically either.)

I asked Martin what he liked about the Clash in particular as opposed to other new wave bands. His reply: "Their total physical and psychic resistance to the fascist imperialist enemies of the people at all levels, and their understanding of the distinction between art and propaganda. They know that the propaganda has to be palatable to the People if they're going to be able to (a) listen to it, (b) understand it, and (c) react to it, rising in a People's War. They recognize that the form must be as revolutionary as the content —in Cuba they did it with radio and ice cream and baseball and boxing, with the understanding that sports and music are the most effective vectors for communist ideology. Rock 'n' roll as a form is anarchistic, but if we could just figure out some way to make the *content* as compelling as the form *then* we'd be getting somewhere!

"For the present, we must recognize that there is only so much revolutionary information that can be transmitted in so circumscribed a space and time, and so we must be content in the knowledge that the potency of form ensures the efficacy of content, that is, that the driving primitive African beat and boar-like guitars will keep bringing the audience back for repeated hypnotized listenings until the revolutionary message laid out plainly in the lyrics cannot help but sink in!"

Martin was bright for his age. Not quite as bright as all that, though. Or maybe brighter. Because of course he didn't say that. I made that up. What Martin said was, "I like the Clash because of their clothes!"

And so it went with all the other fans I interviewed over the six nights I saw them. *Nobody* mentioned politics, not even the dole, and I certainly wasn't going to start giving them cues. This night, I got such typical response as: "Their sound—I dunno, it just makes you jump!" "The music, which is exciting, and the lyrics, which are heavy, and the way they look onstage!" (which is stripped down to zippers and denims for instant combat, or perhaps stage flexibility).

As we were all still wandering out, Mick in the middle of a cluster of fans as usual, not soaking up adoration but genuinely interested in getting to know them, about halfway between bandstand and door, the owner of the club began making noises about "bleeding punk rockers—try to have a decent club, they come in here and mess it up . . ."

Mick looked at him indifferently. "Bollocks."

"Look, you lot, clear out now, we don't want your kind hanging round here," and of course he had his little oaf militia to hustle them toward the exits. Finally I said to him, "If you dislike them so much, why don't you open a different kind of club?"

Instantly he was up against me, belly and breath and menace: "What're you lookin' for, some trouble, then?"

"No, I just asked you a question."

You know, it's like all the other similar scenes you've ever seen all your life—YOU REALLY DON'T WANT TO GET INTO SOME KIND OF STUPID VIOLENCE WITH THESE PEOPLE, but you finally just get tired of being herded like swine.

When we got out front a few Teds showed up—first I'd seen in England, really, and I had the impulse to go glad-handing up to them every inch the Yankee tourist gawker dodo: "Hey, you're *Teds,* aren't you? I've heard about you guys! You don't like anything after Gene Vincent! Man, you guys are one bunch of stubborn motherfuckers!"

I didn't do that, though—I looked at Mick and the fans, and they looked wary, staring at indistinct spots like you do when you scent violence in the air and don't want it. They were treading lightly. But then, outside of certain scenes with each other, almost all the punks I've ever seen tread lightly! They're worse than hippies! More like beatniks.

But what was really funny was that the Teds were treading lightly too—they just sort of shuffled up with their dates, in their ruffled shirts and velour jackets and started muttering generalities: "Bleedin' punks . . . shit . . . buncha bloody freaks . . ." Really, you had to strain to hear them. They seemed almost embarrassed. It was like they had to do it.

I had never seen anything quite like it in the U.S., because aside from certain ethnic urban gangs, there is nothing in the U.S. quite like the Teds-Punks thing. We've got bikers, but even bikers claim contemporaneity. The Teds seem as sad as the punks seemed touching and oddly inspiring—these people know that time has passed them by, and they are not entirely wrong when they assert that it's time's defect and not their own. They remember one fine moment in their lives when everything— music, sex, dreams—seemed to coalesce, when they could tell everybody trying to strap them to the ironing board to get fucked and know in their bones that they were right. But that moment passed, and they got scared, just like kids in the U.S. are mostly scared of new wave, just like people I know who freak out when I put on Miles Davis records and beg me to take them off because there is something in them so emotionally huge and threatening that it's plan "depressing."

The Teds were poignant for me, even more so because their style of dress made them as absurd to us as we were to them (but in a different way—they look "quaint," a very final dismissal). They looked like people who had had a glimpse and were supping at the dry bone of that memory forever, but man, that glimpse, just *try* to take it away from me, punk motherfucker . . . Not that the punks are trying to infringe on the Teds; just that unlike the punks, who pay socially for their stance but at least have the arrogance of their freshness, the Teds looked like people backed into a final corner by a society which simply can't accept anybody getting loose.

In America you can ease into middle age with the accoutrements of adolescence still prominent and suffer relatively minor embarrassment: okay, so the guy's still got his sideburns and rod and beer and beer gut and wife and three kids and a duplex and never grew up. So what? You're not supposed to grow up in America. You're supposed to consume. But in Britain it seems there is some ideal, no, some dry river one is expected to ford, so you can enter that sedate bubble where you raise a family, contribute in your small way to your society and keep your mouth shut. Until you get old, that is, when you can become an "eccentric"—do and say outrageous things, naughty things, because it's expected of you, you've crossed to the other mirror of the telescope of childhood.

In between, it looks like quiet desperation all the way to an outsider. All that stiff-upper-lip, carry-on shit. If Freud was right when he said that all societies are based on repression, then England must be the apex of Western civilization. There was a recently published conversation between Tennessee Williams and William Burroughs, in which Burroughs said he didn't like the English because their social graces had evolved to a point where they could be entertaining all evening for the rest of their lives but nobody ever told you anything personal, anything *real* about themselves. I think he's right. We've got the opposite problem in American right now—in New York City today there's a TV talk show host who's so narcissistic that every Wednesday he lays down on a couch and pours out his insecurities to his analyst . . . *on the air!*

You guys strike me as a whole lot of people who laugh at the wrong time, who constantly study the art of concealment. Then again, it occurs to me that it could actually be that there is something irritating me that you don't suffer from—which is certainly not meant as self-aggrandizement on my part—but that you've been around awhile, have come to wry terms with your indigenous diseases, whereas we Americans got bugs under our skin that make us all twitch in Nervous Norvusisms that must amuse you highly. But even here there is a difference—at our best we recognize our sickness, and struggle constantly to deal with it. You're real big on sweeping dirt under the carpet. So it's no wonder that, like Johnny Rotten says, you've got "problems"—more like boils bursting, I'd say.

And now, as I get ready to close off, I feel uncomfortably pompous and smug—I'll be back with the payoff next week, the sum of what I see in this whole "punk" movement, for anybody who wants to hear it—but here I sit on what feels like a sweeping and enormously presumptuous generalization on not just the punks but your whole country.

Well, then, let the fool make a fool out of himself, but I'll tell you one thing: the Teds are a hell of a symptom of the rot in your society, much more telling in their way than the punks, because the punks, much as they go on about boredom and no future, at least offer possibilities, whereas the Teds are landlocked. You cocksuckers have effectively enclosed these people, who are only trying to not give up some of their original passion in the interests of total homogenization, in an invisible concentration camp. Your contempt stymies them, so they strike out at the only people who are more vulnerable and passive than they are: the punks.

The almost saintly thing about the punks is that for the most part they don't seem to find it necessary to strike out with that sort of viciousness against anybody—except themselves.

So to anyone who is reading this who is in a position of "status," "responsibility," "power," unlike the average *NME* reader, I say congratulations—you've created a society of cannibals and suicides.

PART THREE

Recent history is the record of the vast conspiracy to impose one level of mechanical consciousness on mankind and exterminate all manifestations of that unique part of human sentience . . . which the individual shares with his Creator. The suppression of contemplative individuality is near complete.

The only immediate historical data that we can know and act on are those fed to our senses through systems of mass communication.

These media are exactly the places where the deepest and most personal sensitivities and confessions of reality are most prohibited, mocked, suppressed. . . .

A few individuals, poets, have had the luck and courage and fate to glimpse something new through the crack in mass consciousness . . . the police and newspapers have moved in, mad movie manufacturers from Hollywood are at this moment preparing bestial stereotypes of the scene. . . .

How many hypocrites are there in America? How many trembling lambs, fearful of discovery? What authority have we set up over ourselves, that we are not as we Are?

—Allen Ginsberg, "Poetry, Violence, and the Trembling Lambs"

We're still standing around in front of the club, and Mick Jones and I have been talking to three fans who've hitchhiked from Dover for the gig. They're invited back to the hotel in the more or less loose way these things happen, and Mick looks at me: "Lester, can you put them up in your room tonight?"

It's two girls and a guy and my room is small but they're nice and the conversation's been good so far so I say sure if they don't mind sleeping on the floor. We all climb in the van and immediately Mickey, the driver, begins to bitch about having to carry extra people.

He's not the most sanguine guy in the world but it's been a long drive from Bristol and cats like him got no stage to let it out on. So I try to mollify him a bit, telling him he's like Neal Cassady (because on those long stretches of motorway he is).

"Yeah," he snaps. "I'm drivin' a *star!*"

When we get back to the hotel the surliness escalates. I'm wandering around the lobby trying to locate some beer, so I miss the first part of the trouble. The fans, Mickey the driver, Mick's friend and traveling companion Robin, Paul Simonon, and Nicky Headon sitting there, and the sandwiches are flying as usual, so at first I don't notice what's going on. But when I sit down in my chair I realize that most of the sandwiches are being thrown by Mickey and Robin and the male fan.

I look around at the fan, who seems to be wearing bits of tomato, egg, lettuce, mayonnaise, and bread all over his body and who is shrinking back in his chair in the most abject humiliation. Confused, I hand him a beer and tell him it's all right.

Mickey: "It is *not* all right!" He leaps up and runs across to us, pummeling the fan with his fists. The kid tries to roll up in a ball. A moment later Robin is over; first he grinds the remainder of the sandwich glop all in the kid's hair and clothes, then he's grabbed a cushion off one of the chairs and is smothering his face in it. Finally everybody sits down, and an ugly silence falls.

I don't want to get my face punched in, but finally I've got to say something. I look at Mickey, speaking calmly. "Why are you acting like such an asshole?"

"What's an asshole?" he demands.

"There are all kinds," I say. "You just know one when you see one."

"That little fucker fucked up my jacket!"

He indicates a small stain on his windbreaker.

"So what?" I say. "If you're gonna start throwing sandwiches you've gotta expect stuff like that."

"We didn't start it—*he* did," says Mickey.

"Oh," I say, knowing full well it's a lie.

Another even nastier silence. Finally I say, "Well, I'm sorry about your jacket. You must value it a lot."

"Fucking right I do."

"Would you have punched one of them if they'd stained it?" I ask, indicating Paul and Nicky, who are still sitting there in silence.

"Yeah." Then he starts in on me, verbally, trying to incite whatever he can. I won't bore you with the details.

After a few minutes, Robin stands up and asks me if I want to go up to Mick's room. After everything that has just happened, I can sit there and say, "Yeah, that sounds pretty good." I look at Liz, one of the girl fans.

"Wanna go up and see Mick?"

"No," she says.

So the three fans and I head for the elevator to my room. Somehow, only when we get there does the full sense of the scene just past hit me. "I guess they're hypocrites, aren't they?" says the kid with food smeared all over him. The girls are incensed. It won't be until tomorrow that it occurs to me that I've been reading *The War Against the Jews,* trying to figure out how a whole nation could stand by and let atrocities happen, yet I sit there somehow *refusing to perceive* for several minutes that someone sitting right next to me was being verbally abused and physically brutalized for no reason at all.

By the time we get up to my room the kid is already making excuses for the Clash. "I'm not mad at anybody," he's saying. "It's not the band's fault."

By this time I'm seething. "What do you mean? They sat right there and let it happen! I sat right there and let it happen! What gives anybody the right to do shit like that to you?"

I curse myself again and again for not having acted. Because now I'm sitting in my room, heart pounding, nerves which I've pushed to the breaking point by now pacing myself on this tour twitching, uptight, and itching to smash somebody in the face. I realize that that *goon* down there has only infected me with his own poison but there is nothing I can do about it except try vainly to cool out.

The girls are enraged at the Clash, the kid is slowly admitting to his own anger past utter mortification, and we keep hashing it over and over until we realize that's not going to do us any good. So the conversation turns to other things. The kid works in a hotel in Torquay, a really swanky place, and regales us with stories of some of the foibles and antics of famous guests such as Henry Kissinger and Frank Sinatra. He tells us what pigs most of the big-name rock groups that have stayed there are. The only guests who are worse than the rock stars, he says, are the Arabs. When the rock stars leave, the rooms are decimated; when the Arabs leave, they're decimated and full of bullet holes. Which of course brings us right back to tonight's incident.

"What they don't realize," he says, "is that when they throw food around like that, it's somebody like me who's got to get down on his hands and knees and clean it up."

Which means somebody like the Clash themselves. I suppose I'm going to seem very moralistic about this, and I don't mean for this incident to dominate this story, but if I close my eyes it will not go away.

I recall the first time I read about the Clash, the cover story

NME ran last spring, being a little surprised when it was said that on their first tour they were (already?) tearing up hotel rooms. I mean even then it struck you a bit odd, coming atop all their righteous rhetoric. If somebody screws around with you, fine, smash 'em back if you want. But random destruction is so . . . *asinine*. And so redolent of self-hate.

I suppose there's no basic difference between the Clash trashing hotels and their fans leaving beer mug shards all over concert-hall floors, it's all just the product of frustration and who cares. But some things you just gotta see as a package deal. Meaning that the nature of any enterprise at all levels is defined by what's coming down from the top. What's at the top with most of the big rock groups is diseased, so their whole operation reflects the sickness, down to the employment of brutal thugs to keep the fans away from them in the name of "security" (whose?). What's at the top in the Clash organization seems so basically good, moral, principled, it's no wonder that except for this incident everything has seemed to run smoothly on this tour, everybody has seemed so happy.

When Led Zeppelin or the Stones tour everybody's got to suffer to compensate for the indulgence of the big babies at the top, so all kinds of minor functionaries and innocent bystanders can get ground into shit. But even Led Zeppelin don't invite their fans back to the hotel *and then* beat them up.

At about 4 A.M. one of the girls said to the boy fan, "Looks like you've got a shiner." You could begin to see the discoloration in his right eye. By the time they left, it would have turned into a purple lump half an inch thick and the width of a shilling.

I sat up all night with them, getting to know them in that transient, pleasant intimacy common to travelers. We exchanged addresses and warm goodbyes and they left to hitchhike back to Dover in a mild drizzle around 7:30 A.M. The scene with Mickey had left me too wound up to sleep and we were all supposed to show in the lobby at nine for the drive to Birmingham. So I showered, dressed, packed and went down for breakfast, where I met and talked with a guy named John who was replacing Mickey for today's drive. Which was fortunate, because I would have hopped the first train to London rather than spend another few hours in a van with that shithead.

In fact I didn't say anything on the drive to Birmingham. I figured there was no point in getting into what could be a prolonged argument with anybody in a small enclosed space. But as soon as we checked into the hotel that afternoon, I called Mick's room and asked if I could come over. It had been eating at me since it happened, and I had to get it out of my system. Mick, Robin, and Paul were there, and I repeated what had happened. They didn't seem particularly concerned. When I asked Paul why he hadn't done anything, he said, "Mickey's just that kind of bloke; you don't want to get in his way. Besides, it seemed like it was all in fun—I'ave a tussle with me mates every once in a while."

I pushed the issue, and when I was done Mick said, "Well, I feel as if I've just had a severe reprimand."

"Yeah," said Robin. "You sound like my father."

I told them I didn't mean to set myself up as judge and jury. But you could see that Mick was upset; more than anybody else in the Clash, he loves the group's fans. After a short depressed silence, he said he was going out for a walk, got up and left the room.

The mood at the Birmingham concert hall was ominous. Clash road manager Corky was handing out "I WANT COMPLETE CONTROL" buttons to the kids standing in the door, and police were confiscating them as soon as they got inside. The mood of the crowd was ugly—they gobbed all over Richard Hell even more than usual, and he started gobbing back, which was a mistake.

When I walked into the dressing room Joe Strummer immediately confronted me: "Lester, what's all this shit you're raisin' then?"

"You mean about last night?"

"Yeah. That guy was a bleedin' little ligger . . ."

Rather than tell him he was wrong and get into a hassle just before showtime, I left the dressing room. Out in the hall Mick came up to me, obviously still concerned. "I've heard four different stories about what happened last night," he said, "but the main thing is that it better not happen again."

Later there was a party in a disco above the hall, and I spoke briefly to Bernie Rhodes. I told him I loved the group and liked Mick the best. He sighed, "Yeah, but Mick's my biggest problem . . ."

The real problem, of course, is how to reconcile Mick's attitude toward the fans with the group's escalating popularity in some realistic manner. Meaning that eventually you have to draw the line, and who's going to decide when and where it's to be drawn? Without this one-on-one contact with their audience, the Clash would seem as likely to fall into elitist alienation as most bands preceding them, but if it gets to the point that several thousand people want into your hotel room you've got to find some way of dealing with it. I certainly don't have the answer—all I know is that total access is as unreasonable as Zep/Stones—style security can be fascistically offensive.

In spite of tension between police and audience, the band had played a great set, channeling all the frustration into a liberating mass seizure. I couldn't help comparing this, especially in the light of most of the publicity accorded punks in the dailies, to the last time I was in Birmingham, for Slade in 1972. At that show I'd been warned not to take my tape recorder into the audience because they'd surely break it; they didn't, but they did smash every seat in the house, fights broke out everywhere, and Dave Hill was injured by flying shrapnel.

Of course, that *was* your standard football audience, and what's a little authentic violence in the face of a generation five years on who would seem to prefer rebellion by clothes and hairstyles?

Speaking of which, I experienced a revelation of sorts at the after-gig party. I am loath to confess it, but I must say that try as I might I have never been able to find punk girls sexy. Somehow that chopped hair will just douse you every time, never mind the thought of trying to kiss somebody with a safety pin through her mouth (by the way, I didn't see a single safety pin through the flesh the entire time I was in England)—but now, in the disco upstairs, with Don Letts manning the turntable, alternating punk and reggae at mind-melting volumes, a whole pack of punkettes got out on that dance floor and started pogoing away and . . . well . . . suddenly it all began to make real tight *sense* . . .

In fact, it was one of the highlights of my trip. I tried dancing a little bit, but mostly I just had to stand there and stare and stare, as one girl in black leather did James Brown steps, while Ari Up of the Slits, in all sorts of rags and a fishnet shawl, hopped high-footing around the dance floor like some mix of spider and strutting ostrich, and the drummer from the Lous first walked around the floor on her knees, then got down on all fours and walked the dog for real as my eyeballs and then brain fell out a little at a time.

I suppose all you English tots are used to this sort of thing, but for this American it was Todd Browning's *Freaks* doing the Cretin Hop in the hypno-tantalizing pulsating flesh. Like, if anybody starts asking me about the *sociological significance* of all this punk stuff I'm just gonna flash back to that Lous drummer down on all fours marching in circles, recalling most vividly her face as she did so: the fact that it was serene, *blank,* unconcerned, *un-self-conscious.*

• • •

Much the same sort of thing strikes me next night, when for my last night on the tour, I attend a gig in Coventry with fellow rock critic Simon Frith. Simon, his wife Gill, and I are surrounded by these strange children, the age difference somehow even more accentuated when there are three of us instead of just me blending with the geeks.

We note things like nonfunctional zippers sewn into the middle of shirts, and I'm almost passing out on my feet after six days of three hours' sleep a night on the road when suddenly something very strange runs over me. It's a kid moving through the crowd in a jagged mechanical pivoting careen, like a robot with crossed circuits, staring fixedly at nothing I can see, certainly not seeing me as we collide and he spazzmos on. When I ask Simon what in the hell that was he says they do it all the time— "Curious, isn't it?"—and when I ask if such a gait might be the by-product of amphetamine abuse he laughs: "This is no pill scene. Most of these kids have never had anything stronger than stout." (The Clash, contrary to reputation, are not into speed either, at least not on the road.) Then we stare for a moment at the pogoing army, and Simon says, "Very tribal, isn't it?"

That it is. Between the Voidoids' and the Clash's sets, the PA broadcasts "Anarchy in the U.K.," and the whole audience, pogoing wildly, sings the entire song. I reflect how such a sight must strike terror, or something, into the heart of a middle-aged policeman looking on; but then I recall Slade getting their audience to sing along to "You'll Never Walk Alone" in '72, and the symmetry is inescapable. I *know* about the dole, I recognize the differences, but I wonder just exactly what, in the end, we can all understand this thing to be about.

When the Clash come on in Coventry, Joe repeats a little speech he first tried out in Birmingham: "Listen—before we play anything, we'd like to ask you one favor: please don't spit on us.

We're just trying to do something good up here and it throws us off our stride." I was glad to hear it, because what gobbing really represents to me, besides nausea, is *people doing what they think is expected of them rather than whatever it is they might really want to do.*

Which of course *should* be what the new wave is against.

Or rather, the converse should be what it's all about. At it's best new wave/punk represents a fundamental and age-old utopian dream: that if you give people the license to be as outrageous as they want in absolutely any fashion they can dream up, *they'll be creative about it,* and do something good besides. Realize their own potentials and finally start doing what they really want to do. Which also presupposes that people don't want somebody else telling them what to do. That most people are capable of a certain spontaneity, given the option.

As it is, the punks constitute a form of passive resistance to a slick social order, but the question remains as to just what alternatives they are going to come up with. Singing along to "Anarchy" and "White Riot" constitutes no more than a show of solidarity, and there are plenty of people who think this is all no more than a bunch of stupid kids on a faddist's binge. They're wrong, because at the very least all of this amounts to a gesture of faith in mass and individual unrealized possibilities, which counts for a lot in an era when there are plenty of voices who would tell you that all human behavior can be reduced to a formula.

But if anything, more than fashion and what usually amounts to poses is going to finally come of all this, then everybody listening is going to have to pick up the possibilities with both hands and fulfill 'em themselves. Either that or end up with a new set of surrogate mommies and daddies, just like hippies did, because in spite of whatever they set in motion, that's exactly what, say, Charles Manson and John Sinclair were.

The paradox for me is that the punks, in their very gentleness behind all the sneers and attitudes copped, are lambs—and believe me, I'm with the lambs over the bullies and manipulators of this world all the way—but what are lambs without a shepherd? Rastas aside, I don't want no Jesuses in *my* Promised Land, and if I didn't find it at the end of my road with the Clash I did catch a glimpse of it, on that road, in the way they acted towards women, and ultimately towards themselves, every day. Meaning that even if we don't need any more leaders, we could do with a lot more models. If that's what the punks really amount to, then perhaps we actually do have the germ of a new society, or at least a new sensibility, that cuts through things like class and race and sex.

If not, well . . . I started talking to a girl who knew Simon and Gill, who I figured was a student in one of Simon's classes. She was very fresh, very wholesome, very young in a jacket covered with buttons bearing groups' names, and very miffed that the Clash had asked the audience not to spit on them. "After all," she said, "*they* started it!"

"But look," I said, "they play better when you don't."

"I don't care! I just want to jump up and down! That's all my students want, too!"

I blinked. "Your *students*? Wait a second, how old are you?"

"Twenty-four. I'm a schoolteacher."

Honestly, I couldn't help myself.

"Then . . . but . . . what are you doing here? I mean, why do you like the Clash?"

"*Because they make me jump up and down!*" And she pogoed away.

THE LAST BROADCAST

By Greil Marcus

Originally appeared in the Village Voice *January 31, 1984;*
Music *magazine (Tokyo) January 1986;* Artforum *February, 1986;*
revised January, 1992

A s the number two British punk band, the Clash began as
the Rolling Stones to the Sex Pistols' Beatles, but good
and bad were reversed in punk. As the Beatles, as those
who set the terms of the new game, the Sex Pistols demanded
everything and damned everything—knowing they would be left
with nothing, they played and sang as if they didn't care. The Clash
criticized, always leaving an opening: the Sex Pistols were wreckers,
they were partisans. The Sex Pistols were symbolist, with every
meaning left open and uncertain, utopia and hell in a single,
unstable body; the Clash were rhetorical, voice to flesh. If the Sex
Pistols—or anyway Johnny Rotten—truly were committed to the
destruction of rock 'n' roll not only as myth but as fact, the Clash
were committed to changing rock 'n' roll, to taking it over, to
becoming the Number One Band in the World ("The Only Band
That Matters," their American label said, after the Sex Pistols dis-
integrated). The explanations the Sex Pistols offered when inter-
viewers asked them why-are-you-so-angry turned into the Clash's
songs, songs about boredom, autonomy, lust, power; the Clash
took the true anarchy and the real nihilism the Sex Pistols offered
and rationalized it, made it seem reasonable.

The Clash latched onto received ideas, but they soon made those
ideas their own, and were changed by them—or anyway Joe
Strummer was. It was never clear if he wanted to be a star or if

he wanted everyone to hear him: in the rock tradition Strummer was so tied to, the difference between the one and the other was never clear. With a giant multinational corporation behind them, the Clash toured the U.S.A. (1977: "I'm So Bored with . . .") again and again.

In 1982 they finally cracked the American Top Ten: made it twice with *Combat Rock* on the album charts and the indelible "Rock the Casbah" on the singles list. Most assumed that the Clash were working for nothing else, that the heresies of 1976 London punk were merely the old clothes of bad dreams, but the band's success seemed to shock Strummer. If the Clash had scored their hits, if large numbers of people were finally happy to listen to what the band had to say, Strummer seemed to have decided that that meant the Clash were no longer saying anything. With work on the boards, he disappeared in Paris, then reappeared with his head shaved. Drummer "Topper" Headon quit; the group was unraveling. Strummer called a meeting, got bassist Paul Simonon's vote, and kicked guitarist Mick Jones out of the band.

Jones had been a founder; he had asked Strummer to join him. As guitarist, singer, and co-writer, many saw him as far more central to the Clash's success than Strummer, but in a way that was the point. Jones's noisy love songs ("Train in Vain," "Should I Stay or Should I Go?") had been the Clash's most effective bids for mainstream airplay before "Rock the Casbah" (a sardonic, up-from-the-Muslim-streets reply to the Ayatollah Khomeini's ban on music in Iran, and written by Topper Headon); Jones's voice lacked Strummer's rough edges, his promise that any song could go in any direction, anytime. Strummer detected a spiritual flaw behind the style; despite the punk attempt to destroy the star system, Strummer announced, a pop star was all Mick Jones had ever wanted to be. He was a fake, a revisionist; he had to go.

Strummer and Simonon recruited three new members: drummer Pete Howard, rhythm guitarist Vince White, and lead guitarist Nick Sheppard, the latter both twenty-three-year-old "ex-punks" who affirmed they'd grown up on Clash music. As a band ("The Clash") they played a few shows; hope against hope, their American label even brought them back to the USA.

It was, for a night, a trip worth taking. "This isn't *white* reggae," Strummer shouted, introducing "Police and Thieves." "This is punk *and* reggae. There's a *difference*. There's a difference between a rip-off and bringing some of *our* culture to *another* culture. You hear that, Sting?"

It was 21 January 1984. It had been eight years since the Clash formed, six years and one week since the Sex Pistols played their last show in San Francisco, and the Clash were back in town not as "The Only Band That Matters" but as the only punk band left. "What we play now is what we can do," Strummer had said in 1979. "It wouldn't be fair to do ranting music because we've mastered a time change. So there's just no point." "We started to think we were musicians," he told Joel Selvin, a San Francisco critic, before the new Clash show. "When we made the first record we knew we weren't. It's a bad think to think; it's irrelevant, not to the point."

To a happy, not quite sold-out crowd in a dumpy, medium-sized hall, the Clash played ranting music. Keeping Strummer's promise to Selvin, they "went back to where we went wrong, and then forward again." Against an industrialist backdrop and eight television sets flashing images of present-day social disaster, Strummer shook, scowled, smiled, and sang as if he and his audience had a life to make within a world they'd already lost.

The band was ragged, Nick Sheppard played too many Mick Jones licks, and such rock-star flimsy as if leaps from the drum riser or floodlights in the crowd's face was still part of the show. The only identifiable new song was the hopeless, "We Are the Clash," which only added credence to the old rumor that the favorite song of Bernard Rhodes, the Clash's original and now returned manager, was "Hey, Hey, We're the Monkees." Still, I'd never seen Strummer more exhilarated, or more convincing. In 1978 in Berkeley, "I'm So Bored with the U.S.A." was a gesture of contempt to a bourgeois audience; this night it was offered to the audience as their own, and they took it. Some of *our* culture to *another* culture.

Still, almost everyone was sure it was the end of the road. As time passed, Strummer gave increasingly confused interviews about "rebel rock," changing the world, the special role he had to play in that change, England's turn to the right under Margaret Thatcher, the collapse of the punk community and the possibility of reinventing it, social injustice, fascism, the end of the world, and when there might be a new Clash album. He wasn't saying anything terribly different from what he and many more had said in 1976 and '77—but in London in '76 and '77, the old rock 'n' roll dream of "taking over the world" hadn't meant topping the world's charts, it was supposed to mean making the charts irrelevant, and then proving that the charts and graphs and ledgers that governed the structures of everyday life—the hierarchies of education, work, family, bureaucracy, politics—could be made just as irrelevant. Now, though, with Thatcher's brutal, popular Tory rule, the oppressions punk had fought when it gave birth to itself—the oppressions of false leisure, false work, false entertainment—seemed like the playthings of childhood, and Strummer sounded like a crazy old man.

In May 1985, in the UK, the new Clash, the five of them, showed up in a parking lot outside of a hall where the Alarm, a newly popular group, were playing a sold-out show. Strumming acoustic guitars and tapping drumsticks against each other, they were busking—playing for small change. Before 1976, Strummer had been a subway singer, a thick-fingered guitar banger—that was where he got his name. In interviews in the 1980s, he talked often about "going back to the roots," but no one could have guessed he'd meant going back so far. It was a bizarre reversal, a testament to how desperate Strummer was to dramatize that punk had meant what it said when it said it would destroy all heroes. On their early tours of the UK, the Clash sometimes brought their fans back to their hotel and let them sleep in their rooms; now, playing the Isley Brothers' (or the Beatles') "Twist and Shout," their own "Garageland" (from the Clash's first album), or "Stepping Stone" (the Monkees again—the Sex Pistols had tried it, too, once), the Clash asked the curious who gathered to hear them if the fans could, you know, put them up for the night. In this moment you could see Joe Strummer's whole future: on some dank London corner, the drunken bum calls out to passersby. "Hey, you wanna hear 'Rock the Casbah'? It was a hit, it was a hit, ah, in . . ."

As the band chanted in the parking lot, you could see the Clash's past. On the back sleeve of "White Riot," the Clash's first single, there was a rough collage of photos (ugly public housing blocks surrounded by rubble; cops; a band) and words. Along with quotes from the Brighton Beach youth culture riots of the mid-1960s (a Mod: "I haven't enjoyed myself so much for a long time . . . It was like we were taking over the country"), one could read something more suggestive:

that there is, perhaps, *some* tension in society, when perhaps overwhelming pressure brings industry to a standstill or barricades to the streets years after the liberals had dismissed the notion as "dated romanticism," the journalist invents the theory that this constitutes a clash of generations. Youth, after all, is not a permanent condition, and a clash of generations is not so fundamentally dangerous to the art of government as would be a clash between rulers and ruled.

The explanations of

Out of this blind fragment of a found manifesto, the Clash had made a career. In advance of any sort of pop career, the words took in the inevitable dismissal, or failure, of any attempt to use rock 'n' roll to dramatize a clash between rulers and ruled: As far as almost everyone was concerned, no band could signify more than a transient clash between generations, a present-day (now long past) version of a sixties beach riot between Mods and Rockers, new fans of the Who, and the Small Faces beaten bloody by fans of Bill Haley and Gene Vincent. Teddy Boys who kept the faith were relics whose whole lives were based on the conviction that they had heard the truth and would kick in the faces of anyone who suggested it might be incomplete.

In other words, with that old manifesto now playing against the idea that an old band could make itself new, Strummer, well into his thirties as he spoke—as the new Clash made noise for coins, and then made a new record and asked people to buy it—was precisely the old fart punks had dumped when "White Riot" first hit the stores. *Cut the Crap,* the new Clash album was titled, and the words were thrown back in Strummer's face. *You* should talk, said the British reviews. Go away! Who wants to hear what a dead man has to say! Stop reminding us of what you failed to do the first time around!

On the terms punk set for itself, it would change the world or it would be nothing. In a certain sense, Strummer was never a real rock 'n' roller, because he trusted neither fun nor money; thus the chart success of the Clash had to mean nothing to him. You could draw two different conclusions from the failure of punk to change the world and its sometime success on the charts: you could conclude that the punk critique of everyday oppression and spectacular entertainment was wrong—or you could conclude that it was correct, and the enemy more invisible, than even the most conscious punks had dared to think. Drawing the first conclusion, you would, if you were Strummer, try to find a place in the record business; drawing the second, you would try to find a new way to say the same old things. And of course it is the second path Strummer has chosen.

Cut the Crap seems to be set in a riot—not the idealized "White riot/Wanna riot of my own" of the 1976 Clash, not their "LONDON'S BURNING WITH BOREDOM NOW!," but a far more prosaic affair, tired, too familiar, the everyday bad news of New Britain. A new king of riot: As the strict re-division of British society into a capitalist and serving classes proceeds, it becomes plain that redundancy and civil disorder are not merely costs of this project, but linchpins. Under Thatcher, redundancy is not simply economics: It is social exclusion organized as spectacle. Those who are cut out of organized social life make up a third class, which is used to terrorize those who still retain their places into a thank-god-it's-them-instead-of-me acquiescence, which is silence, and that silence has no force without some noise in the streets.

This is power as culture: a form of speech that has answered all questions in advance. Behind the Labour government of 1977, which administered What Is as a final social fact, punk could discover a negative: welfare security as spiritual poverty. With Thatcher, who administers What Could Be (you can be anything, she says, which means, you can also lose everything), oppositional culture can only discover an affirmative. It can only agree, and agreement is a further silence. As the redundants riot, the ranter grabs a passing clerk by the collar and tells him the truth: "You could be next!" "Right, mate," says the clerk. "That's why I'm keeping my nose clean. Hey aren't you Joe Strummer?" As public speech, both the riot and the Clash's new music have been contained before the fact.

Thus Clash's new riot, too, sounds like a kind of silence: an exhortation in place of drama, inspirational music for "rebel rockers." "CLASH COMMUNIQUÉ OCTOBER '85," it says on the inner sleeve. "Wise MEN and street kids together make a GREAT TEAM . . . but can the old system be BEAT? . . . no . . . not without YOUR participation . . . RADICAL social change begins on the STREET! . . . so if you're looking for some ACTION . . . CUT THE CRAP and get OUT there." The new songs, the new music, aren't much more convincing. A wash of ambient mass media noise, an old-fashioned punk guitar sound communicating not as a revival of a period style but as a new discovery, an occasional rhythmic jump—too soon, it all seems lost in a shoving match between skimpy lyrics and football-match chants of vague slogans. More than anything, *Cut the Crap* sounds like a transfer from the Clash to Big Country—a band that scored a good, rousing hit with the self-titled "Big Country," a teary approximation of early Clash— back to the Clash again. *Cut the Crap* sounds less like failed "rebel rock" than like failed pop music.

And out of this comes one true moment, "This Is England." Released as a single, it had a strange jacket: on the front, a Mohawked punk couple wander through Piccadilly Circus, blank-eyed and scared of the sleaze, country mice finally arriving in the big city to find out what punk is, seven years too late: "24 HOUR ETERNAL SUNSHINE STRIP STRIP STRIP," "SEX STYLE SUB-VERSION," "DISCUSSION DISCO." There's no one else on the street. On the back, there are lots of people on the streets, black-and-white shots of 1950s men and women finally shrugging off the privation of the postwar period and shopping, buying, smiling, "IT'S NEW," "GET IT," "LAST FEW DAYS SALE," and, square in the middle, a collage from old painted postcards, Buckingham Palace, the Queen in her carriage, a hand raised to hide her face.

"Who will buy my potatoes?" asks the voice of a small child; a drum machine kicks in, slowly, firmly; synthesizer chords lift the music, hold it in, refuse to let it move through any melody, to find

any rhythm; a punk buzzsaw guitar rides down, sounding wonderful, alive, free, then beaten. Strummer begins to sing, to talk,
walking through the riot like his own tour guide, nearly mute for
all his words. As the riot takes place it's already over; he is singing
the ruins, and the passion in his voice, the despair, the plain desperation to make you understand, is like blood frozen on a corpse.
The corpse is the singer: It's the country. "This is England," an
anonymous male chorus says over and over, and again and again
Strummer comes off the chorus to try and tell you what it is:
"Land of a thousand stances." Images of random violence, of official murder, pass by; nothing connects. The singer flees; he's
trapped. An incident comes to life with detail, then vanishes as
allegory.

> *On a catwalk jungle*
> *Somebody grabbed my arm*
> *A voice spoke so cold it matched the*
> *Weapon in her palm*
> *This is England*
> *This knife of Sheffield steel*
> *This is England*
> *This is how we feel*

England is a nowhere, but all possibilities of feeling seem
present in the way Strummer sings that last line, here in the voice
of another, throughout the rest of the song in his own. "THIS IS
ENGLAND," echoes the chorus, and then Strummer is solitary,
bearing down on the following words so hard he makes them
vibrate, the solitary "we" so painful and strange, pressing with
such force that all that's come before, the Clash's whole career, all
the great songs, your favorite, seems trivialized by this quiet, still
negation, the patent, the physical gap in the "This" of "This is how

we feel," a frightened hesitation between the "th" and the "is," a break in time that carries the full weight of what Strummer is saying: carries it, and suspends it, leaving you hanging, unready for the fact that after a few minutes the record, like other records, simply fades out.

Postscript: Shortly after the release of *Cut the Crap,* the three new members quit the band; it never re-formed. *Cut the Crap* was never released in the United States. "This Is England" has been excluded from all Clash retrospectives, greatest-hits collections, and CD-boxed sets.

THE
Rebel
WAY

THE REBEL WAY:
ALEX COX, JIM JARMUSCH, AND DICK RUDE ON THE FILM WORK OF JOE STRUMMER

By Antonino D'Ambrosio

For me the problem with writing a novel is that I would not want to be content to be the author. I would want to be the character.

—Rogerio Duarte

Not to be admired. To be believed.

—Jean Cocteau

Strummer: What are you going to do with yourself?
Ray Gange: I don't know.

—From the film *Rude Boy*

S tanding on the edge of a diving board, Strummer strikes a silhouetted defiant rockabilly pose for the cover of his first official solo album *Earthquake Weather*.[1] The cover foretells the isolation and ensuing fall from "top to bottom" Strummer's life had taken after the Clash shut down in 1985. He was, for the first time, venturing out on his own, an intimidating undertaking for a performer who throughout his career enjoyed the collective comfort of a band. Restless and a bit lost, Strummer carved out a briefly idiosyncratic film career as both actor and composer, with his most prolific period covering four years up to 1989. After that point, Strummer entered what Dick Rude—the actor, director and longtime friend of Strummer—told me was his "dark night." [2]

As a teenager, Strummer became fascinated with cinema including Hollywood gangster and cowboy pictures as well as politically radical films like Gillo Pontecorvo's *Battle of Algiers* and *Burn*. Marlon Brando, Montgomery Clift, and George Raft were a few of the screen actors who would later serve as models in helping shape the Clash's rebel persona. For young filmmakers of the day, the rise of punk and it's mix of bold music, brash personalities, and theatrical live performances presented exciting cinematic opportunities. For a group like the Sex Pistols, the music was initially secondary to their posturing, as they seemed to be characters from *A Clockwork Orange* come to life.

The Clash was different in that they offered politically charged music buoyed with a raw charisma and delivered via fiery live performances that offered a message of hope rather than misery. The group also looked the part in clothes pieced together and rife with political slogans written across them. For example, Strummer stenciled PASSION IS A FASHION onto his boiler suit and controversially wore a Brigade Rosse (Red Brigade) T-shirt.[3] This made them a dynamic subject for film.

Early Clash film work would include a feature-length political film and some short films that foreshadowed music videos. Still, music videos, MTV, and the revolution in filmmaking it would cause was years off.[4] Even so, for aesthetically conscious and politically active bands like the Clash, film was a natural step towards getting their music and message out to a larger audience With this in mind, the Clash set about making a film that aimed to capture the simmering social unrest of mid-1970s England and that would also place the band squarely in the middle of the political and popular culture fray.

Set against this backdrop, the Clash began participating in an ambitious film project, *Rude Boy*. The film would merge the Clash's political radicalism, unique aesthetics, and raw performances in hopes of achieving the ultimate agitprop film. But when it was released in 1979, the film was a haphazard mix of Clash concert footage placed over a disjointed narrative that attempted to deal with the issues of the day like racism and state repression. As Strummer pointed out, *Rude Boy* is not a good film and is not interesting to watch for most of its two-hours-plus running time. "*Rude Boy* does not even seem to have the participation of the Clash," Rude explained. And according to Strummer it did not.

Rude Boy is set in 1977 London and opens with a long scene where the police and protestors square off as the National Front attempts to march through an Afro-Caribbean community. It follows the hapless Ray, played by Ray Gange, a disaffected youth who becomes a Clash roadie. From the opening performance of "Police and Thieves," this plot device serves to give the filmmakers, Jack Hazan and David Mingay, a great opportunity to film concert footage of the Clash in their electrifying prime. The film tries but fails to capture the political and social unrest of the time despite using actual footage of social unrest and fascist-group demonstrations. Far more effective at highlighting the groups political ideals are their performances. We see them performing a blistering set at the Rock Against Racism event, Carnival Against the Nazis in 1978.[5]

As the film unravels, the only scenes that are engaging in addition to the live footage are those few moments where Strummer attempts to offer the unsympathetic and errant Ray a political education whether it be while drinking in a pub, washing his Brigade Rosse T-shirt in a hotel room, or playing "Let the Good Times Roll" on a piano. The film is not the agitprop work that the Clash hoped it would be, but rather equal parts documentary, social commentary, and concert film. When released in 1980, the Clash did dissociate themselves from the film as it seemed like more of an attempt to exploit their enormous success and popularity rather than offering anything more substantial. In *Punk Productions,* Stacy Thompson explains, "but for all of the film's attempts to link the band to the ongoing racial and political clashes and violence occurring in London in the late '70s, it stops well short of ever suggesting that any identifiable effects resulted from this particular intersection of punk, race, and politics."[6]

While the release of *Rude Boy* did not live up to what many had hoped from the Clash, the band was entering a stage in their career of unprecedented success and influence, soon assuming the mantle of the world's greatest rebel rock band with the release of their next record *London Calling.* Making their way to America once again in 1981 in support of *Sandinista!,* the Clash played a three-week stretch of shows on Broadway now known as the Bonds Residency. They would play seventeen shows during this residency, attracting thousands of people from divergent sectors of American society including two emerging pop culture icons who were huge Clash fans: Martin Scorsese and Robert De Niro who listened to the Clash incessantly, particularly during the filming of *Raging Bull.* Peter Biskind writes that Scorsese "would go into his trailer, put on the Clash at top volume, and sit there revved up by the music, pacing back and forth."[7] Scorsese hoped to cast the Clash in his newest project *Gangs of New York*. The admiration was mutual—Strummer later shaved his head into a Mohawk à la De Niro's Travis Bickle in *Taxi Driver* for the Clash's punk rock guerrilla phase.

When it became apparent that Scorsese would not get *Gangs of New York* produced, he shelved the project and began working on his dark satire *The King of Comedy*[8] Strummer and his bandmates make a fleeting appearance as "street scum." The Clash also had prepared to produce their own film while in New York with Don Letts, the Rastafarian DJ at the Roxy Club in Covent Garden and close associate of the Clash. Letts was a talented young filmmaker who made *Punk Rock Movie,* a Super-8 film documenting the 1977 London punk scene. He was traveling with the Clash to New York City to shoot a video for "This Is Radio Clash" and film the short documentary *Clash on Broadway*.[9]

Much of this footage appears in the Letts directed documentary *Westway to the World,* released in 2000. At the center of Letts' film are the charming and often heartbreakingly honest interviews given by each member of the band. Intercut with exceptional concert footage, the documentary follows the band from their celebrated rise to their cheerless end with fascinating anecdotes spotlighting the group's originality and influence. Jones, Simonon, and Headon each offer thoughtful historical accounts but it's Strummer that steals the show as he movingly speaks about the music and the politics that drove the band.

At one point Strummer explains, "I quickly realized that either you became a power or you were crushed . . . and that we were trying to grope in a socialist way for some kind of a future where the world is a less miserable place than it is." The film is neither nostalgic nor sentimental and serves two important roles as a historical document and revelatory primer for the uninitiated. Strummer concludes the film by discussing the band's demise after Jones's departure and the sadness of an opportunity squandered. "We weren't parochial. We weren't narrow-minded. We weren't little Englanders," he says. "At least we had the suss to embrace what we were presented with, which was the world and all its weird varieties."

While *Westway to the World* is a look backward, *Let's Rock Again* is a moving glimpse into Strummer's new life and the bright future that was ahead. Directed by his friend Dick Rude, the film was meant as a vehicle to get his new music out to a larger audience and to serve as a memoir. Spending an afternoon in New York City with Rude, best known for his role as Duke in the film *Repo Man,* I learn that the film is an intimate, loving portrait of a person that Rude describes as his "brother, best friend, mentor, hero . . . he remains all things to me." The film began after Rude went to Strummer's Somerset farm in an effort to convince him to document the then impending *Global A Go-Go* tour.

Let's Rock Again was filmed over a period of about seven weeks and it took eighteen months to complete.

Strummer was resistant at first, telling Rude, "I'm not interesting" and that filming him would be like making "a home movie." He tried to encourage Rude to make another documentary about an old woman in Rude's apartment building in Los Angeles. "That would be much more interesting," Strummer told him. "No one's gonna wanna see this." Strummer finally relented, not knowing that his decision would have such enormous consequences. And while the film does serve to promote his new music, it takes on an entirely different tone, symbolizing a life loving music and a musician loving life.

Rude's film, which had only two screenings both at the 2004 Tribeca Film Festival in New York City, has no official release date and is still in search of a distributor. A strange twist of irony to be sure, since Rude and Strummer had hoped that this film would help get his new music out. In the film Strummer tells an interviewer that *Rock Art and the X-Ray Style,* the first album he recorded with the Mescaleros, lost money and that he worried he was taking these young musicians down the road of failure. "I don't know if they realize what they are in for," he quietly tells one interviewer. I ask Rude if the other members of the Clash had a chance to watch his film. "I had private screenings both for Mick and Paul," he tells me. "They each said, 'Wow, I wanna be like that' . . . they did not know the man he really was, how pure he was . . . the person he had become after hitting the bottom spiritually, he was realizing his true self."

Let's Rock Again opens with a quick but powerful montage of Strummer's days with the Clash. It is a perfect complement for the scenes ahead where Rude captures Strummer's performances with the Mescaleros in all their glory. "When people see this film," Rude told me, "especially all those who would not normally appreciate Joe, they get sucked in to the person he was . . . they come to love him."

Rude catches Strummer behind the scenes and offstage almost like he was unaware that he was being filmed. Relaxed and disarming, Rude tells me it was "like we were just hanging out . . . once he committed to the project he was open and accessible," Rude says.[10] The moments on film with the band—at the time, Martin Slattery, Tymon Dogg, Scott Shields, Antony Genn, and Pablo Cook—displayed a real unity. Rude explained that he initiated some of the scenes including those that find Strummer traveling to a local Atlantic City radio station in hopes of getting on the air to promote his show and the new album, or Strummer handing out homemade flyers to people walking along the board walk. Both scenes elicit a strong reaction from viewers, often times of pity and sympathy. One person at the screening asked Rude, "Was Strummer bitter or angry that he had fallen on such hard times?" Rude takes umbrage to this narrow viewpoint. "When people respond like that they are missing the point . . . in those scenes, I see a man who is doing something he loves with the wonderment, energy, and enthusiasm of when he was a young musician and playing with the Clash."

Rude poignantly adds that "while he was alive and had trouble getting his music on the radio, people were like 'so what?' and now that he is gone there is a desperation to fill this void instead of being in that moment when he was here and enjoying his music." In the end, *Let's Rock Again* achieves this, and more significantly, helps us deal with Strummer's loss as not a tragedy but as a celebration of an artist who leaves behind a legacy that can never be duplicated. "There is only one Joe Strummer," Rude says, "and since the days of the Clash there has been no group that has even come close to doing what they did." For Rude, what remains most important is to not lose sight that Strummer's music and message will influence generations to come.

Rude first met Strummer during the production of Alex Cox's *Sid and Nancy*. Strummer was recording two songs for the film's soundtrack. Rude was in London to write the sequel to the 1984 cult classic *Repo Man*, which was directed by Cox and starred Rude along with Emilio Estevez and Harry Dean Stanton.[11] The sequel was never produced but a scene from the script became *Straight to Hell*. Shot on location in Spain in 1986 this spaghetti Western parody starred Strummer, Rude, and Sy Richardson as bumbling hit men who decide to rob a bank. The film features many cameos from musicians including Elvis Costello who plays a waiter who is never without a tray of coffee.

In all, Cox worked with Strummer on three film projects and each were bold political and cultural statements. Cox describes

Straight to Hell as a political response as the "Reagan/Thatcher maniac front was working overtime to destroy the Sandinista revolution by any means. Thatcher had even attempted to criminalize the word 'Sandinista'—hence the Clash album of the same name. It would be a mistake to underestimate the power of the punk movement at that time: The Clash, the Jam, the Pistols, and their successors were almost the only beachhead many of us had against a tidal wave of reactionary politics."[12]

Cox told me Strummer "was a brilliant film composer, who got better and better as we worked together. He was interested in being an actor as well, but in the case of *Walker,* used that as a way of being immersed in the production and the place . . . I think by that point he'd realized he was a composer and musician rather than a thespian." Cox describes *Walker* as "a comedy about how badly Americans behave abroad." The film follows William Walker, a nineteenth-century American adventurer who becomes a soldier of fortune and eventually dictator of Nicaragua.[13] "Walker was such an unpleasant character, a coward, and a liar," Cox adds. "You can't make a film about that seriously because he's an idiot." Undoubtedly, Strummer's committed anti-imperialist stance and his support for the Sandinistas and other Latin American revolutionaries explains the film's remarkable soundtrack. Cox's film fit perfectly with his political sensibilities and as Cox confirmed, "I think *Walker* is one of the best film soundtracks ever composed, a pity it's no longer available."[14] Rude agrees, describing Strummer as "not confident as an actor" but his "soundtrack work is genius."

Interestingly, Strummer was not credited with playing anything on the *Walker* soundtrack, only singing. Strummer told Bill Flanagan of *Musician* magazine in March 1988, "I couldn't credit myself playing because I was afraid of getting sued by Sony, to be honest. I got permission from CBS/Sony to sing on it. See, I can write it, conduct it, produce it, okay? I can do all that and have it on any label quite freely. But should I sing on it or play, then some deal has to be made. So because *Walker*'s on Virgin I made a deal for the singing with CBS/Sony. Then when I began to compile the credits I thought, Anything I've done I better not put on there, 'cause for all I know there may be a separate deal for *playing* it. It could open a can of worms, right? So I just put down 'Vocals' but in fact I'm probably playing some rhythmic instrument on every track, whether it's piano, guitar, or marimba."[15]

Nevertheless, critics who believed that Strummer was incapable of producing good music without Mick Jones as a reassuring partner were impressed with the *Walker* soundtrack. Charles Shaar Murray, who had years before in a column derided the Clash as a garage band and therefore became the motivation behind the song "Garageland," wrote that it was "a remarkably elegant, loose-limbed, and accomplished set of ersatz Latin themes spiked with delicate country touches."[16] And *NME*'s Gavin Martin explained, "You may be a little stunned and staggered at first (I was) to find the man with the demon bark and three-chord bite has composed every note here. But from lustrous samba percussion, through flamenco horns, and country inflections, it's all gorgeously effective and superbly detailed."[17]

David Byrne, who won an Oscar along with Cong Su for their score of Bernardo Bertulucci's *The Last Emperor,* echoed these sentiments. After accepting the Oscar, Byrne told the press he believed that Strummer should have been given the award for his work on the *Walker* soundtrack. Rude explains, "Strummer could explore both darkness and light in a way few musicians could and that's what makes *Walker* and also *Permanent Record*[18] such compelling work."[19]

"Because he was a talented artist in another area—music—he realized that you could not do things halfway, you have to be studied," Rude adds. "While he had that powerful charisma he was not studied enough to be an actor . . . he was a hack like me." Although many felt Strummer possessed a natural, unforced ability as an actor, Strummer was the first to admit that this period of acting was more a cathartic experience rather than a serious attempt to become a full-time actor. "I played myself," Strummer amusingly told me referring to his 1989 role in Jim Jarmusch's *Mystery Train*. "It was my best performance."

Mystery Train is Jarmusch's discerning examination how various outcasts, outsiders, and foreigners view America. Jarmusch sets the film in Memphis, Tennessee using the American obsession with Elvis Presley as a grim metaphor to what passes for America. Jamrusch gives us three charming vignettes each offering a markedly unique perspective. In the first, we follow a young Japanese couple essentially on a pilgrimage to Memphis to explore the city where their American rock heroes (Elvis and Carl Perkins) once roamed. From the young Japanese hipster couple we meet Luisa, an Italian widow. Memphis now serves as an allegory for loss and renewal with Elvis appearing as her spiritual guide, promising comfort and hope. Finally, we encounter Strummer's Johnny in a bar, a Brit caricature of a 1950s rockabilly outlaw who goes by the nickname "Elvis." In fact, Johnny is a small-time crook wallowing in desperation as his wife has left him with only his brother-in-law, played by Steve Buscemi, to console him.

Jarmusch's Memphis in *Mystery Train* is equal parts exciting, mythical, and dangerous. Yet, the film's allegorical narrative offers a more critical analysis of a country as a paradox using the city that became famous for Elvis and rock 'n' roll as a stand-in for America. As each vignette intersects at a hotel that counts Howlin' Wolf's night clerk and Cinque Lee's bellhop as employees, the film plays on the troubling contradiction of a once thriving and bustling American city that is now hollow and gray, mostly inhabited by African-Americans who live with the legacy of a white man who became famous for performing Black music.

Strummer's performance in *Mystery Train* is engaging and clever. Jarmusch, an innovative director, does well in placing Strummer in this part and getting out of his way. Jarmusch describes Strummer "as being so incredibly valuable to me, both as a friend and for all the things he created." He adds that while bands like the Sex Pistols and the Ramones were about "reduction," Strummer and the Clash took "everything that flowed into their hearts and souls . . . grabbed onto that essence and used it to make it a part of themselves." In a final gesture of Jarmusch's affection and admiration for Strummer, he took part in the filming for the video of "Redemption Song." The video was shot in New York City and followed the creation of a mural painting dedicated in Strummer's honor on a wall on East Seventh Street. The mural consists of an image of Strummer in 1950s rebel rock pose with slogans "The Future is Unwritten" and "Know Your Rights" over a red, gold, and green flag emblazoned with the Lion of Judah, a symbol of power and mercy in the Rastafarian religion.[20]

In the late 1980s, Strummer became involved in the Rock Against the Rich tour, which was an attempt to inject class analysis into the political struggle by promoting issues like the redistribution of income and other socialist economic policies. He also played a prominent role in the Free Nelson Mandela concerts organized by Amnesty International.[21] Dick Rude describes Strummer's politics "as having strong views that he was willing to change" but overall it was "about taking care of his brother and of justice." Strummer believed in certain political issues "so strongly he felt they needed to be repeated," Rude tells me. Alex Cox added that Strummer's "motto might have been 'one mustn't grumble'— which about personal things he never did" and that "he pursued politics as hard as he could for as long as he felt he could." Finally, both Rude and Strummer himself describe Strummer "as an exemplar of the Rebel Way." The "dark night" after the Clash and his brief flirtation with acting and soundtrack work was a time of creative reflection and political renewal. In the end, Strummer best summs up this period and more specifically his life's work: "To someone who says to me, 'You were the spokesman for your generation and you fucked it up,' I say, yeah, but we tried—whether we succeeded or failed is immaterial—we tried."

BE BOP A LULA HERE'S JOE STRUMMER

By Ann Scanlon

Originally appeared in Sounds *April 2, 1988*

J ust within earshot of the barrow-boy cries on London's Notting Hill market is a cramped café, offering whiskey-laced coffee and early morning refuge to anyone who needs it.

For the past four years, Joe Strummer has stared into an empty cup, half listened to the crackle of a caffeine-stained wireless and reflected on a broken past and perpetually uncertain future.

As the former leader of one of one of the most influential bands of the last decade, Strummer had plenty to think about.

And it took an awful lot of coffee before he was able to understand how the Clash had allowed such anger, passion, and street sensibility to dissolve into complacency, confusion, and parody itself.

"The Clash were fucked by success," he realizes now. "We were singer/songwriters and the better we did our craft—and we tried to do it real good—the more it removed up from the frame of where we were writing from."

But it wouldn't be Strummer to wallow in coulda-always-been-a-contender contemplation for ever. Armed with the hard learned lessons of the past twelve years, he's back in the ring with an impressive soundtrack, *Walker,* and a clear vision ahead.

Until recently, it was Alex Cox who provided the main outlets for Strummer's brooding madness. When the latter gatecrashed a *Sid*

145

and Nancy party in '86, Cox invited him to work on the score and Strummer ended up writing the central song, "Love Kills."

A few months later, Cox gave Strummer a lead role in his spaghetti spoof *Straight to Hell* and subsequently asked him to appear in *Walker.*

Shot in Nicaragua, Cox's fourth movie outlines the life of William Walker, the American soldier who declared himself president of Nicaragua in 1855.

Unlike *Straight to Hell,* which revolved around a small clique of the director's friends, *Walker* drew on a huge pool of Hollywood stars and features the talents of Ed Harris, Miguel Sandoval, and Marlee Matlin.

Strummer's acting capabilities are hardly stretched as Faucet the dishwasher or as a battle extra.

"If I had any less of a role then I wouldn't be there at all," he says. "It would be best if we had it on video so I could press pause and say, Look, see that guy holding his hat running through the back of the battle scene—that's me!

"Although I do have another scene where I dive into a river with a rope and try to lasso these naked women who are washing clothes in the water."

Strummer and his *Straight to Hell* co-star Dick Rude were initially written in as comic relief to the serious storyline but, as *Walker* was cut from its original three hours to half that length, most of their efforts ended up on the cutting room floor.

"At some point Alex decided that he had to reach the *Rambo* audience, which you can understand. But really his audience is the people who'd go up to the Gate cinema or the Scala, we could have sat and enjoyed a two-and-a-half-hour *Walker,* and now it seems to fall between the two stools.

"I think Alex started with both a great script and crew of actors. They were real professionals, no complaints, no tantrums, Ed

Harris would sit down in the dirt with the extras, but everything was still very uptight.

"As soon as we got there it was (adopts phony drawl), *Right, this is dead serious. This is a five-million-dollar* picture and personally I didn't enjoy the ten weeks we spent there."

That said, Strummer was glad of the opportunity to visit Nicaragua and—just as on *Straight to Hell,* he had preferred to "method out" and sleep in a battered Dodge—so himself and Dick Rude skipped the luxuries of Managua's Hotel Intercontinental for a rented house in Granada.

"Nicaragua was just like being in a Gabriel Garcia Marquez book. There's nothing to do except sit outside on rocking chairs, rocking the mosquitoes away. You'd sit there in the afternoon and feel so clear in the mind that it was like being on a different planet."

Because they were filming in the south, the *Walker* crew were well out of the war zone. But Strummer—who once dealt in the polemics of "Sandinista" and the more specific "Washington Bombs"—still maintains his support for the Sandinistas.

"Nicaragua is a country with nothing, and the Sandinistas are the first to admit that they've made every mistake in the book. But when they took over from Somoza (the dictator who was deposed in 1979), the first thing they did was to teach everyone to read and write and make sure that there was some sort of medical care.

"There's a guy called P. J. O'Rourke who writes in *Rolling Fucking Stone* and represents the typical, Hey, dude, let's party segment of America and probably doesn't even know where Nicaragua is. Anyway, he went down there to slag it off, and of course he can go into a supermarket and see all the empty shelves, but he's not talking about the real issue which is that America supports any kind of fascist dictator so long as he ain't a commie."

It was while *Walker* was being edited in Granada, that Cox asked Strummer to write the score.

"I banged the stuff off in two weeks. I had my trumpet, violin, myself, and two suitcases in this house, and every day I'd take a couple of new songs to Al."

Less straightforward, however, was the actual recording when Strummer had to explain his arrangements to more than a dozen musicians in a San Francisco studio.

"That was incredibly nerve wracking. I felt completely paranoid all the way through the first side because the Clash would just record, Bang! Bang! And that was it.

"There's a song called 'Omotepe,' which I wrote with one finger on the piano, and when I explained it to the pianist I was almost apologizing for its simplicity. But she just said, I think that's tough, and gradually I began to feel better.

"But it was only when we cut the second side country style that it was more like rock 'n' roll and I could say, *This* is how it goes, boys. We'd do ten takes: a slow one, a long one, a fast one, a funny one—that's the way rock 'n' roll was made."

On completing *Walker* Strummer returned to London and, within weeks, a guest appearance to the Pogues at Camden's Electric Ballroom led to a three week tour of the States with them.

"It was funny how it happened," he smiles. "I'd met Jimmy The Red, a well-known drinker around Notting Hill, and he was telling me that he'd been to Narcotics Anonymous, had given up everything and was feeling great.

"So I decided to knock drinking on the head for a month, went home and was sat there feeling all smug with my new decision when the phone rand and the Pogues' manager Frank Murray said, Joe, you're gonna come to New York with us in three days time."

Standing in for ailing Pogues guitarist Philip Chevron refueled his enthusiasm for playing live.

"There's something about thrashing an instrument to the limit and that's what really appealed to me about the Pogues—the sheer physicality of the music. I'd just done *Walker* and I loved the way we could really rock the house with a tiny little thing like a mandolin, rather than bludgeoning everyone into submission with a huge wall of sound.

"Philip Chevron is a *fantastic* rhythm guitar player, and it was scary enough to learn all that stuff let alone try and play it at nine hundred miles per hour."

Four days after the last of these Pogues gigs, Strummer was back in LA writing a score for *Permanent Record*, a U.S. movie dealing with teenage suicide.

This time, he put together the Latino-Rockabilly War, a six-strong band which mixed psychobilly with Latin and jazz, and includes Zander Schloss of Circle Jerks and Poncho Sanchez, one of the most respected Latin/jazz musicians on the West Coast.

"I wrote all the songs in two weeks," says Strummer, "and that's the best way to do it, 'cos we're being too damn precious. There's not enough people pushing themselves to write.

"Instead of rewriting they'll endlessly tart it up and take it to Memphis and take it to New York and take it to this magic mix master or that. Too much money is spent papering over the fact that it's shit in the first place."

Ever since Strummer heard the Rolling Stones' "Not Fade Away," as a ten-year-old in boarding school, he has thought of nothing but rock 'n' roll.

"It's the only thing that's living to me," he claims. "I shall live and die and be judged by it."

God knows, he even sold his marriage vows for it. In 1974 he married a complete stranger, who needed immigration status in order to travel abroad, and used the resultant £100 to buy the black Telecaster that he has used every night since.

"I'd like to get divorced," he shrugs, "but I can't find her."

It's not something that Strummer—now the father of two daughters—things about from one year to the next.

"I've been with Gabrielle for ten years and we don't need a piece of paper to tell us we're together."

And although he now accepts that the Clash have split for good, he and Jones are closer than ever.

"Mick's daughter Lauren and my daughter Jazzi are the best of friends—a terrible duo—so I see him all the time. I see Paul too and I'm goin to go and see Topper who's been detained at Her Majesty's pleasure."

Strummer is curious as to what Topper will make of the recent spate of Clash reissues.

"When I heard that they were going to release 'I Fought the Law' I had a predictable reaction," he admits. "But then I rang up Rob Steiner at CBS and he explained that he was a long term Clash fan but hadn't got 'I Fought the Law' because it was released on the since deleted EP, and now sells for £45. Until then I hadn't thought about it in terms of the audience, and Rob convinced me that he'd made the right decision."

Together with Jones, Steiner subsequently worked out a track listing.

"*Story of the Clash Volume One* was my idea of a joke. I've got no right to assume there will be a second volume, but this double album is made up of all the main stuff and I think we've still got an interesting odd bag that might fit on a single LP in a couple of years' time."

For today, though, Strummer is back in his favorite Notting Hill retreat, staring into another cup of coffee but surer than ever of his next move.

"Sitting here these past four years listening to stuff out of that," he nods in the direction of an old radio behind the counter, "I've realized there's no Bop Message. And I've decided that I'm going to deliver the Bop Message to anyone who'll listen.

"It's nothing to do with bebop, I call it the Bop Message 'cos I'm differentiating it from all the drivel that I hear on the radio, which has no message to me except that some fucker wants to be famous."

It was while Strummer was working with the Latino-Rockabilly War, in a tiny studio in LA, that he fully realized the potential of the Bop Message.

"Most of the studios in LA look like the London Rock Shop, but we found this Mexican place called Baby 'O which was just a simple wooden room. I've got a song called 'Trash City,' which is going to be released as a singled off the *Permanent Record* sound-track, and I asked my friend Jason Mael to bring his Super 8 camera and shoot a video.

"He just shot it as we were recording, and the whole thing cost six hundred fifty dollars. That to me is the Bop Message."

But although Strummer's message and method is simplicity itself, he is only too aware that promoting the Bop Message won't be quite so easy.

"Right now, I'm a one-man operation and it's lovely and clear. I've got nobody to please but myself and that's the way I want to keep it.

"*Walker* sold fifteen thousand copies in America, but there's never been an advert, it's not on the radio, and the film died in a week. So I'm not dispirited by those figures 'cos what that means is that there's fifteen thousand hipsters in America who searched *Walker* out and found it.

"I don't have an extravagant lifestyle to maintain so I can almost operate on that level. Whereas if I was trying to compete on a mega-mega level I'd have to have all these wankers polishing my mix and polishing my haircut. I'm just not interested enough in Joe Strummer to push Joe Strummer the way Madonna must push Madonna."

Strummer might have resigned himself to indie sales figures, but he's planning to return to the road nevertheless.

"Touring is like a drug. You never forget what it was like to be high on that drug, but when someone comes along five years later and gives you another taste, you're addicted again. And on the Pogues tour, I really felt the bite."

"But what really annoyed me," he continues, curling his top lip into the famous snarl, "was that for thirteen numbers the audience would be rocking away, having a great time, but as soon as I stepped up to do 'I Fought the Law' and 'London Calling' all these tossers would suddenly start gobbing.

"I'm going to go back onstage and when I do I'm going to play everything from 'Keys to Your Heart' to 'Rock the Casbah'—I *insist* on playing my back catalog—but the first person to gob at me, I'm gonna jump offstage and have that Telecaster right through the center of their head.

"But," he stresses, "I don't want my songs to be about my hotel rooms or my ego. I'm a one man operation, and I'm not interested in becoming a superstar 'cos you *can't* write."

Strummer's train of though is interrupted by a stray busker who wanders over an unwittingly asks, "Can anyone tune a guitar?"

Within minutes the guitar is at the center of a fully fledged session, a café regular singing while Strummer and his friend Roughler Ray keep rhythm.

"*I am a sincere man,*" echoes Strummer, translating the singer's Spanish, "*the most thing I want in life is to spit my words out into the air.*"

And then he's lost again, keeping time with his teaspoon as simply and effectively as he'd banged out one-finger piano patterns for *Walker*.

Joe Stummer might have been unsure about where he was going or even of what he was doing, but he could never lose sight of himself.

CLASH AND BURN:

THE POLITICS OF PUNK'S PERMANENT REVOLUTION

By Dennis Broe

A sensuous mob, they think/only of food and drink;
They ignore since food is their only goal/the immortality of
the soul.

—"The Migratory Rats," by Heinrich Heine

I have the will to survive
I cheat if I can't win
If someone locks me out
I kick my way back in
—"Hate and War," by the Clash

I f punk came to "tear away the veil," to tell the world, and specifically the staid musical world of '60s rock 'n' roll, whose former dissent was now commodified, that revolution was in the air, though not on the airwaves, then its primary messengers were the Sex Pistols and the Clash. While the Sex Pistols opened Pandora's box, negating, just as the Dadaists before them, the very ground on which their art form stood, it was the Clash who would, just as the Surrealists alchemized the Dadaist energy and turned it into something enduring, with their grounding in the specific moment of the rebellion of pre-Thatcherite English working-class youth, transform the pure negation of the Sex Pistols into an animus that would continue to rebound and grow to eventually take in hip-hop and then the worldwide expansion of a globalized multiethnic revolutionary youth culture. Of course Rotten and Vicious could only be about tearing down the false gods, but Strummer and Jones, one name indicating the endurance of the rock 'n' roll guitar form, the other indicating commonality and the everyday aspect of its followers, would instead point the way toward the potential of lasting rebellion aimed not just at overthrowing the rules of a form that was proving more and more susceptible to co-optation but also at uniting that form with a consciousness that was about not finding a place in the market but shattering the marketplace. Strummer, Jones, and the Clash, most markedly in the first British album and subsequent singles, came not to save the world, but to destroy and then to rebuild it.

This impulse sprang not from preordained theory but from an absolute honesty and identification with their moment, with a Britain which offered little to its working youth and was in the process of de-industrializing, that is, of offering less. Joe Strummer, the diplomat's kid, was the theoretician, and Mick Jones was the street kid who would always "Stay Free" that is, in the terms of one of his greatest songs, stay loyal to his working-class upbringing. In addition, both theory and practice were molded not just by white working-class consciousness but also, and crucially, and most adamantly among all the punk groups, by Strummer and Jones's lasting interest in black forms, particularly reggae, and, in the deeper sense, by their interest in uniting, finding a rapprochement between, not only black and white musical forms, but also black and white working-class consciousness. Their radicalness came, as Dick Hebdige points out, in attempting to bridge this chasm at a moment when commercial interests were starting to move in the opposite direction, breaking down audiences into marketable segments. The Clash, the name itself giving voice to Marx's historical dialectic of change through struggle, also became early commentators on record industry commodification, inscribing their own struggles with their record company, the corporate giant in the pre-conglomerate era, CBS, in their music. That they eventually lost the struggle, succumbing to the temptations of the U.S. market, in an early bout with globalization, in no way diminishes their achievement both in giving expression to an individual moment and in supplying the impetus for the eventual picking up of their torch first by rap in the U.S. and, then, when that would be commodified, by hip-hop across the world.

To identify the way in which punk, and specifically the Clash, helped precipitate a permanent revolution I want to use a remarkable book by the French philosopher Stathis Kouvalakis, *Philosophy and Revolution: From Kant to Marx*. Kouvalakis, through French theorists like Michel Foucault, is concerned with restoring the immediacy of revolution, seeing this process as a rupture that tears down the old without positing a map of the new. What is revolutionary, Kouvalakis claims, paraphrasing Lenin, is the capacity to "recognize the fundamental problem of our time at the time and place of its first appearance . . . [the fact that] every question of the day—precisely as a question of the day—at the same time [becomes] a fundamental problem of the revolution."[1] This capacity to explore the present, to be immediately of it, marks the first Clash album in the way that Kouvalakis argues, in the previous century, characterized the work of the German poet Heinrich Heine and the early work of Karl Marx. Heine turned his back on an age which, as a reaction to the upheaval of the French Revolution, craved "harmony, social peace, and political moderation"[2] and portrayed, in poems like "The Silesian Weavers" and "The Migratory Rats" the insatiable hunger of the workers who in the first poem tell Germany its doom approaches, its "shroud is on our loom" as ominously "we weave."[3] In the second, the workers take the form of rats who destroy everything in front of them and who will not be appeased by politics or philosophy: "Soup-logic only and reason-dumplings/Will silence their hungry stomach rumblings."[4]

The last word though on this state of permanent readiness as permanent revolution came from a Marx just beginning his career in activism and philosophy who wrote that the lack of an exact idea of what the future ought to be "is precisely the advantage of the new trend: We do not dogmatically anticipate the world, but only want to find the new world through criticism of the old one."[5] Marx later crystallized this state of being in the now when he stated in *The German Ideology* that "communism is for us not a state of affairs which is to be established, an ideal to which reality [will] have to adjust itself. We call communism the *real* movement which abolishes the present state of things."[6] Marx, at least the early Marx, remember, was not a Marxist. Whoever suspected, though, that he was at heart a proto-punk?

ENGLISH CIVIL WAR

The Clash emerged at a moment, in 1976–77, well after the end of the sixties, when that generation's rebellion was over, and when another generation's, that in reaction to Thatcherite England, was just beginning. The U.S. Bicentennial in 1976 and the Queen's Jubilee in Britain in 1977 would be springboards for the repression to come in the Thatcher-Reagan era, and the Clash thrashed violently against the encroaching passivity these events promoted. The Queen's Jubilee, celebrating, as Clash commentator David Quantick put it, "twenty-five years of grinding the proletariat's face into the dirt with an iron heel," would be greeted by the

Clash's first album, a veritable compendium of the grief of working-class English youth.[7] Thatcher herself, crowned queen the next year, is to usher in, as Reagan will in the U.S., the post–Fordist era which featured the dissolving of the labor-business pact that had held for thirty years with an attack on the very legitimacy of unions (Reagan's first official act was to smash the air traffic controllers' union) as well as the accompanying large scale exporting of the industrial base of both countries to other areas of the globe in a worldwide corporate "race to the bottom" in order to find the lowest possible wage.[8]

Both the form and style of the first album, simply titled *The Clash,* announced a break with rock 'n' roll as usual and an absolute identification with the fate of the group's audience. This album is one of the great working-class statements of the last century. The Beatles had opened rock 'n' roll content up beyond the love song, but Punk and the Clash restored the purity of the form in their return to the short blunt bursts of the early rock 'n' roll era. The content though was radically different than the silly love songs of early rock 'n' roll. "Janie Jones" ("I'm in love with a rock 'n' roll world . . . I'm in love with Janie Jones world"), the name of a madam the punks frequented, outlines both the attraction and alienation of sex as outlet for the frustrations of the workplace. "Career Opportunities" (". . . Do you want to be, do you really want to be a cop? the ones that never knock") details the deadend that English working-class youth faced, leading an earlier generation back to the grind of the factory as depicted by the working-class character (Albert Finney) giving up his rebellion, getting engaged, and going to work at the end of the 1960s film *Saturday Night, Sunday Morning.* In Strummer and Jones's generation, when the factory itself is disappearing, this frustration leads to the junkie's clutches, and/or the dole, the army or prison, expressed in the song "Hate and War, "the only thing we have today." This critique of dead-end work has its complement, expressed in "48 Hours," in the way the group sees the weekend, the two-day reprieve. Their depiction of "leisure" recalls Adorno and Horkheimer's critique in "The Culture Industry: Enlightenment as Mass Deception," where it is the frantic other of work, recreating in its rote quality the pattern of the factory.[9] This totalizing critique is best summed up in "Remote Control" ("Don't make no noise . . . Don't make no money to get out of here") whose group-chanted bridge is simply the word RE-PRES-SION.

If the album's content is dystopian, its form belies this content and suggests the beginnings of a way out. Its language is cockney, working class argot, so thick as to be often indecipherable for an outsider and with no accompanying words on the album jacket. It celebrates language as the collective wisdom of the working class and makes no pronunciation concessions to the American market, as British groups often do. The choruses are often anthemic, sung or chanted by the group, not just by the front man, Strummer. They represent the collective element in the music that both challenges the standard rock 'n' roll division of lead singer and band and presents the chorus sentiments as group (or class) rather than individual statements. Musically, Jones' guitar slashes through the Clash's early tunes in staccato bursts of anger, a buzz saw that destroys the intricate harmonies of rock in its now fossilized stage. Yet, in key moments, especially in "Police and Thieves" the guitar plaintively, here in an unadorned solo, plays the melodic line and in a deeper way not only echoes Strummer's anger and hurt in the vocal, but also suggests that there are reservoirs of feelings beyond anger and hurt which may yet be tapped.

There was still another layer though to the Clash, a layer which, though it manifested itself imminently, that is, grew out of the specific conditions of their moment, would enable their revolutionary message to resound across the world. This was their connection to Caribbean youth in Britain through reggae. Strummer had always shown an interest in black musical forms and black politics, with an early song in his band the 101ers (named after the address of an illegally squatted house where the band lived) being a rhythm and blues riff about a "big blue policeman" and his "little black book."10

The defining moment of this connection occurred at the Notting Hill Riots in 1976. Strummer and the group's base player Paul Simonon watched as black youth threw bricks at cops expressing their frustration that would be so much a part of the album the Clash would write in the wake of this event. "White Riot" ("I want a riot, white riot, a riot a' me own"), their signature song, was written in solidarity with the event. The John Bulls running on the cover of the first album to quash the actual black riot are, in the imagination of the band, alternately running to quell the rebellion the Clash urge on their audience. The secret history of punk is that the movement was born not out of the stick-it-in-your-face attack on the Queen's Jubilee waged by the Sex Pistols ("God Save the Queen and Her Fascist Regime") but rather out of a transposing into white circles of the anger evidenced by black youth at Notting Hill the year before.11

Reggae, as Dick Hebdidge puts it, not only "carried the necessary conviction, the political bite so obviously missing in most contemporary white music" through its "aesthetics born of suffering,"12 but also, through its use of patois, a language spoken "beneath the master's comprehension," made no concession to an outside audience and seemed to be, much as the working-class punks conceived themselves, a "foreign body which threatened British culture from within."13

Both black and white youth were in the crosshairs of the British imperial system, but among the punk bands it was the Clash who perceived this most directly. In "Police and Thieves" ("in the street, fighting the nation with their guns and ammunition") the Clash take Junior Murvin's melancholy reggae song and infuse it with punk anger through Strummer's accusing vocals and Jones's slashing guitar. It's the only song on the first album in which the Clash go into a "jam," the only song over three minutes, or as they later say in "Hitsville in the U.K.," over "two minutes fifty-nine." In the song proper and the chanting over the rhythm that extends the musical interlude at the end of the song, the Clash carve out a space not only for a reconciliation of black and white youth, which in its liberal moment begat punk's Rock Against Racism, but which also attempted, in its more radical moment, to forge a bridge across the interracial chasm that would lead both groups to see their common class enemy and take action against it. The later "White Man in Hammersmith Palais" expresses this sentiment literally, but also suggests in its irony that the time for its coming to fruition may have passed: "White youth, black youth, better find another solution (other than random violence), Why not call up Robin Hood and ask him for some wealth distribution?"

The Clash's interplay with reggae persisted throughout their career, with Jones and Strummer writing about their trip to Jamaica in "Safe European Home" (on *Give 'Em Enough Rope*) and using both the ska beat and the language of Jamaican toasters in their later ode to working-class solidarity on *London Calling*'s "Wrong 'Em Boyo" ("It's wrong to cheat a tryin' man"). The interplay was acknowledged on the reggae side when studio impresario Lee "Scratch" Perry, who engineered the Clash's "Complete Control," had their likenesses inscribed in a mural in his Black Ark recording studio in Jamaica and later when Bob Marley responded to the Clash's creation of what was termed "punk dub" by recording his own "Punky Reggae Party."[14]

`CAREER` `OPPORTUNITIES`

The second way, besides their representation of the milieu of working-class youth, that the Clash pursued their immanent critique was as artists, in their reaction to their own marketing and commodification by the record industry. Like the Sex Pistols, the Clash participated in a generalized questioning by the punk movement of all phases of the record company mediation between the groups and their audience. The Clash continually made their dealings with this marketing machine an issue in their music.

In "Garageland," in responding to an infamous review by the orthodox musical press claiming they should be locked in the garage they came from with an engine running, the band viewed this homicidal suggestion as a badge of honor. "We're a garage band, we come from garageland," Strummer snarls on the chorus, then he fills in the class aspect of what it means to be a garage band: "We don't want to know where the rich are goin'. We don't what to know what the rich are doin'."

Two later singles extend their critique of the musical industry. When CBS released "Remote Control" as the first single from their debut album without consulting the band, they wrote "Complete Control," perhaps their greatest song. The song starts with a series of orders by the record company each of which beginning with "They say," equating the corporate "they" with the other powerful forces over the lives of working-class youth detailed in the song's predecessor "Remote Control." Here the Clash pose their most formally collective alternative to this control in the music itself which, with its fast-clipped singsong pace and raunchy call and response meter, is designed to duplicate the feeling of the band on the road; out there, together, taking on all comers. The song also introduces the note of irony in characterizing the culture industry which will be picked up in their next musical encounter with it. They catalogue the ways corporate conglomerate CBS is attempting to manage them and conclude by snarling at CBS's "complete control even over this song," recognizing that even their attack against the record company will be used by it for profit.

Finally, in "White Man in Hammersmith Palais," the last great song from their early revolutionary period, they deal with the larger question of commodification. Noting the process of punk becoming commercialized in a way that is echoed later in rap's old school/new school debate ("The new groups are not concerned with what there is to be learned. They're always fightin,' looking for a good place under the lightin'"), they then address the larger issue of the power of a corporate media that is just beginning to accelerate the process of centralization. In so doing they also raise the issue of the dawning penchant for product placement. "They (the punks) got Burton suits/Hah, ain't it funny/Turning rebellion into money." The question of cultural cooptation is the central problematic that both the punks and those who follow them in rap and in global hip-hop will deal with and it is the Clash that raise that question most directly and eloquently.

The next phase of their career, post-1978, is their interaction with the American market, an interaction that, in the end, destroys them. The changes start in the second album, *Give 'Em Enough Rope,* where Blue Oyster Cult producer Sandy Pearlman teaches them how to adapt their critique to the American market, where violent overthrow is indicated, not stated, and where class consciousness must be concealed, as Dick Hebdige says, in style. The album is still interesting and Jones manages in "Stay Free" to use the trope of the love song to describe the parallel between him and a buddy who ends up in jail. The "Stay Free" of the title means literally his hope for his ex-con mate and metaphorically his consciousness that to live a working-class life and not adapt to other values is to stay free.

The next album *London Calling* is pitched to the American

market. It's a perfectly awful mish mash of musical styles, only finally redeemed in the throwaway uncredited last song, "Train in Vain" which proved that the group was capable of writing a perfect pop song. The distance traveled between the first and third album can be measured by "London Calling," the title track, which suggests a phony, Hollywood blockbuster, post-Armageddon city, a fantasy dystopia which contrasts sharply to the first album's "London's Burning" a celebration of the possibility of immanent revolution and of a potential utopia realizable because of the recognition of the dystopic elements of the present. The accommodation to the American market, and to their own global marketing, reaches its nadir in Strummer-Jones's last album together, *Combat Rock*. "Rock the Casbah" which peaks at number seven on the American charts, ostensibly about democracy in the Middle East, goes on to become one of the anthems of the American troops in the first Gulf War, where the song is easily translated as a rationale for an imperial attack on the oil resources of that region.

The Clash eventually succumbed to a commodity process which in its present moment is all encompassing. As John Harris says, "Put bluntly Anglo-American popular music is among globalisation's most useful props . . . . mainstream music, whether it's metal, rap, teen-pop, or indie-rock, cannot help but stand for a depressingly conservative set of values: conspicuous consumption, the primacy of the English language, the implicit acknowledgement that America is probably best."[15]

STAY FREE

But the spirit of the first Clash album and the early singles lives on and migrates. If for punk, reggae is a "present absence,"[16] a form around which much of punk composes itself, then for rap, beginning in the Bronx in 1979 a year after the end of the first

Clash period, punk was a present or structuring absence as well. Punk taught rappers that they could challenge the record industry and create hits outside the system, that music with a rawer edge could succeed, and that revolutionary immediacy was possible in a commercial art form. Chuck D, the leader of the most politically and culturally conscious rap group of the era, Public Enemy, credited punk with "showing me that music can be a powerful social force and . . . must be used to challenge the system."[17]

At the same time rap in the U.S. was domesticated, transformed in the marketplace into the raunchy but apolitical gangster rap, the movement spread across the globe and returned again to the local immediacy of British punk in the 1970s and American rap in the 1980s. As Tony Mitchell relates in *Global Noise,* models and idioms from hip-hop in the U.S. have combined in other countries with "local musical idioms and vernaculars to produce syncretic combinations of African-American influences and local indigenous elements." This form is promoting a worldwide culture of rebellion that, paradoxically, grows out of an absolute commitment by its artists to expressing the local conditions of their repression. Global rappers, the children of Chuck D, but also of Strummer and Jones, in this punk/hip-hop nation include antiglobal communists in Italy, Basque separatists in Spain, Maori street rappers in New Zealand, and the militant Islamists of the Palestinian rap group Shehadin (Martyrs) who advocate armed opposition to Israeli oppression.[18]

By adamantly defining themselves in their early work as being of their place and time, the Clash were conversely able to take part in what Hegel termed "world spirit," the advancing of humanity forward on a revolutionary path, or what Ismael Reed, in describing how black music spreads black consciousness and rebellion, labels simply and unequivocally, "The Jazz."

A BROTHER IN REVOLUTION:
WOMEN IN PUNK DISCUSS JOE STRUMMER'S INFLUENCE

By Amy Phillips

I t was my first year of college. We were listening to *London Calling*. I said, "Man, how could anyone not love this band?"

"I don't like them," said a woman I didn't know.

A male friend commented, "Yeah, girls don't like the Clash."

"That's absurd!" I exclaimed. "I love them!"

"You," he scoffed, glancing at my plain, loose-fitting clothes, scraggly hair, and un-made-up face, "you're not really a girl."

If being a girl means being boy-crazy, fashion-obsessed, and not a Clash fan, then I'm guilty as charged. But if it means having the right bodily equipment, and being stirred by the spirit of punk to work to bring down the sexist state, well, that's another story. When Joe Strummer shouts "Anger can be power!" in "Clampdown," the first image that pops into my head is of the thousands of protesters at the March for Women's Lives in Washington, D.C., in April (and no, that has nothing to do with the Indigo Girls' horrendous version of the song on the *Burning London* tribute album). Like all great art, the Clash's music is open to interpretation. You take what you want from it, and you leave the rest. It's inspirational, but not unproblematic—especially for women.

Growing up a punk fan in a post-Clash world, I've been conditioned to think of 1976–1982 as a Golden Age, and Joe Strummer an immaculate saint (let's forget anything after '82). I saw him in concert once, on the tour supporting his 1999 album *Rock Art and the X-Ray Style*. Even then he was untouchable, seemingly deserving of only my utmost admiration and respect, not my criticism. I could imagine finding fault with Strummer no more than I could picture dissing Martin Luther King, Jr., or Mother Theresa. He was a rock 'n' roll hero, but not like Bob Dylan, the Rolling Stones, or any of those stuffy old codgers. I had no problem criticizing them. But Joe, he was different. He was *ours*—our patron saint, our guiding light, our foundation on which the canon was built.

When I set out contacting female musicians for this project, I expected to receive nothing but fawning, reverent responses to my questions about Strummer's influence on their lives and work. But these women were smarter than I was, and they knew him as a living, breathing force of nature, not a saint. "Joe was a guy who appreciated women," artist and journalist Vivien Goldman, who chronicled punk's beginnings as a writer for *Sounds, New Musical Express* and *Melody Maker,* tells me. "Recently I was talking with this girl from Kid Creole and the Coconuts and she said—I hope I'm not blowing anything when I say this—they would go out on the road with [the Clash] and they would make notes of really good chat-up lines that guys gave. And Joe came out on top. It was Joe who had the best chat-up line."

Joe Strummer using cheesy come-ons to pick up girls? It blew my mind. Women didn't always just fall at his feet without any effort on his part, because he was, you know, *Joe Strummer*? Apparently not. "He made a lot of jokes," says Ari Up, former lead singer for the pioneering all girl band the Slits. "He was big on making pranks." Pranks? The lead singer of The Only Band That Mattered, the voice of Britain's angry young underclass, the keeper of the punk rock flame, did stupid things to get people laughing? It made him sound almost . . . human.

Both Goldman and Up speak of how supportive Strummer and his bandmates were of their female contemporaries, at a time when it wasn't particularly fashionable to do so. Being a first-generation punk was hard enough, what with the majority of British society antagonizing the entire nascent subculture, but being a female punk was almost unbearable.

"It was ghastly then," Goldman says. "It was so difficult, being one of the few females. I'm not saying we didn't have a lot of fun, but it was rough. It was a boys-only club. But the Clash's attitude towards chicks was deep. They were really out there being young lions, young warriors."

Up adds, "We had the whole world against us. We were literally chased on the street. We had to walk with people like Joe or Paul [Simonon, the Clash's bass player] as bodyguards. They really were the support system of the Slits. It was so important that we had people like the Clash around us to survive all the sabotage and outcasting that was going on."

In 1977, the Clash embarked on their first nationwide head-lining trek, the infamous White Riot tour. They brought the Slits along as a support act, despite the fact that the group, comprised of Up, guitarist Viv Albertine, bassist Tessa Pollitt, and drummer Palmolive, had only previously played three live shows together. As journalist and one-time Clash manager Caroline Coon noted in her book *1988: The Punk Rock Explosion,* the Clash paid the Slits' expenses, and shared their tour bus with the girls, much to the chagrin of the driver. "The bus driver had to be bribed every day just for us to get on the bus," Up recalls. "It was OK for the boys to be bad—the Clash were tearing up hotel rooms, throwing stuff, going insane. Don Letts stuck his naked ass out the window! But we didn't do any of that stuff, and we were banned from the bus. It was the middle ages. A total witch-hunt environment. We weren't doing anything, just being childish and female and wild and free as females could be at the time, but not necessarily outrageous or disgusting. And that was offensive to people."

Coon wrote, "What they [the Slits] represent is a revolutionary and basic shift of female ego from one which is biologically defined to one which is made strong by an assertive, mainstream role in society. Thus they are far more 'threatening' than the male musicians they are touring with." But the Clash didn't feel threatened. "They weren't just our friends," Up explains. "They were our brothers in revolution. Because we were so isolated from the rest of the world, that made it an even stronger brotherhood."

The Clash continued to make a point of choosing local acts featuring female members to support them on their tours, and collaborated with women like Ellen Foley and Janie Jones on musical projects. Even their treatment of groupies seems to have been enlightened. Goldman recalls, "They used to have their followers, some of whom were male, some of whom were female, and they would just sort of posse up, and let them crash on the floor of their hotel room, let them travel on the bus. There wasn't some sort of weird sexual subtext. It was all curiously innocent, in retrospect. Not that nobody had sex ever, but it was, you know, kind of a camaraderie." Australian aboriginal rights activist Gary Foley, who accompanied the Clash on tour, is quoted on his Web site as saying, "No doubt there were young women who turned up at the shows and were keen to bed him, but he always deflected them from those sorts of thoughts and tried to encourage them to think about local political issues and engage them in broader political questions."

All in all, Strummer seems to have been a fairly upstanding gentleman who treated ladies as equals. It makes sense that the women who knew him personally would shower him with praise (reverent or not). But what explains the e-mail responses I received from musicians who weren't close to him, who only knew the man through his public persona and his work? Penelope Houston, singer for the Avengers, wrote, "I was a fan of the Clash, but not him [Strummer] in particular. He struck me as leaning towards the somewhat humorless pro-working class Brit who's got a soapbox in his back pocket." "The Clash were one of those bands that I always thought was a little too mainstream for my punk rock sensibility," explained Black Flag bassist Kira Roessler. "The really underground stuff was more my speed. I was a bit of a punk rock snob I guess. They always seemed like a straight rock band, nothing new or different except the way they dressed (which wasn't that punk anyway)." Garage-rock revivalist Holly Golightly, Kleenex/Liliput guitarist Marlene Marder and no wave icon Lydia Lunch all agreed that Strummer's music had not affected their lives in the least. Sue Gogan, vocalist for the Derelicts and Prag Vec, posited that in her case, the influencing may have gone the other way around: "The Derelicts had a much more political approach than [Strummer's first group] the 101ers, and I think that the Clash picked up on that."

As the replies filled my inbox, I realized that my image of Joe Strummer as founding father and patron saint was completely out of line. This was punk rock I was dealing with, not ancient history. Punk is all about destroying the canon, cutting idols down to size, sticking safety pins in bloated golden gods. By putting Strummer on a pedestal, I was treating him just like Dylan or Jagger; I was perpetuating phony Beatlemania as phony Clashmania. Joe himself certainly wouldn't have stood for it.

But maybe there was more to it. I remembered that college conversation as I read an email from Lora Logic, X-Ray Spex saxophonist and Essential Logic frontwoman: "Speaking personally, I think the Clash emanated a very male energy that kind of passed me by. Great band, but not really an influence on the women I knew."

Male energy! That explained everything. It was what was made the Clash attractive and repulsive simultaneously, and what ensured their place in the rock 'n' roll continuum. It was what the groupies fell for and the followers wanted to harness. And what groups like the Slits, X-Ray Spex, and Kleenex/Liliput stood in sharp contrast against.

In their 1995 book *The Sex Revolts: Gender, Rebellion and rock 'n' roll,* Simon Reynolds and Joy Press wrote of the Clash, "It's not that their songs are misogynist, but rather that they seem to have nothing to say to, about, or for women. You can count on one hand the number of songs in their immense oeuvre that are addressed to or even passingly refer to a woman, while there are endless anthems exhorting (the) 'boys' to action." It's true: there's "Janie Jones," "Julie's Been Working for the Drug Squad," "you" in "1-2 Crush on You," "baby" in "Brand New Cadillac," the female alluded to in "Protex Blue," and not much else.

"The Clash's music is amongst the most chaste rock'n'roll ever created: hoarsely hollered insurrectionary anthems, carried by martial, unsyncopated rhythms," Reynolds and Press continued, "'We had group discussions,' recalled singer Joe Strummer, 'Bernie [Rhodes, the Clash's manager] would say "An issue, an issue. Don't write about love, write about what's affecting you, what's important." One of the few songs about a relationship with a girl, Mick Jones' "I'm So Bored With You" was misheard by Joe Strummer as "I'm So Bored With the USA", and so he wrote an anti-American lyric for it. You couldn't ask for a more dramatic example of the way punk learned the art of rejection from mod put-down songs, and metamorphosised misogyny into militancy."

Certainly, girls can be militant. We want to overthrow The Man, too—probably even more than boys do. And when a group like the Clash creates a militant world in which we're ignored, well, some of us will form our own gangs and start riots of our own.

The Clash may have been, as Ari Up says, our "brothers in revolution," but their exclusionary lyrics revealed the limits of their vision. Take away all the trappings, and the Clash were a good old fashioned boy band, no different from the Rolling Stones: "The emotional framework behind the Clash—bored boys breaking loose and letting rip—was actually as traditional as they come," wrote Reynolds and Press.

Despite all that male energy, the Clash still managed to inspire quite a bit of women throughout the years. The list of female musicians who have covered their songs runs from old-school Canadian punks the Dishrags to pop divas Kylie Minogue and Annie Lennox. The post-riot-grrrl trio Sleater-Kinney, frequently described as heiresses to the "Only Band That Matters" throne, are vocal about the debt they owe to the Clash. Drummer Janet Weiss told *Rolling Stone* that Joe Strummer was one of her heroes, "Not because he is an infallible genius, but because he chose the path of his own personal truth."

Perhaps journalist Judy McGuire put it best, in a *Punk* magazine tribute to Strummer, when she wrote, "I was a painfully shy, depressed, awkward teenager the first time I heard them. They taught me about politics, to think for myself, to question authority, and to become a better, more informed person. Their lyrics gave me the courage to stop caring what other people thought about me and to always be true to myself."

When it comes right down to it, the Clash were a great rock 'n' roll band, and Joe Strummer was a great rock 'n' roll star. You don't have to be male to appreciate that, you just have to be human. Because that's what Strummer was, above all else. Not a saint, or an icon, or a god. Just a human.

ALWAYS PAYING ATTENTION:
JOE STRUMMER'S LIFE AND LEGACY

By Charlie Bertsch

A sked to define "punk attitude" in a 1999 interview, Joe Strummer begins by critiquing clichés. "Punk ain't the boots or the hair dye." But then he stops. Everybody says that. Even if it's true, the statement is itself a cliché. He isn't content to pass reflex off as thinking. "I've been asked to define it many times so I've actually thought about it for a couple of seconds." Interviewing rock stars comes pretty close to the proverbial task of herding cats. Wary of being cornered, they rival politicians in their ability to speak in negatives. But Strummer is generous to a fault. He constructs a scenario. "Say that you come in here and the music sucks. I don't care if the guy is big and in a bad mood. The first thing I do is go up to him and say 'Change that music!' I do it in a cool way though but I don't sit here fuming, getting sick and having to leave in twenty minutes. I go straight in, see what's wrong and I fix it. If we're meeting some new couples, the second someone lights a cigarette, I grab an ashtray and it'll be there while's everything's going on. Everyone else there will be standing around while their ashes fall off."[1]

This is one way of explaining the do-it-yourself approach. Don't stand around waiting for someone else to take care of things; take care of them yourself first. But Strummer stresses the point differently than most people who have written about punk. He downplays the individualism in DIY. This isn't a selfish do-it-yourself approach but a do-it-yourself *for others.* "I like to be completely aware of what's going on at all times, even if it's four in the morning. She needs a chair or he needs a beer. There's no long wait 'cause I've already clocked it." His DIY ethic is emphatically ethical. "In fact, punk rock means *exemplary manners to your fellow human beings.*" It's hard to imagine a definition of "punk attitude" more sharply contrasted to Sid Vicious's raised middle finger. Yet that archetypal gesture only tells part of the story. In another interview from the end of his career, this time for *Unpop,* Strummer recounts the story of the time the Sex Pistols opened for his first band, the 101ers. "They were walking through the dressing room, and the last guy in line was wearing an Elvis Presley gold lamé jacket, and I said 'Hey, where'd you get that from?' And he went, 'Oh, this jacket? I'll tell you where I got it from. This store up there in Camden.' And he was really nice and cool about it. And that was Sid Vicious, [who] at the time was kind of a hanger-on."[2] From his earliest fame until the day he died, Strummer's conversation was peppered with good words for the people he considered comrades. Even at his most combative, he was more interested in building up a community of rebels than in tearing down those who failed to make the grade.

Surely this explains why the Clash, far and away the most successful first-generation punk band from a commercial standpoint, have never received their full due from music historians. It's easier to tell the story of punk as a break with tradition, a refusal to play the games of the music industry, a transcendental "No" screamed at the powers that be. Although the sand in Strummer and Mick Jones's voices captured that spirit of resistance as well as anything, the band's openness to rockabilly, reggae, and the mundane melodicism of the Brill Building exposed them to criticism. If the purpose of punk was to be unpalatable to mainstream audiences, the Clash erred on the side of tastiness. Surprisingly, the biggest spoonful of sugar came from the band's politics. Their left-wing exhortations were what distinguished them most sharply from the Sex Pistols, the Buzzcocks, and the Ramones and were also, in large measure, what ended up making them more popular.

Instead of encouraging listeners to revel in their alienation, Clash songs called them to overcome it. They invited you to join the party without inquiring into your past or making demands on your future. That meant making room for fans of Elvis, the Beatles, Bruce Springsteen, as well as disaffected youth caught up in the backlash against sixties-style peace, love and understanding. It's precisely this inclusiveness that Greil Marcus highlights in his 1978 piece reporting on the sessions for the band's second album *Give 'Em Enough Rope*. "If the Sex Pistols were frankly nihilistic, asking for destruction and not caring what came of it, the Clash are out for community, the self-discovery of individuals as a means to solidarity, a new 'I' as the means to a discovery of an old 'we.'"[3] Tellingly, however, Marcus went on to produce a massive book centered on the Sex Pistols, *Lipstick Traces: A Secret History of the Twentieth Century*, but has written relatively little about the Clash. Too earnest, too popular, too easy, the Clash became one of those acts—Roxy Music is another—that many people love, but few love to discuss.

Maybe this is a good thing. The bloodrush you get listening to Strummer's cry of "London's burning!"; the brutish chords of "Guns on the Roof"; the pause-littered path of "Clampdown" can only be done partial justice in words. And Lester Bangs already hit the redline in that foolhardy endeavor way back in 1977. He describes Strummer's inspired performance one night as, "a fury unleashed on the stage and writhing in upon itself in real pain that connects with the nerves of the audience like summer thunderbolts." In the face of this overwhelming intensity, bouncing up and down struck him as a hopelessly inadequate response. "It's not your class system, it's not Britain-on-the-wane, it's not even glandular fever, it's the cage of life itself and all the anguish to break through which sometimes translates as flash or something equally petty but in any case is rock 'n' roll's burning marrow."[4] Yet as sublime as the Clash could be in the heat of the moment, their real legacy wasn't records or concert performances, but the remarkable ability to realize their values in the mundane stretches between storms. Bangs understood. He had seen the band at their hotel-trashing worst, but it didn't matter. "Here at last is a band which not only preaches something good but practices it as well, that instead of talking about changes in social behavior puts the model of a truly egalitarian society into practice in their own conduct."[5]

It's hard to imagine a tougher standard to measure oneself against. That Joe Strummer resolutely refused to settle for a more modest one, even at the height of the Clash's fame—they played New York's Shea Stadium, for goodness' sake, just like the Beatles—testifies to his steely political will. When a band gets that big, though, problems of scale emerge for which the DIY ethic is ill-equipped. Every new piece of equipment, every roadie required to set it up takes the concert tour out of the realm of the common man. By the time they released their scathing third single "Complete Control" in September 1977, the Clash already understood the depth of the trouble: "On the last tour my mates couldn't get in/I'd open up the back door/But they'd get run out again." Yet the band pressed on in its quest for world domination for five more years, willing to forsake the intimacy of a personal relationship with their most devoted fans for the promise of reaching listeners who probably wouldn't have given them the time of day on the street. All successful major-label acts confront this paradox. But its pressures must have been overwhelming for a populist punk band like the Clash.

Punk has struggled with the contradictions of popularity ever since the Sex Pistols first made the headlines. As the 1970s came to a depressing close, the artiness of post-punk drew in the community's borders. And a little later, hardcore militarized them. While the Clash was cracking the Billboard Top Ten for both the album *Combat Rock* and the single "Rock the Casbah," uncompromising bands like Black Flag, Hüsker Dü, Minor Threat, and the Minutemen were reconquering the rocky highlands of punk for true believers. In its relentless deferral of the simple pleasures of pop music, hardcore functioned much as bebop had within the jazz world of the 1940s. Independence became the watchword as the resolutely anticorporate magazine *Maximum Rock and Roll* and its followers reshaped the terms of debate. Do-it-yourself metamorphosed into a synonym for don't-do-it-on-a-major-label. The collective identity that the Clash had struggled so hard to inspire solidified into a relatively stable "we," but at the expense of connections to the wider world. Although few artists had the nerve to overtly trash the Clash, the band's financial success and corporate backing made them a poor fit within the interconnected local scenes of second-generation punk. Perhaps this explains the development of bands like the San Francisco Bay area's Operation Ivy, which came so eerily close to capturing the special Clash sound that they almost seemed like a cover band on a politically correct independent label.

After the dissolution of the Clash, Strummer kept a low musical profile for several years, focusing his attention on the world of film. When his first solo record, 1989's underrated *Earthquake Weather,* did poorly in the marketplace, he was held captive by the recording contract with Epic—now a division of Sony—that he had inherited from the Clash. Even if this silence was purely an accident, the forced hiatus kept him above the fray during the new wave of discussion about "selling out" that accompanied the unexpected commercial breakthrough of Nirvana in 1992. Kurt Cobain was not as overtly political as Strummer, but they shared a desire to instigate social change. Unlike Cobain, however, Strummer never let himself be paralyzed by self-doubt. The difference between them was partially a matter of context. Strummer didn't grow up at a time when the purity of self-marginalization was highly valued. Although he and his bandmates may have lamented the Clash's position in the industry, he never felt the need to beat himself up for signing to a major label. "Complete Control," after all, was not a one-off 45 for an obscure indie label, but a major-label single like its predecessors. The band's critique of corporate machinations was a matter of content rather than its mode of distribution. More broadly, Strummer didn't waste much time beating himself up for anything. His generosity extended to himself. That may sound like a curious formulation. But in a world where self-loathing is a prime motivational tool, Strummer's ability to fuse attentiveness with contentment stands out.

Once Strummer figured out how to extricate himself from his contract with Epic, he turned to an independent label. An imprint of the American independent label Epitaph, Operation Ivy and Rancid frontman Tim Armstrong's Hellcat was the perfect political and musical fit. While Strummer probably could have landed a major-label contract if he had wanted, he recognized the advantage of working with people who truly respect your work. But his decision also represented an endorsement of the third and fourth-generation punk acts signed to labels like Epitaph. As good as Strummer's new music was—the Mescaleros records are sounding better with age—this willingness to make connections within a punk community radically different from the one that gave birth to the Clash was every bit as important. In nearly every interview he conducted after forming the Mescaleros, Strummer took pains to give props to younger artists, some of whom weren't even born when he started performing. An interview published by the resurrected *Punk* magazine after his death is a good example. "I'm into all the new punk. I like to hear Green Day on the radio. It's a lot better than the other shit they play in England, let me tell you that. I just toured with the Offspring and got really tight with them. And my favorite group of the moment is Hepcat, from LA. They're the best ska band ever born in the United States of America, bar none."[6] The names change, depending on the interview, but in each case Strummer clearly has a sense of who needs a chair and who needs a beer.

He was always paying attention. That's what makes some of his more controversial moves so interesting to ponder. When an interviewer for the fan Web site www.strummersite.com asked him about the use of "London Calling" in an American television commercial for Jaguar, he took full responsibility. "Yeah, I agreed to that. We get hundreds of requests for that and turn 'em all down. But I just thought Jaguar . . . If you're in a group and you make it together, then everyone deserves something. Especially twenty-odd years after the fact. It just seems churlish for a writer to refuse to have their music used on an advert and so I figured out, only advertise the things you think are cool. That's why we dissed Coors and Miller." It's surely no accident that, even though Strummer's own career had been reborn on an independent label, he chose to praise major-label punk bands like Green Day, the Offspring, and even Blink 182—a fave of one of his daughter's—along with his labelmates. While he steadfastly promoted the virtues of independent record labels, underscoring the artistic bankruptcy of the corporate conglomerates that own the majors, he cheerily undermined the ideologues demand for purity. "Putting your music to an advert is a compromise. But a good advert with cool music can turn on a lot of people. I know when I'm watching TV and you get a good ad, it's an up."[7]

Joe Strummer never lost the ability to imagine his listeners' lives, the sort of people who feel the burdens of the moment ease, however slightly, when they hear a good song on a commercial. He never lost it because he was always listening to music himself, because he listened to what his fans told him before and after his shows, because he was always a good listener. Although he only made it to fifty, Strummer was old and famous enough to have been tempted by the prospect of retreating to the mirrored walls of the self-satisfied mind. But he never gave in. That's why we owe him an incalculable debt, not only for his prodigious musical legacy, but for staying true to the carefully crafted self he made famous in the Clash, the middle-class diplomat brat John Graham Mellor transformed into the proletarian hero Joe Strummer. He showed us how to get big without going soft. And he showed us how to stay big without becoming too hard. Because he recognized that there was equal danger in bending over backwards and refusing to bend an inch. Either way, you're liable to end up broken. Joe Strummer knew how to stay in one piece. His greatest gift to us is not any particular song or story, but the way all his songs and stories were bound together by the clarity of his consciousness. Even after his death, he's paying too much attention to let any ashes fall.

WHITE RIOT OR RIGHT RIOT: A LOOK BACK AT PUNK ROCK AND ANTIRACISM

By Antonino D'Ambrosio

And the society that spawned them
Just cries out who's to blame?
And then wraps itself in the union jack
And just carries on the same
> —"The Few," by Billy Bragg

At the height of the White Riot tour an earnest political journalist asked me, "What are you going to do with all the energy of your audience? How can you harness it? What do you think happens to it?" I said, "It slides under the door and out of the hall."

> —Joe Strummer

T he scene was utter mayhem. Or at least that's what the newspaper headlines blared the next day. The frenzied crowd gathered at London's Rainbow Theatre in May 1977 to see the Clash ripped chairs from their moorings and threw them at the stage. "Playing the Rainbow that night," Strummer said, was the equivalent of "playing Madison Square Garden . . . we knew that punk had arrived."[1] Coming on the heels of much civil unrest throughout England, including a recent spate of IRA bombings, the Clash's full-throttle performance was a statement that it was time to find purpose and create "the movement." Punk was not swearing on TV, like the Sex Pistols famously did only a few weeks before, but becoming an active agent for collective social change, echoing the nineteenth-century poet Rimbaud's invocation to "change life."[2]

Freedom, both personal and political, was the driving force behind their performance that night. They issued a spirited declaration, telling all that the Clash were going to take charge in the all-important struggle ahead; anything was possible if you were willing to stand up and fight. The song that "kicked things over that night," as Strummer said, "was 'White Riot.'" The Clash wanted to destroy racism and spread the message of unified rebellion. This song was their rallying cry, which aimed to transform Clash followers from passive concertgoers into a guerrilla army tired of "going backwards" and willing "to take over."

Yet a closer look at punk's approach to antiracism reveals that it was far from effective. In some instances, it did more to breed racism and ultimately undermine any serious attempt to bring together conflicting multiracial, ethnic communities, and working-class whites.

The Clash certainly tried to lead the antiracist charge within the punk movement. They took a prominent role in Rock Against

Racism and were committed supporters of the Anti-Nazi League.[3] There were a number of reasons for the group's anti-racist activism but the primary reason stems from the influence of Strummer and Paul Simonon, the Clash bassist. They both greatly admired Afro-Caribbean music (reggae, dub, ska), particularly Simonon. Both had spent their youths living closely with multiethnic communities.[4] The respect that members of the Clash felt for the music influenced their interest in and concern for the struggles of Afro-Caribbean communities in England. This attitude reflected in a broader sense the general influence of blacks within English culture following World War II. This influence would become a key component in shaping the punk movement's antiracist activism. Conversely it would also greatly limit and weaken the movement's scope and value.

Beyond the fact that some of the Clash's music was laced with reggae rhythms and ska beats or that they covered important reggae songs like "Police and Thieves" and "Pressure Drop," the group's anti-racist political message was not easily conveyed to their listeners. Two songs that the Clash recorded early on—"White Riot" and "White Man in Hammersmith Palais"—reveal the ambiguity of their multiethnic message. In the latter song, Strummer describes his experience with Simonon at a reggae event at the Hammersmith Palais, recounting the duo's disappointment in the performances, and his realization that unity between the Afro-Caribbean people and white punk youth seemed nearly impossible. In the song, Strummer describes the fighting and robbing as counterproductive and ultimately dangerous as it further splintered blacks and whites. The true enemy was the State, as Strummer wrote in the following lyric:

> *Dress back jump back this is a bluebeat attack*
> *'Cos it won't get you anywhere*

Fooling with your guns
The British Army is waiting out there
An' it weighs fifteen hundred tons

To a certain degree, the ambiguities of "White Man in Hammersmith Palais" does work in the song's favor as the listener gets the sense that Strummer is making a plea for true unity. "I was really trying to get at the division between the black rebels and white rebels and the fact that we got to have unity or we're just going to get stomped on," Strummer explained nearly a decade later.[5]

"White Riot" was written after Strummer, Simonon, and the Clash's manager Bernie Rhodes were caught in the middle of a riot between the police and Afro-Caribbean youth gathered at the Notting Hill Carnival on August 30, 1976. In the song, Strummer cries: "Black people gotta lotta problems/But they don't mind throwing a brick/White people go to school/Where they teach you how to be thick." While discussing the song Strummer said, "our goal was to prod those people who were complacent and comfortable . . . it was important to join the struggle with those groups being beaten down and who were willing do something about it . . . 'cause we all were being beaten down . . . we had to realize we were all in the some boat and unity was a necessity or we would get smashed."

To complicate matters, England was on the cusp of a period of intense political and social conservatism that would dominate the country for the next two decades. The reactionary build-up was creating a hostile, violent environment in which many were choosing sides in the escalating conflict between marginalized communities and the white power structure. The Tory Party effectively seized the opportunity to lure working-class white youth to join their party, blaming immigrants and racial minorities for the terrible economic conditions. And in terms of racial violence, the

National Front was not alone. The violent Anti-Paki league directed their abuse at the South Asians who were rapidly populating cities throughout Northern England. For this reason, "skinhead" came to embody anti-Asian hatred and much of the neo-fascist music was basically anti-Asian rants.[6]

But it was the the National Front, a sinister, neofascist hate group on the rise who draped its racist and xenophobic beliefs with the Union Jack, that was successful in building a small but significant electoral base amongst disaffected white working-class voters.[7] As Strummer mentioned, the same misery that caused people like him "to search for positive solutions," stirred feelings of anomie and hatred among others who ultimately "chose the route of fascism." The neo-fascist punk band Skrewdriver became the cultural face of white supremacy, proudly taking up the flag to wage a race war. Their music, described as Racialist, helped spread a message of hate while recruiting English youth to join along.[8]

Even among listeners of the Clash, Stiff Little Fingers, and the Jam, the not easily discernable anti-racist message caused confusion resulting in a gross misinterpretation of the artist's intention. Roger Sabin explains, "in terms of song lyrics, anybody who used the word 'white' could be asking for trouble."[9] As a result, songs like "White Riot" became anthemic favorites of the National Front and were given much press in their magazine *Bulldog*. Furthermore, the incorporation of fascist iconography into their aesthetic by some bands/musicians including Joy Division (who took their name from Hitler's military brothel), Siouxsie and the Banshees (who performed wearing swastikas and singing about the Nazis), and even Mick Jones and Paul Simonon who were in a group called the London SS before they founded the Clash, sent a troubling message to their audiences.[10]

The myopia of the antiracist punk movement was further revealed by their indifference to and participation in other forms of hate crimes. The racism directed against Asians, Hispanics, and Jews was essentially ignored.[11] Rock Against Racism tried to organize events in areas highly populated by Asians, for example, but these events generally failed thanks in large part to the racist blunders of the bands involved including Sham '69 and Adam and the Ants.[12] Songs like "White Riot" and the Stiff Little Fingers' "White Noise" were certainly illustrative of the tenuous line some musicians walked in an effort to promote a specific ideal of unified rebellion.[13] These songs held a romanticized view toward the struggles of oppressed Afro-Caribbean and black communities believed to possess a music, style, and approach to life that was exciting and therefore should be celebrated. Asians, Jews, and other minorities were not represented, begging the question: How does supporting a certain community's music or culture make one anti-racist? Of course, the alliance between punks and the Afro-Caribbean community became the stuff of myth when Bob Marley recorded "Punky Reggae Party" immortalizing the supposed unity:

> *Rejected by society*
> *Treated with impugnity*
> *Protected by their dignity*
> *I face reality*
>
> *new wave, new craze*
> *new wave, new craze*
> *new wave, new craze*
> *new wave, new craze*
>
> *Wailers still be there*

the Jam, the Damned, the Clash
Wailers still be there
Dr. Feelgood too, ooh

Norman Mailer's *The White Negro* offers some historical context to this romanticized view of racial struggle and the specific fixation on the "coolness," and "hipness" of "rebellious" blacks. Superficially, Mailer's book comes across as macho posturing and Beat-era rhetoric.[14] Ultimately, a bewildering fetishization of an aggressive African-American response to a history of persecution is what lies at the heart of Mailer's *The White Negro*. For that reason, Mailer contends that white communities must appropriate "blackness" in order to effectively revolt against repressive American society.

The thematic similarities between *The White Negro* and songs like "White Riot" are rooted in the general belief that blacks are ideal symbols of oppression and are thus perfect models for resistance to state oppression. Strummer explained that "White Riot" was "a call to kick things off," a favorite expression of his, and to bridge the "divide between black and white youth." Mailer intended to reach white ethnics, intellectuals, and most importantly artists who he believed were excluded from society like blacks. Furthermore, *The White Negro* asserted that the appeal of black struggle would deliver whites, namely white hipsters, from the drab conformity of the 1950s.

The outgrowth of Mailer's ideas stem largely from the Beats, from Kerouac to Ginsberg, who wrote romantically about blacks and their struggle. James Baldwin quotes Kerouac in *Nobody Knows My Name*, "wishing I were a Negro feeling that the best the white world had offered was not enough ecstasy, not enough life, joy kicks, darkness, music, not enough insight."[15] Mailer adds that "blackness" offers a staid, conservative society liberation.

White hipsters and the like needed to take on, from Mailer's stand-point, the sexual freedom and hostility blacks seemed to possess towards the society that subjugates them. This combination would be the force to propel "hip" white society into action. For Strummer, it was clearly more of a case of class and recognizing the need for class struggle. Poor working-class whites needed to understand that their lot in life was tied to building relationships with other marginalized communities instead of separating themselves based on socially constructed (not political) differences.

Both Mailer and Strummer believed that at the heart of their work was a demand for critical self-examination and an evalua-tion of the circumstances that have created the sense of individual complacency and inability to stand against tyrannical society. Mailer argued that the severe treatment of blacks throughout American history has fostered a consciousness that is best described as part-psychopath. "Hated from the outside and there-fore hating himself," Mailer wrote, "the Negro was forced into a position of exploring all those moral wildernesses of civilized life which the square automatically condemns as delinquent or evil or immature or morbid or self-destructive or corrupt."[16] He con-cludes by declaring, rather ridiculously, that we must emulate this part of the Negro and "encourage the psychopath" in oneself."[17]

Shortly after publication of *The White Negro,* James Baldwin wrote a response aimed directly at Mailer, a friend, called *The Black Boy Looks at the White Boy.* He first rebukes *The White Negro* for demeaning and pathologizing racial minorities and then argues that it is dangerous for anyone to adopt "blackness" as a means of political self-transformation, particularly if white ethnic minorities are attempting to wear the mask of "blackness" in an effort to appear stronger in the face of oppression.[18]

Baldwin points out that Mailer's thesis is defenseless when one takes into account that the majority of black Americans were hard-working, conservative, Christian citizens not displaying any of the quixotic qualities Mailer so greatly envied. And moreover, to consider the struggle of blacks as "cool" or "hip" is unwise. "But why should it be necessary to borrow the Depression language," Baldwin writes, "of deprived Negroes, which eventually evolved into jive and bop talk, in order to justify such a grim system of delusion."[19] Mailer's assertion that the "psychopathic hipster personality" would lead to a joyous transcendence outraged Baldwin who countered that these personality distortions were a sign, not of joyous transcendence, but of "humiliation and suffering."[20]

Still, social upheavals including the Civil Rights movement did lead some young whites to identify with and emulate black activists such as Malcolm X, Stokely Carmichael, Huey P. Newton, and Martin Luther King, Jr. They became the heroic models for would-be white subversives. And this is what occurred in the antiracist punk movement with respect to Afro-Caribbean musicians like Horace Andy, Sly and Robbie, and Toots and the Maytals, and especially Jimmy Cliff and Bob Marley. I often wondered what exactly was going through the minds of all those who sang along to songs like "White Riot"? Did the followers of the Clash understand that they were calling for a unified rebellion or were they hearing a completely different, more sinister message? Punk as a subculture was not impervious to the larger society that it existed within—the societal values, stereotypes, and ideologies concerning race were difficult to dispel in a three-minute song or even a series of well-intentioned concerts.

David Widgery's *Beating Time* makes the case that Rock Against Racism and the Anti-Nazi League found a perfect ally in the punk movement. In spite of that, these and other historical accounts are more revisionist and to a degree disingenuous. In America, the response to racism by the punk community made that of England's look like the new Civil Rights movement. Lester Bangs addressed this in the essay *The White Noise Supremacists,* a sharp indictment of the rampant racism within the New York City punk scene originally written for the *Village Voice.* He recounts countless examples of prominent musicians who adopted a "racist chic" and "racist cool" attitude. Ivan Julian, one of a handful of Black musicians in the New York punk scene at the time, told Bangs. "It's like a stance . . . a real immature way of being dangerous."[21] Bangs also recounts Nico of the Velvet Underground's explanation of Island Records dropping her from the label: "I made a mistake. I said in *Melody Maker* to some interviewer that I didn't like Negroes. That's all. They took it so personally . . . although it's a whole different race. I mean, Bob Marley doesn't resemble a negro, does he? . . . He's an archetype of Jamaican . . . but with the features of white people. I don't like the features. They're so much like animals . . . it's cannibals, no?[22] In the end, Bangs concludes that Rock Against Racism and other attempts "at simple decency" could never work in a scene that shows little tolerance and even more indifference to racism.[23]

The situation Bangs discusses has become the norm as punk and pop music in general steers clear of politics, especially when in relation to race and class with notable exceptions that today include Bad Religion, NOFX, and Anti-Flag.[24] Strummer and the Clash remained undaunted if not a bit bruised back in England and dedicated themselves to continuing what they started. "The media scrutiny was intense," Strummer told me. "Any time we made any kind of statement or played a benefit show it would be manipulated and distorted to the point that they were literally putting words in our mouths . . . it took the steam out of us and made us at times somewhat reluctant to speak out."[25]

Strummer then explained, "but when Margaret Thatcher started using race" and was ingeniously employing a racist rhetoric into her campaign, "the media, for the most part, did little to challenge her." Thatcher went on to become Prime Minister from 1979 to 1990.[26] Her government did its best to rollback or eliminate many social programs that the 1945 Labour government had inaugurated. It also expanded police powers against immigrant and racial minority communities; one of the results, arguably, were the riots in England's inner cities during the long hot summer of 1981.

Linton Kwesi Johnson, "the true Rude Boy" as Strummer called him, described those involved in events like Rock Against Racism as nothing more than "liberal racists."[27] "In the seventies, sections of the white left in this country were trying to exploit the conditions that blacks found themselves in and trying to win us over to their various ideological positions. They saw us as victims. We had an analysis that we were not victims. We had a history of struggle and resistance against British colonialism, which in a sense was being continued in this country. We needed to build independent organizations that could carry our struggles, our hopes and our aspirations forward."[28]

Crass, the definitive radical punk band, supported Kwesi Johnson's position.[29] In the song "White Punks on Hope," the group took on the Clash and those in the punk scene with uncompromising, critical directness:

> They won't change nothing with their fashionable talk,
> All their RAR badges and their protest walk,
> Thousands of white men standing in a park,
> Objecting to racism's like a candle in the dark.
> Black man's got his problems and his way to deal with it,
> So don't fool yourself you're helping with your white liberal shit.

However, Kwesi Johnson did have a more nuanced approach about what needed to be done. "I believe in humanity, that all races have more in common than they do different," he continued.[30] "If you're not thinking in international terms in the twentieth century you're backward" and Strummer shared this view completely as evidenced by his most recent creative and political activity. Kwesi Johnson felt that some, like Strummer and the Clash, were sincerely trying to do something to move forward and felt that alliances could be built among some groups and organizations at the time. "We did not see ourselves as separatists," Johnson explains. "We felt that, given the particularities of our historical experience, we needed to organize ourselves independently as a force and to build alliances with progressive white organizations."[31]

Looking back, Strummer felt, that despite the many missteps and contradictions, there was a sincere attempt to respond to issues of racial injustice. Something had to be done and somewhere along the way people understood his message and changed the way they thought and acted. Even so, his "most recent work takes into account a much more global perspective and with it a more thoughtful approach to not only racial injustice but ethnic and immigrant discrimination." Then he paused and looked at me and said, "When the music you are playing is considered a danger, a threat and then you combine it with a message of justice it can't not be allowed to stand . . . you will be crushed by those who are against this political view and also by many who say they are with you."

YOU CAN'T Have A REVOLUTION without SONgs

YOU CAN'T HAVE A REVOLUTION WITHOUT SONGS[1]:
THE LEGACY OF VICTOR JARA AND THE POLITICAL FOLK MUSIC OF CAETANO VELOSO, SILVIO RODRIGUEZ, AND JOE STRUMMER

By Antonino D'Ambrosio

Victor stood in the stadium
His voice was brave and strong
And he sang for his fellow prisoners
Till the guards cut short his song
His hands were gentle, his hands were strong
　　—"Victor Jara," by Adrian Mitchell

As every cell in Chile will tell
The cries of the tortured men
Remember Allende, and the days before,
Before the army came

Please remember Victor Jara,
In the Santiago Stadium,
Es verdad—those Washington Bullets again
—"Washington Bullets," by the Clash,

When Joe Strummer first stepped out onto a London stage he was a 1970s version of the 1920s and '30s dust bowl musicians who first stirred his imagination as a young boy. Before playing in the pub-rock band the 101ers, Strummer had spent time "busking" in the London streets and tube working alongside Tymon Dogg.[2] Performing with Dogg helped Strummer hone a musical sensibility that would endure throughout his entire life. The 101ers were a London music scene favorite and Strummer, who had long hair, wore jeans, boots, and a checkered shirt began calling himself Woody after Woody Guthrie, one of his musical and political heroes. Guthrie's influence on music and politics was profound and serves as both the model and foundation for all of Strummer's work. He was a cultural pioneer— mixing traditional music with emerging musical styles and forming compositions that were injected with radical political lyrics taking on the cause of the dispossessed.

At the time of his death it seemed that Strummer had come full circle. With a distinctive worldview and artistic vision, his newest recordings had a fury reminiscent of the Clash and a maturity gained from hard fought battles won and lost. In the years beginning with the release of *Rock Art and the X-Ray Style* recorded with his new band the Mescaleros, Strummer was climbing hard to fully join the ranks as one of contemporary music's most compelling political musicians.[3] Building on what he started with the Clash, he incorporated scores of world musical styles to create new music that once again carried his unique subversive wit and humanist politics.

"That's bullshit dumb," Joey Ramone once remarked about groups like the Clash who decided to use their music as a vehicle for political activism.[4] "If anything," he continued, "punks should have no politics or be right wing."[5] Not only was Strummer up against a political and social environment that rejected much of what he had to say as nothing more than dogmatic leftist rhetoric, he also had to contend with a music scene that felt his exploration and mixing of different musical styles was "un-punk." The rampant hostility and affected negativity that so dominated punk with slogans like NO FUTURE made for great press.[6] Punk became and remains to a large degree, a reactionary music, a trivial reflection upon societal problems whether alienation or heartbreak.[7] It's what the record companies like because there is some profit to be made with little risk. Don't challenge the kiddies to think about their reality in any critical way that may engage and empower them. Make them feel even worse about their lot in life. Commercialize hopelessness. Commodify self-loathing. As Strummer sang, turn rebellion into money. And lot's of it.

Strummer certainly did have his moment with the Clash and his success, many believed, weakened any political stances he took.[8] "I think I self-consciously destroyed it all," he remarked to me, "Once Jones was gone the Clash were no more . . . and with Reagan and Thatcher . . . there was no room for questioning and even less tolerance for protest music." It is true that the once celebrated "Only Band that Mattered" was about the music and the message and without the two, success and all the rest of it did not matter. So Strummer floated a bit for the better part of a decade and returned on his own terms. The music and message were tied tightly together again in what ultimately became his last stand.

In a life that was filled with ironic twists, Strummer was entering his prime five decades into his life. All that had come before was a long rehearsal for the next stage in his creative-activist life. Before his death, Strummer was influencing new musicians all around the world with his impassioned blend of inspired new music and political activism. "He showed me that music could be a very powerful political tool," Manu Chao explained, "we should not be willing to compromise, and take the necessary step forward to fight injustice with art."[9] Manu Chao is a gifted musician, who in many ways is an heir to Strummer's creative-activist legacy. Crafting music incorporating a wide-range of musical styles, Chao expands upon the work he started with Mano Negra, which named itself in honor of an Andalucian anarchist group. Spanish natives who immigrated to Paris, Mano Negra combined rai, rock, rap, and flamenco to create a style they dubbed "Patchanka."[10]

Strummer's influence on the *Rock en Español* and the World music movements and, to a lesser degree, hip-hop and reggae, continues to be extensive. Café Te Cuba, Tijuana No!, Los Olvidados, Maldita Vecendad, Spaccanapoli, and Anouk are artists ranging from Africa, Europe, and South America who cite Strummer, the musician and political activist, as a primary influence. The self-effacing charm and intellectual maturity Strummer the songwriter revealed in his later recordings is rooted in his appreciation of the political folk of Brazilian Caetano Veloso and Cuban Silvio Rodriguez, musicians dedicated to uplifting the repressed peoples of the world.

For Strummer, the vanguard socio-political movements of the 1960s and early 1970s played a huge role in his development as a both a musician and an activist and both Veloso and Rodriguez played a significant role in fostering the change. "May '68 was a moment that showed me that anything was possible," Strummer told me, "and what followed in the '70s was just a mess . . . we needed to get behind something and when punk broke I had something I could not only get behind but be a part of . . . you see we were part of this post World War II generation . . . there was a great deal of disaffection . . . we wanted no part of what was being offered to us, which seemed to be dead-end jobs that did very little for the working class . . . and we were frustrated because we had no voice in a political system that was more a tool for the ruling class"[11]

Strummer watched as people were rebelling against right-wing dictatorships and scoring some short-lived democratic victories in France, Chile, and to a lesser degree the United States. He also witnessed the role music played in helping to bring about these historic political changes. In the late 1960s, these emerging, exciting artists including the Last Poets and the MC5 in the United States, Leo Ferre in France, and Mercedes Sosa in Argentina were in effect bold composers arranging a new revolutionary soundtrack.[12] Not too soon after, Strummer would find himself part of the next wave of politically active musicians introducing new music to the world that was electrifying and determined to change things.

Caetano Veloso was a member of this emerging group of radical musicians. Regarded as the father of *Tropicalismo*, the Brazilian musical movement of the 1960s, which he created together with Gilberto Gil at the beginning of the Getulio Vargas military dictatorship, Veloso was radically altering the face of modern music. Shortly before this time, Silvio Rodriguez had joined together with other musicians to form the *Movimiento de la Nueva Trova* (New Ballad Movement). La Nueva Trova had its roots in la *Nueva Cancion* (New Song) movement.[13] This development was in many ways part of an international wave of political folk singer-songwriters that included Phil Ochs, Pete Seeger, Joan Baez, Roy Brown, and Victor Jara. Yet for political folk artists including Pablo Milanés and Sara González it was difficult to get recorded, played on the radio, or have concerts in most venues. In what became another key element of political folk, they took it upon themselves to create their own forum in order to get the music out. Casa de las Américas,[14] the literary and cultural center of Cuba, became this forum and their refuge. "La nueva trova and what some of these musicians were doing" Strummer explained, "went a long way to helping us organize protests like Rock Against Racism, the Anti-Nazi League, Rock Against the Rich, and the Red Wedge."

One of the key contributors of la Nueva Cancion was Victor Jara. Jara had taken political folk music to astounding heights in the early 1970s describing his role as an artist as "an authentic creator and in very essence a revolutionary . . . a man as dangerous as a guerrilla because of his great power of communication."[15] As Strummer remarked, "Jara's music went beyond protest music, it was revolutionary music." His music and performances were significant in helping Salvador Allende and his Popular Unity Party ascend to the presidency in Chile in 1970.[16] Jara's music is filled with his love for the struggles of the indigenous and working people of rural Chile with "La Plegaria de un Labrador (A Farmer's Prayer)" and "El Manifiesto (The Manifest)" being two of his most renowned songs. The song "Angelita Huenumán" is a good example of Jara's support of the hard working Chilean people from which he came:

> Angelita, in your weaving
> there is time and tears and sweat,
> there are the anonymous hands
> of my own creative people

With his music, theatre, and poetry, Jara was a cultural hero in the eyes of the Chilean people. It is no wonder then that his performance at the Stadium of Chile capped Allende's campaign for office. In 1971 Jara wrote, "In every place where we perform we should organize, and if possible leave functioning, a creative workshop. We should ascend to the people, not feel that we are lowering ourselves to them. Our job is to give them what belongs to them—their cultural roots—and the means of satisfying the hunger for cultural expression that we saw during the election campaign."[17]

Unfortunately, Allende's time as Chile's president was violently cut short when on September 11th, 1973, General Augusto Pinochet, with support from the CIA, orchestrated a violent and ultimately successful coup d'etat of the democratically elected government.[18] Tens of thousands were rounded up and placed in the Stadium of Chile. Here, they became known as the *desaparecidos* or disappeared.[19] Many were brutally tortured, and murdered. Victor Jara found himself among them and while in captivity his hands were broken by the guards who then presented him with a guitar telling him to try and play now. With smashed hands, Jara took the guitar and performed the Popular Party anthem.[20] Shortly after torturing Jara the military murdered him with a machine gun and then dumped his body in a mass grave. Survivors of the imprisonment managed to smuggle out bits and pieces of Jara's final unfinished composition, which ended with the lyrics "silence and screams are the end of my song."[21]

Those that deny "music and politics should not be mixed," as the Scottish political folk musician and Celtic songwriter Dick Gaughan says, "[should] tell that to the CIA and their thugs who murdered Jara because his repertoire didn't suit their interests."[22] Gaughan adds that Jara's "People's music, folk music if you will, is very dangerous stuff! It is subversive to acknowledge that ordinary people actually have a culture with artistic merit. This gives the lie to those who would like us to think that the poor are poor because they are stupid."[23] Strummer adds, "Jara's murder is just part of a long history of trying to destroy revolutionary music and the potential it has to mobilize people."

Veloso can certainly attest to that as he had his own encounter with state repression in 1968. Veloso along with Gil were arrested by the Vargas dictatorship for "disrespecting the national anthem and Brazilian flag."[24] After a brief imprisonment, they were forced to leave the country where they were exiled to England. Still this did not stop Veloso as it bolstered his resolve to continue to speak out making him a defiant hero in the eyes of many Brazilians. The exile was a critical mistake on the part of the Vargas dictatorship for it allowed Veloso to introduce himself to a new audience in England and Europe while exposing the troubling political situation in Brazil.

Strummer borrowed heavily from Veloso both thematically and stylistically through his career with many examples found on the Clash album *Sandinista!* and much later on his solo record *Global A Go-Go*. At the heart of Veloso's Tropicalismo was a cultural movement whose aim was the reevaluation of traditional Brazilian music and the incorporation of non-Brazilian musical styles. The movement pushed Brazil into a new era of pop avant garde but it more importantly challenged the dominant socio-political order of the day. Veloso's impact is revealed in the beautiful "Algeria, Algeria (Happiness, Happiness)," a song recalled in Clash songs like "Know Your Rights." "I'm going without handkerchief, without papers/Nothing in my hands or pockets," Veloso sings, alluding to the tightening repression imposed by the Vargas dictatorship on the Brazilian people's everyday lives, which included carrying documentation at all times or suffering the consequences of arrest or worse.

"Algeria, Algeria" was, in part, influenced by another Brazilian political musician, Chico Buarque, a politically outspoken and popular performer often described as Veloso's rival.[25] Buarque's "A Banda" was the spiritual, musical, and political inspiration for "Algeria, Algeria." "A Banda" depicts a Brazil that is slipping away:

My long-suffering people
Said goodbye to their sorrows
To see the lands pass by
Singing songs of love

Both songs were compelling declarations of the need to recognize the serious political and cultural problems gripping Brazil during this time and quite a few of Strummer's newest recordings including "At the Border Guy" and "Bummed Out City" are reminiscent of this political theme. Veloso and the Tropicalistas were resisting the introduction of mass consumer culture into Brazilian society and the dictatorship's attempts to curry favor with the United States. "What is good for the United States is good for Brazil," Juracy Magahaes, minister of foreign affairs under Vargas, famously declared.[26] Veloso was deeply troubled by this and the threat it posed to Brazilian culture while dismayed by efforts of the Brazilian left to respond to these and other issues.

Veloso realized that the left was easily distracted by sectarianism rather than solidarity. Again, these are beliefs that Strummer shared with Veloso and he immortalized them with the Clash song "White Man in Hammersmith Palais," a song that challenged punks and nonpunks, black and white youth, and marginalized communities to join together rather than fight one another. Frustrated, Veloso joined with Rogerio Duarte,[27] who believed that to truly fight oppression you must first come to remove "the embryonic forms of oppressive structures within the very groups fighting against it."[28] Veloso found himself unpopular for this stance but pushed forward to establish *Esquerda Festiva*

(Festival Left)[29] as a more thoughtful response to the political turmoil gripping Brazil.

As Veloso was trying to use his music to rebel against the Vargas regime in Brazil, Silvio Rodriguez became captivated with the revolution in Cuba and angered about the country's subsequent isolation perpetuated by the U.S. led embargo once the Batista dictatorship was overthrown. Living in Argentina at the time, he was inspired by the political folk music of "the voice of the silent majority," Mercedes Sosa.[30] Sosa was the driving force behind la Nueva Cancion movement, and the first to experiment with traditional music and mixing rock 'n' roll. "Sosa was the mother of rebel music," Strummer explained, "she had the courage and will to produce something radical and paid a huge political price for it . . . her work continues to challenge me to this day."

Soon Rodriguez, like Jara, became an important voice in freedom and justice movements throughout the Americas as he became the heir to the legacy left behind by Jara's death. He is considered by many to be the current voice of Latin-American rebellion, a position he respectfully downplays: "that people identify so well with my songs is for the very fact that they recognize their own lives."[31] Rodriguez adds, "many people describe me as a poet who sings, but what I am really doing is inviting everyone to join my band, which is the band of the Revolution and of beauty."[32] Rodriguez's music is interesting in that the political message is not as clear as Strummer's and his musical style is much more esoteric than Veloso's. As Strummer pointed out, it is the very nature of the mysticism, poetry, and innovative use of language that expands the boundaries of societal consciousness on all things political and cultural in Rodriguez's music.

The song "Unicornio" has come to define Rodriguez's political folk. The poetic imagery is a beautiful subterfuge for a message of human struggle. Rodriguez sings: "My blue unicorn got lost yesterday/but I only have one blue unicorn/and even if I had two/I'd only love that one." While "Unicornio" captures Rodriguez the mystic, other songs including "Nuestra Temo (Our Story)," "No Hacen Falta Alta (You Don't Need Wings)," and "Sueno de Una Noche de Verano (A Midsummer Night's Dream)" showcase Rodriguez the steadfast humanist and radical. These recordings have much in common with Strummer's recordings on *Rock Art and the X-Ray Style* and *Global A Go-Go*. It is music that serves to confront the tired uniformity of popular culture and speaks to those who are culturally disenfranchised. Even now what is most evident in the music of Veloso, Rodriguez, and Strummer is their unyielding accountability to produce work that celebrates culture as the true foundation of a free society.

Paramount to each of these artists were their feelings of responsibility to "turn people on to something new." With his two first albums, Strummer showed that he was composing "genreless" music, creating records that moved effortlessly from honky-tonk to cumbia to Balkan to Celtic to Arabic music. In his bio on *Global A Go-Go* Strummer explains that "Shakhtar Donetsk," the album's spiritual and cultural anchor, "is the name of a Ukrainian football team and I just knew there was a good story in there. We don't know what's going on beyond our own neighborhood, that's what it's saying. The song is about the movement of peoples and exiles and economic fugitives. Refugees add to our culture. They bring talents and abilities with them. So it's a song calling out for some more intelligent leadership in the world."

Indeed, fashioning a music that is political yet enchants the listener allowed for each musician to boldly delve into areas of life and society that most performers never dare to explore. With his final posthumous album, *Streetcore*, Strummer returned to hard-driving rock 'n' roll evocative of his finest work with the Clash while creating a spiritual and rebellious record. "Where the hell was Elijah," he sings in "Get Down Moses," demanding to know where the prophets have gone who promised salvation. "[You gotta] get down Moses," he continues, "Once we were free/The recipe for living/Is lost in memory." It is an album of recollections, connections, and faith, channeling every disparate musical influence from bits and pieces of past Clash songs like "The Call Up," to lyrical touches suggestive of Dylan, Springsteen, and Woody Guthrie. In the track "Arms Aloft," Strummer may have penned the truest description of the spark that fuels his political spirit:

> *Falling back in the garden*
> *of days so long ago*
> *somewhere in the memory*
> *the sun shines on you boy*

> *May I remind you of that scene*
> *We were arms aloft in Aberdeen*
> *The spirit is our gasoline*

Significantly, the one chief distinction between Strummer's political folk and that of Veleso, Rodriguez, and Jara, is that the others were all products of sweeping political movements. In each case, the musicians cast themselves into the middle of the political fray and this served to inspire them to create. It is important to understand that the social and political movements of the 1960s from the civil rights movement in the U.S. to France in May '68 provided a compelling forum for artists to originate work that was distinctly political. Just as "you can't have a revolution without songs," it is true that you can't have songs without a revolution. While punk was a social movement, it was chiefly a marginalized subculture dominated by reactionaries that did little to change the dominant political culture. Strummer, the eternal seeker and optimist, spent a lifetime creating music in hopes of placing it within a larger social movement.

In the end, the political folk music of these musicians advances a tradition of what Veloso explains as "liberating people to see a broader perspective, enabling a new un-dreamt critique of an anthropological, mythic, mystical formalist, and moral nature,"[33] thus creating a condition of freedom with music that establishes a dialogue with the outside world. These musicians serve an important function in our society, particularly when many people find themselves further isolated and at risk in a world that seems to be teetering on the edge of disaster. They craft a soundtrack of our rebellion and give us the courage to conceive of a grand intervention in the future of the world. It is, after all, as Veleso describes, a right that at once begins to be lived as a duty.

CLASH OF THE TITAN

By Joel Schalit

Originally appeared in Punk Planet *magazine, January/February 2000*

I was ten years old when the Clash's first record came out, living a short walk from the epicenter of the first highly publicized punk rock explosion: King's Road, in London. Even for the smallest, youngest, and least hip of awkward immigrant children like me, it was impossible not to have known who the Clash were. Like the Sex Pistols, they were literally everywhere: on BBC radio, in London's weekly entertainment magazine, *Time Out,* on television shows like *Top of the Pops,* even on the pages of conservative newspapers like *The Daily Telegraph.* But at the time, it was very difficult to understand why the British media fixated upon them so strongly.

In contrast to Lydon and company, the Clash's first two records weren't the kind of radically conceptual artistic statements meant to start cultural revolutions like *Never Mind the Bollocks* or the Pistols' posthumously released *The Great Rock and Roll Swindle.* Instead of denouncing the music industry as a monolithic authoritarian political structure, albums like *Give 'Em Enough Rope* were simply really great rock records that you could dance to. They escewed the Pistols' antipolitics in favor of a more traditional American folk music liberalism, filtered through the sensibilities of four young men raised on British pub rock, nostalgic for the days of protest singers like Woody Guthrie, the Weavers, and early Bob Dylan.

Like the MC5, the early Clash were all about resurrecting the hyperbole of radical street politics, romanticizing riots, rebellion, and at times even sold school revolutionary violence. The brashness of their early songs helped give this nostalgically radical stance a lot of fasionable weight, but the band consistently failed to explain where it was really coming from. Were they Marxists? No. Were they Leninists? No. Were they anarchists? Definitely not. Were they upwardly mobile rock and rollers who coopted revolutionary slogans in order to gain market share? Maybe, that depended on what side of the punk fence you stood on. If you were in a band like Crass, you definitely thought they were bourgeois. Accomodationists. "We're Crass, not the Clash!" they declared. But if you were someone like Billy Bragg, the Clash opened punk's door to the Communist Party.

While their politics may not have been expertly defined, there was no denying that the Clash had a real axe to grind. No matter how stylized and image-conscious that proverbial axe was, many people felt that the Clash helped demystify much of the tension underlying the Britain of their day. Regardless of how clueless they were about their politics, the Clash's first two records successfully anticipated the crisis of the British welfare state. To the imminent election of Margaret Thatcher, the failure of the Labour government to address growing income discrepancies, and Britain's inability to recognize the existence of an increasingly multiracial immigrant society, the Clash's emotional political drive added the sense of melodrama necessary to raise consciousness about the way the UK was deteriorating.

However, the real significance of the Clash's work did not become apparent until 1979's *London Calling*, followed by 1980's even more magisterial *Sandinista!*. Over the course of producing these two albums—and an occasional twelve inch—the Clash moved beyond the nihilistic political straight jacket of Sex Pistols-inspired British punk to develop one of the most politically sophisticated critiques of American imperialism to have ever surfaced in rock 'n' roll. They went after everything, from American consumer culture writ large across the face of the globe, to the Middle East and even the Nicaraguan revolution. It not only made artistic sense, but was politically valid too.

Yet what's difficult to figure out about these records is how they expressed their politics musically. Instead of simply delivering political sermons, i.e., "Know Your Rights," the Clash's utopia was embedded in how they synthesized the musical forms of England's emerging multiethnic culture, melding dub and reggae with punk rock and pop, experimenting with hip-hop and New York's burgeoning post-disco remix culture. Metaphorically speaking, it was all there. Regardless of how many other artists engaged in similar international maneuvering during the '80s (The Talking Heads, Peter Gabriel or Paul Simon, to name a few), the Clash added an explicitly progressive political dimension to their global explorations that was firmly rooted in the '60s Left. Whether the band actually understood the implications of what they were doing is beside the point. The fact is that they pulled it off, and in doing so, the Clash helped give punk radicalism its first overtly multicultural set of artistic sensibilities.

By the time the Clash got around to releasing its next to final LP, 1982's *Combat Rock,* the band was in total crisis and in deep debt to their record company, Epic, for various reasons, so the Clash decided that it was time to make a hit record. *Combat Rock* succeeded beyond anyone's wildest dreams, making the band a household word in the United States on the strength of the video for "Rock the Casbah," a song about the banning of disco music in post-revolutionary Iran, and a rather awkward opening slot on the Who's Schlitz beer-sponsored premiere farewell tour.

Taking the Clash on tour with them made the Who look like a

bunch of savvy opportunists seeking to have their opening band's countercultural credibility rub off on their rapidly diminishing artistic relevance. However, for a band like the Clash, being taken on an American tour by a band that once smashed their guitars on stage and appeared on album covers mocking commercialism (*The Who Sell Out*), made perfect sense because, having been raised in the '60s, they were the Who's artistic offspring.

No British punk band at the time was more historically self-conscious about analogies like these than the Clash were. They were positioning themselves as inheritors of the '60s rock 'n' roll legacy. Nevertheless, playing "Should I Stay or Should I Go?" in Shea Stadium was a far cry from the riot-plagued Bonds Casino shows that the Clash played in New York the year before with the Bad Brains.

While reams have been written about what happened to the band after the Combat Rock tour, the only thing relevant is that the Clash began to fall apart. Having lost drummer Topper Headon before the tour began, Strummer's primary songwriting partner Mick Jones was forced out. The only surviving original members were Strummer and bassist Paul Simonon.

In a way, it's kind of fitting for the band to have lost it after the Combat Rock tour. Anyone who accomplished what the Clash did with that record was bound to suffer, especially if you consider the album's political significance. Based loosely around Strummer's concept of what he called an "urban Vietnam," *Combat Rock* was a highly overproduced but nonetheless jarring record that tried to see the emerging world order of the 1980s through the eyes of the African-American ghetto. It was a colonial battlefield, where the American military acted as world gatekeeper and the experience of Vietnam was being repeated in all of the world's ghettos. A grandiose and highly ambitious gesture, yes, but the commercial success of such an outrageously conceptual political album outweighed the band's subsequent interpersonal failures.

The Clash went on to record one more album, 1985's *Cut the Crap*, but by then, it was clear that aside from that record's only memorable track, "This Is England," everything was pretty much over. The group disbanded not long thereafter. Band members went on to pursue solo projects of various kinds: Mick Jones' better-than-average Big Audio Dynamite, Paul Simonon's barely passable Havana 3AM, and Joe Strummer's short-lived but illustrious career acting in Jim Jarmusch, Alex Cox, and Aki Kaurismäki films. However, Strummer took a ten-year break from recording his own albums.

Constrained by contractual problems with Epic over the next decade, Strummer made only one solo album, 1989's distinctly unmemorable *Earthquake Weather*, while contenting himself to play sideman in friends' bands, like the Pogues, Big Audio Dynamite, Shaun Ryder's brilliant, cynical dance act, Black Grape, and the all-star comedy band with artist Damien Hurst, Fat Les.

How fitting then that after a decade, Strummer would come forth with his best album since *Combat Rock, Rock Art and the X-Ray Style,* issued by Rancid frontman Tim Armstrong's Hellcat Records. The first of three full-lengths issued by the label over the next three years, *Rock Art* is a slightly inconsistent but otherwise beautiful record that reestablished Strummer's significance as a songwriter in leagues with the likes of peers such as Patti Smith.

In the midst of a Fall 1999 promotional tour of the U.S. to plug the record, I got a chance to speak to Strummer while he was visiting his new label's office in Los Angeles. When I picked up the phone at the appointed time, and the publicist asked "Punk Planet, are you ready to rock," the only thing I could think of was how far away rocking was from my mind. I wasn't going to rock. I was going to talk to Joe Strummer.

Joel Schalit: One of the ironic things I noted with your record coming out now is that when you were in the Clash, there was no one else taking as much of a critical stance towards American imperialism and American cultural and military hegemony than you. Yet you issued your first full-length record in ten years at a point when American world power is at its highest. The Cold War is over, the Soviets have been defeated. America is literally *every-where*. It's more present in Europe, it's more present in the Third World. How do you feel about your timing? I find something poetic about it.

Joe Strummer: You have to understand that I'm a European. You guys did a great job from the '30s until now. Everybody loves American culture in Europe. You've done a great job of putting it out over there—we're all *steeped* in it. We get all your shows and we have all the films that you have, but we tend to get them a bit later than you. I think they show American films quicker in Tel Aviv than they show them in London. But what we like in Europe is the *good* American culture, not the generic one.

Joel Schalit: That bias is definitely reflected in the specific types of American culture you've personally appropriated as an artist.

Joe Strummer: I'd like to kick for a minute this scene they've got here in Hollywood where they re-edit films according to the audience's reaction sheet. That's not art. Obviously they'd laugh at me for even suggesting such a thing, but American films between the '40s and '70s *were* art. They were mass entertain-ment, but they were also art. Now they police audiences by changing a film every week to suit the latest screenings. Obvi-ously it makes monetary sense—studios are making a fortune off of this method. But when you're seventeen, you want to see something grown up, not made for your benefit. When you're sev-enteen, you want to stretch a bit, you want to enter the grown-up world. You don't want everything to be tailored for your tastes. This is a danger, I think.

Joel Schalit: You can definitely see your new record as being an example of what you're saying popular art ought to be about. It has nothing to do with American popular culture in the sense that you're describing it. I think that's inherent in *Rock Art's* global feel—not in the sense of a Peter Gabriel record, but in the manner of a Clash record. In that sense, your work still maintains an implicit critique of American imperialism.

Joe Strummer: That's true. As long as we keep entertaining the people, we'll be doing good.

Joel Schalit: I've been listening to your work since 1978, when I was in the fifth grade. One of the things I've always noticed about your songwriting is that you've always had a very ambivalent relationship with the United States.

Joe Strummer: [Laughs] It's love and hate!

Joel Schalit: On the one hand you've been very critical of American politics and foreign policy. But on the other hand you've so thoroughly assimilated American pop culture.

Joe Strummer: Certainly, yeah. But let's point out that the British government is just as bad as the American government.

Joel Schalit: That's true. So what's your take on Tony Blair?

Joe Strummer: I came up with this nickname for him the other day. I thought, lets call him Tony Baloney, he's a lot of baloney, yeah. I told my friend, "We're going to get this into the national language within twelve hours." So I went to this Clash party after they showed the Clash film [a BBC documentary on the band] and I drew on my T-shirt "Lets get rid of Tony Baloney—the Tuscan Liberation Front," because Blair goes on holiday to Tuscany.

So I wore the shirt into the party, and all these journalists were there. They all asked me "Where'd you get that shirt?" I told them that I'd just come back from Fashion Week in Milan, and that everyone was wearing them. All the reporters immediately got out their notebooks and wrote everything down that was on my shirt. We got it in the first edition of the *Evening Standard* the very next day. Twelve hours later! [laughs]

Joel Schalit: There's not too many Tuscan guerrilla groups.

Joe Strummer: "Fronta Liberazione di Toscana!" But it was all spelled wrong. I write it in Italian and misspelled everything, but no one knows it.

Joel Schalit: I'm sure the British press totally ate that up. I know what you mean about Blair, he's totally fucking noxious. I just read the text of his speech to the recent Labour Party convention . . .

Joe Strummer: Oh no! It's terrible. We're never going to ret rid of him. Blair's machine is so perfect that I reckon that if we can get rid of him in fifteen or twenty years, we'll be lucky.

Joel Schalit: It seems to me that Blair is a charismatic leader in the tradition of Margaret Thatcher—that seems to be what he's deliberately going after.

Joe Strummer: They've learned from the American machine. In fact, its even more chillingly machine-like than the Americans have got it so far. Labour has certainly learned from them. You can't even have an opinion in the party. Say you're an MP [Member of Parliament] and you go, "Hey Tony, I think that policy sucks," the Labour Party would go, "Dock that guy's card. Get rid of him." There's no debate there. It's terrible. We don't have any debate. We don't have any dissension. Blair might as well be Stalin.

Joel Schalit: And yet Blair portrays himself as a radical democrat spreading multiculturalism and human rights around Eastern Europe, like all of his posturing during the war in Kosovo, for example.

Joe Strummer: Exactly. Maybe we've come to realize that all leaders want is power. They couldn't give a damn what they say or have to do to get it. But this is quote a hard thing to come to terms with. What are we going to do now?

Joel Schalit: It must be an interesting experience for you, coming from the same generation as Blair. You guys are very close in age.

Joe Strummer: Oh, I know. I'm bewildered by this Blair development. We're all very confused right now in England.

Joel Schalit: Is there an alternative?

Joe Strummer: That's why I was saying its going to take twenty years to get rid of Blair. There is no alternative. We're all standing around flapping our arms going "What are we going to do now?" I don't know. Its going to be interesting. At least it's a comedy . . .

Joel Schalit: Do you think it'll be good for the British counter-culture?

Joe Strummer: I think so, definitely. Comedians are having a great time with him. Every cloud has a silver lining.

Joel Schalit: Yeah, it's true. Margaret Thatcher was great for punk rock.

Joe Strummer: We should make her an honorary punk rocker. I should go over to her house in Chelsea and give her a pink wig or something.

Joel Schalit: Doesn't she have one already?

Joe Strummer: [Laughs] That's true.

Joel Schalit: I know a lot of people have criticized the Clash over the years for not having thought out their politics very carefully. For example, you never aligned yourselves with any particular political parties in Britain, yet you wore Italian Red Brigade T-shirts. Or how once the band broke up, you went on the Rock Against The Rich Tour sponsored by Class War, an organization dedicated to violent revolution, *after* you'd become wealthy.

Joe Strummer: It was all my fault.

Joel Schalit: [Laughs] To an outsider, this sympathy for violence made sense, especially given the kind of street imagery that the Clash always employed. How did you respond to being criticized for adhering to double standards at the time? Where do you see your politics fitting in? Does it have a framework?

Joe Strummer: Right now I realize that in Britain, my vote is useless. We'll never get rid of Blair because there is no alternative to him. So I ask myself what I've got, and I find that I have a dollar bill in my pocket. So I'm going to vote like that. I'm going to shop locally—that's how I'm going to use my dollar bill—as a vote. I'm not going to give it to the corporations?

Joel Schalit: You're going to support small business . . .

Joe Strummer: Putting my money into records and food, anything I'm going to try and buy. I think of my dollar bill as a vote. Every time I spend it in a small, independent local spot, it's like one less dollar I'm giving to massive global corporations. The only vote we've got is the dollar bill in the pocket. Obviously you're going to have to take your kids to McDonalds when they're screaming, but this is what I want to push myself to do.

Joel Schalit: I understand what you're saying, but how then does it feel to be working with Mercury Records in Europe? They tend to symbolize a lot of the things you don't like.

Joe Strummer: At least they had the guts to come forward with me. There must be a lot of companies in Europe, but every man jack of them went, "Get out of the office." But Mercury said, "This is pretty good." I have to respect them for that, because it was looking pretty bleak.

Joel Schalit: It doesn't seem like your politics to have been about typically punk things like being independent. Rather, your music has consistently proffered some kind of radical multiculturalism symbolized by your early experiments synthesizing dub and reggae with rock 'n' roll. To me that's a pretty identifiable political position.

Joe Strummer: Don't forget that our entry into hip-hop culture was back in 1980 with "Magnificent Seven." It was a huge hit in New York that summer on WBLS. I want to point out that because we always get passed over in these hip-hop histories. Whoever puts together these accounts just hasn't done their onions.

Joel Schalit: Right, I agree. Such accounts tend to attribute the kinds of breakthroughs that the Clash pioneered to groups like the Beastie Boys. Not to diss them, but that's generally what's assumed.

Joe Strummer: Nineteen years ago we entered into hip-hop culture. *Nineteen years ago!* So lick upon that! [laughs]

Joel Schalit: The first time I heard "Radio Clash" was on a black radio station in New York back then.

Joe Strummer: That's incredible. Stuff like that doesn't happen any more.

Joel Schalit: You also experimented a lot with remixing in the early '80s.

Joe Strummer: And it still sounds good too. When you hear that "Radio Clash" remix, it sounds like some guy just did it down the block.

Joel Schalit: The experimentation and international slant that the Clash took seems to have come—or at least been influenced by—your own background. I've been reading a lot about your personal history and your background recently. You grew up all over the world. I read that your dad served in the British Foreign Service.

Joe Strummer: That's right. I was born in Ankara, Turkey. I spent a couple of years there, followed by Cairo for a couple of more years. We also lived in Mexico City for a couple of years, followed by this fairly boring town in Germany called Bonn. Then I went to boarding school in England. My parents went on to move to Tehran. They spent five years in Iran.

Joel Schalit: Hence "Rock the Casbah."

Joe Strummer: [Laughs] Then they went to Malawi, in central Africa.

Joel Schalit: That certainly explains the cosmopolitanism of your musical arrangements. On that tip, you employ a bit of Arabic on the new record, especially in the song "Yalla Yalla." You want to tell me what that's about?

Joe Strummer: It came out of the idea of a bunch of us coming down the street in London, in top form, shouting, "Yeah, we're free." I found out that in Arabic it means, "Come on, let's go." When I came up with the song's chorus, I wondered if I'd had it stored away somewhere in my brain and it just popped out. But what the song is about is that freedom is gone and we're fucked up in Britain. All we've got to do is fight with each other on the streets after dark. When they close all the bars at eleven, it can get kind of grim out on the street. So "Yalla Yalla" is a story starting with Adam and going through "C'mon, lets cut out of this scene. Let's go grooving." If there's some culture happening in Glasgow 600 miles away, we're going to go 600 miles—there's no object. And then it gets to the freedom verse, "Yalla Yalla Yalla Yallah."

Joel Schalit: It's interesting that you're talking about freedom. It seems to me that a search for freedom (particularly given your contractual problems with Epic) led to your transition to film after the dissolution of the Clash. Some people saw that as a radical break in your career at the time, but it made metaphorical sense because there's a real cinematographic quality to your songwriting.

Joe Strummer: Seeing people work in front of cameras, people who'd been thinking about it all their lives, makes you realize that you can't really jump in on a game. You might get lucky though. There are exceptions, like Tom Waits, who can easily move between the two roles. And there are other actor-singers who can do it great. But for myself, I figured that I have to really own up that there's no way to be better than these actors because they've been thinking about acting since they were born. I don't think you can catch up on that; I think you have to respect that. I'm just going to stick to plugging the guitar in and trying to make something interesting with that. Leave the acting to the actors. Personally, that's my hope.

Joel Schalit: Nonetheless, you got to act in some seminal indie films.

Joe Strummer: I had my go and appreciated it.

Joel Schalit: Then let's get back to music. I bet that one of the things which must amuse you making rock 'n' roll after all these years is how people still fight over what's "punk." I distinctly recall how much shit you took for making *Combat Rock*. That bore many parallels with what Nirvana had to deal with nine years later. When *Nevermind* came out and the shit hit the fans, it was though no one could remember that the popularity of *Combat*

Rock triggered many of the same cultural crises about punk going mainstream as Nirvana later did.

Joe Strummer: What a disaster that was. Poor Kurt Cobain!

Joel Schalit: Do you feel any affinity with the kind of backlash that Nirvana had to suffer?

Joe Strummer: It's just typical, isn't it? Cobain writes a brilliant record and everybody disses him. This is exactly what we had to put up with, way before *Combat Rock* even, back in London in 1977. As soon as you do something really brilliant, obviously its going to attract more from your fellow human beings. As soon as that happens, all of a sudden all of these hipper-than-thou people start railing off at you. These are the kinds of pople you just have to shuck off, because you're going to meet them in any corner of life. Any time you do something good, people are going to come and kick you down for it. You've got to be ready for it at any moment.

Joel Schalit: So for you, that's what the whole discourse about selling out is: Simply jealousy.

Joe Strummer: *Exactly.* That's all it is.

Joel Schalit: I totally understand where you're coming from, especially if you consider some of your more early lyrics on songs like "Hitsville U.K." It's not as though you weren't critical of the process of commercialization. That's why I think it was unfair to flog you for "giving in." After all, you were writing songs about how it sucks to be a commodity.

Joe Strummer: What can you do?

Joel Schalit: I have very mixed feelings about the selling out thesis, particularly in the case of *Combat Rock*, because it was the most explicitly political record to top the American charts since the late '60s. For god's sake, any record that combines spoken word rants with funk and sneaks in Allen Ginsberg into a top-ten album is pretty subversive in my book.

Joe Strummer: That's true, so true. Good old Ginsberg!

Joel Schalit: How did he end up on the record?

Joe Strummer: I used to call him a hustler for a joke. He was just coming to hang out at the *Combat Rock* sessions. He was sitting there with Peter Orlovsky [Ginsberg's lifelong companion, and a poet in his own right]. They'd just sit there and watch us record. After about a week, I just turned around to him and said "You're America's greatest living poet and you're going on the mic now." He said, "Well great, what should I do?" I said "I want the sound of God!" I told him, "You're perfect for the role. I just want you to do the intro to 'Ghetto Defendant.'" I gave him two or three minutes scribbling on the piano and on paper. And then there he was, "Slam dance the cosmopolis."

Joel Schalit: [Laughs] He is acting as though he was an old Beat poet fronting a jazz band.

Joe Strummer: Absolutely.

Joel Schalit: That makes a lot of sense. I remember reading a lot of your press in places like the *New York Times* in the early eighties, and recall how older rock critics were saying that the Clash were resurrecting a particular way of making popular art that they hadn't seen since the mid-'60s. I seem to remember one critic even saying that the Clash were essentially modern contemporaries of the former Beat generation, and this was well before Ginsberg had collaborated with you.

Joe Strummer: For me, the Beats were the only game in town. During the '60s, England was probably more like the '50s were in America, but we carried it on longer. The Beatniks were exactly what we needed. The 1965 Beat poet's reading at the Royal Albert Hall blew the lid off of everything—that was the day that the old culture died in England. We already had the Beatles and the Stones. When they hired the Albert Hall, the jewel of normal, boring culture and brought in all the Beat poets, including Allen Ginsberg, it brought it all down and turned everyone on. That's when the '60s really began.

Joel Schalit: That makes sense, especially if you consider that in some respects British pop culture can be even more anti-intellectual than American pop culture.

Joe Strummer: Yes, I am completely anti-intellectual. I am pro-intuition and pro-instinct. We've already given too many props to intellectualism. The intellectuals' time is over. They've done nothing for us. They write long, boring philosophy books that no one can understand except themselves. All we've ended up with is a world full of jet airplanes screaming overhead with laser-guided bombs and rockets. I figure that all the intellectuals should go off to an island somewhere and wear wooly clothing.

A MAN THAT MATTERED

By Kristine McKenna

Originally appeared in Arthur, *Spring 2003*

When the Clash first burst on the scene in 1977 I dismissed them for the same reason I've always hated U2. Their music struck me as humorless, self-important political blather that wasn't remotely sexy or fun. Definitely not for me. Nonetheless, being a dedicated punk I had to check them out when they made their Los Angeles debut at the Santa Monica Civic on February 9, 1979, and what I saw that night changed my mind—but onlyjust a little, though. As expected, Mick Jones came off as a typical rock fop who clearly spent far too much time thinking about neckerchiefs and trousers. Joe Strummer, however, was something else. With the exception of Jerry Lee Lewis, I'd never seen anyone that furiously alive on stage. Legs pumping, racing back and forth across the stage, singing with a frantic desperation that was simultaneously fascinating and puzzling, he was an incredibly electric presence.

At the press conference following the show that night, LA's ranking punk scribe, Claude Bessy, jumped up and snarled, "This isn't a press conference—this is a depressing conference!" (Jeez, tempers always ran so high during that first incarnation of the punk scene! Who knows why the hell we were all so crabby!) I remember that Strummer looked genuinely hurt by the comment. Mind you, he was a working-class Brit so he wasn't about to start sniffling in his sleeve, but he didn't cop an attitude either. I was

229

touched by how unguarded and open he was—and I was certainly impressed by the man's vigor. I wasn't surprised when I subsequently learned that Strummer ran three marathons without having trained at all. His preparation? "Drink ten pints of beer the night before the race and don't run a single step for at least four weeks before the race."

That first show at the Santa Monica Civic didn't transform me into a Clash fan but Strummer interested me, so when the band showed up in 1981 in Manhattan, where I was living at the time, I decided to see what he was up to. The Clash had booked a nine-show engagement at Bond's, an old department store on Times Square in Manhattan, and this turned out to be not a good idea. The place wasn't designed to handle the crowds the band drew, and the engagement turned into a nine-day standoff between the band and the fire marshals. I attended three nights in a row and can't recall them ever actually making it to the stage and performing. But then, that was business as usual during the glory days of punk, when gigs were forever being shutdown, aborted, abruptly canceled. This was political theater, not just music, and nobody embodied that idea more dramatically than the Clash.

Cut to June 14 of the following year and I finally saw the Clash succeed in completing a full set at the Hollywood Palladium in Los Angeles. By then, I'd finally begun to appreciate the breadth and fearlessly experimental nature of the band's music, and Strummer was at the peak of his powers as a showman at that point. The huge hall was packed, and it was as if Strummer was a maestro conducting this undulating mass of sweaty people, and could raise or lower the pitch at will. Boots, beer bottles, and articles of clothing flew through the air, and people leapt on stage then leapt back into the arms of their friends, while Strummer stood at the microphone stoking the fire. Somehow he managed to keep the proceedings just a hairbreadth short of total chaos for two hours. It was a commanding display from a man who clearly knew his job and knew his audience.

Following the break-up of the Clash in 1985, Strummer charged head-on into a busy schedule of disparate projects. He acted in several independent films and composed six film sound-tracks, including one—for Alex Cox's lousy film of 1988, *Walker*—that was remarkably beautiful. I wrote an admiring review of the score for [now defunct] *Musician* magazine, and a few months after it was published Strummer was passing through LA and invited me to lunch in appreciation for the supportive words. We were to meet at a Thai restaurant on Sunset Boulevard, and though I was nervous on the way there, he put me at ease the minute we met. Strummer was such a genuine person that it was impossible to feel uncomfortable around him—I know it sounds corny, but he truly was a man of the people. He was funny and generous in his assessments of people, but he didn't sugarcoat things either. He had no trouble calling an asshole an asshole when it was called for. The thing that ultimately made Strummer such a spectacular human being, however, is so simple that it barely seems worth mentioning: he was interested in people. He wanted to hear your story and know what was going on in your neighborhood, he asked how you felt about things and was an empathetic listener—he paid attention! The other thing I imme-diately loved about him was that he was an enthusiast and a fan.

Just how big a fan he was became clear to me a few months later when he guest-hosted a radio show I had at the time on Santa Monica radio station KCRW. My show was at midnight on Sat-urday, and KCRW's studio is hard to find, so our plan was to meet behind the Foster's Freeze at Pico and 14th at 11:00 P.M. He roared into the parking lot exactly on time in a car with four pals, and the lot of them tore into the record library at the station looking for the records on Strummer's playlist. His plan was to play all the records that shaped his musical taste as a teenager in the order that he discovered them, and the show he put together was equal parts history lesson and autobiography. Included in the far-flung set were tracks by Sonny Boy Williamson, Lee Dorsey, Captain Beefheart, Bo Diddley, Hank Williams, and loads of fabulous, rare reggae and dub. His loving introduction to the Beach Boys' "Do It Again" brought tears to my eyes. Several fans crashed the studio when they heard him on the air and realized he was in town, and he welcomed them all. It was a wonderful night. He had fun too, and as he thanked me and said goodnight, he kissed me on the cheek and I blushed.

Strummer spent the next ten years struggling to re-start his career post-Clash and stumbling repeatedly. "The only thing that got me through was sheer bloody-mindedness—I just won't quit!," he told me when I interviewed him in October 2001. We were talking on the occasion of the release of his second album with his five man line-up, the Mescaleros, *Global A Go-Go*, which was rightfully hailed as the best work Strummer had done in years. He was happy with the record, and when I saw him perform at the Troubadour a few weeks after we spoke, he seemed happy in general.

"I've enjoyed my life because I've had to deal with all kinds of things, from failure to success to failure again," Strummer told a journalist from *Penthouse* magazine in 2000. "I don't think there's any point in being famous if you lose that thing of being a human being."

That's something that was never a danger for Strummer. During that last interview, I asked him what the great achievement of punk rock had been, and he replied, "It gave a lot of people something to do." Though I loved the complete lack of self-importance in that answer, however, this isn't to suggest Strummer ever broke faith with punk. "Punk rock isn't something you grow out of," he told Penthouse. "Punk rock is like the Mafia, and once you're made, you're made. Punk rock is an attitude, and the essence of the attitude is 'give us some truth.'

"And, whatever happens next is going to be bland unless you and I nause everything up," he added. "This is our mission, to nause everything up! Get in there and nuase it out, upset the apple cart, destroy the best laid plans—we have to do this! Back on the street, I say. Turn everything off in the pad and get back on the street. As long as people are still here, rock 'n' roll can be great again."

The following conversation took place on the eve of Strummer's final U.S. tour, during the winter of 2001–2002. He died of a heart attack at the age of 50 on December 22, 2002.

Kristine McKenna: You say the great achievement of punk rock was that "it gave a lot of people something to do." What was its great failure?

Joe Strummer: That we didn't mobilize our forces when we had them and focus our energies in a way that could've brought about concrete social change—trying to get a repressive law repealed, for instance. We're stuck in a kind of horrible holding pattern now, and it seems to me that the only way to change it is if we get hipsters to stay in one place long enough to get elected. The problem is that no hipster wants to get elected.

Kristine McKenna: I saw the Clash several times during their U.S. tours of the late '70s and early '80s, and I remember the sense that something profoundly important was at stake at those shows, that they were about something much larger than pop trends. What was at stake?

Joe Strummer: In the rush of youth you assume too much—and so it should be—but we felt that the whole machine was teetering on the brink of collapse. Some amazing things went down in Britain during the '70s—the government decided they could disempower the unions by having a three-day week, for instance. Can you imagine that? Monday morning you wake up, and suddenly there's only a three-day week, from Monday to Wednesday. There were garbage strikes, train strikes, power strikes, the lights were going out—everything seemed on the brink, and looking through youthful, excitable eyes it seemed the very future of England was at stake. Obviously, that's very far from the feeling these days, when everything's pretty much smugly buttoned down.

Kristine McKenna: Has England recovered from the Thatcherism that dominated the country during the years you were with the Clash?

Joe Strummer: It will never recover—and now we've got Blairism. We are so completely confused. If you think of England as a patient laying on the couch in a shrink's office I'd say it's time for the straitjacket. Imagine the party we had in England when Blair got into office after all those years of Thatcher. Everyone was cheering, "this is the dawn of a new day," but since then we've had no vision or justice. The Blair administration just wants to get into bed with the richest corporations, and the very notion of labor has vanished into the mist. Obviously, the worse it gets, the better it gets for artists, so culturally, England is doing OK. But politically, it's total mixed-up confusion.

Kristine McKenna: What's the proper course of action when everything around you is falling apart?

Joe Strummer: It's not a good idea to run away. You gotta smile, whistle, look self-assured, and try and fix things up a bit.

Kristine McKenna: Given that the Clash's music grew out of a situation specific to England, did it strike you as odd that it was embraced in America?

Joe Strummer: No, because everybody feels the same on a certain level. The Zeitgeist is a real force of nature, and although we don't know how it's transmitted, it's like an invisible tidal wave.

Kristine McKenna: How would you characterize the Zeitgeist now?

Joe Strummer: I think people are feeling a bit cheated and frustrated. They've come to realize that voting is basically useless because either side you vote for has no more than a shade of difference from the other side, and ultimately politics is about nothing but the mighty dollar. So OK, say the people, let's forget politics and get into drugs or skateboarding—anything that passes the time and gives you some sense of freedom. People want to feel free, and it's a hard feeling to come by in this world. People have a right to change their consciousness, too, and in the back of their minds they know they have that right. So people are gonna flout the laws established to prevent them from smoking marijuana or experimenting with Ecstasy, because they know that nobody—especially a politician half pissed on gin—has the right to tell you what goes on in your mind.

Kristine McKenna: You say it's hard to experience the feeling of freedom: do you feel free?

Joe Strummer: No, I do not. If I invited nine friends over to my house and put on an acid house record, and we stood in the garden listening to it, we'd all be arrested and fined a thousand pounds each, because in the United Kingdom it's illegal for ten or more people to listen to repetitive beats—this is in the statute books, "repetitive beats!" People in Britain are much less free than people in many other counties because we've got really repressive laws. All bars there must close at 11:00 P.M., for instance. As to why I continue to live there, I really think all British people have a streak of sado-masochism. I live in the middle of nowhere, so you'd think I could get away with playing a record, but such is not the case.

Kristine McKenna: Why do you live in the middle of nowhere?

Joe Strummer: I've got no idea! If you wanted to be harsh you could describe the area where I live as nothing but an agri-business abattoir—all you see is people wearing masks, riding tractors, and spraying god knows what onto the ground. I'm a townie, and I don't know what I'm doing out there, although it is nice being able to see all the stars in the heavens at night.

Kristine McKenna: As a rule, people tend to resist change; why is this so?

Joe Strummer: Because they're afraid of the new and the unknown, and familiarity is comforting. For instance, when you live out in the middle of nowhere as I do, you really appreciate small things, and one of the things I'd come to appreciate was this small bar not far from where I live. The guy who ran it was cool, he kept the lights low, and there would always be interesting jazz playing when you popped in there. In the middle of nowhere, that's like a gold mine. I popped in the other day and the music was gone, it was brightly lit, and a smiling woman chirped, "Can I help you?" The bar had been sold, so the place I knew no longer exists. Arthur Rimbaud said "some destructions are necessary," and that's a lesson I'm really trying to learn.

Kristine McKenna: An overriding theme in all of your music is personal and political conflict. Why can't people get along?

Joe Strummer: I think fear is the corrupting agent, and I don't know how we can eliminate that. Of course, there's no way to eliminate the most terrifying reality—that we all have to die—but at least the sun shines, and we've got a bit of time, so it's not all sniveling. Maybe if every child in the world was shown a really good time, a new breed of human beings would appear. On the other hand, I believe some people are just born bad—I've met a few of them, too. Whether they were born bad, what happened to them was bad, or it was a combination of the two, by the time they're teenagers you can see they're gonna flip. No matter who loves them or what happens to them, they're gonna smash up the room.

Kristine McKenna: Do you believe in karma, or do some people get away with smashing up the room?

Joe Strummer: Surely karma must be one of the few things we can believe in. Even if it were proved to me that it wasn't in play here on earth, I'd still hope that in another dimension, in the spirit world, it does exist. I do think it operates in this world.

Kristine McKenna: What forces played a role in shaping your sense of morality?

Joe Strummer: My mother was Scottish, and a no-nonsense kind of woman, and maybe I got some vibes from her.

Kristine McKenna: What's been the most difficult year of your life?

Joe Strummer: I took a long breather after the Clash broke up, and I had a really hard time about half way through that. I needed a rest, so I was kind of grateful for the break, but at a certain point I became overwhelmed by a sense of self-doubt. In the music business, an eleven-year layoff is like 111 years, and felt like I'd blown it and would never get up there again. The only thing that got me through was sheer bloody-mindedness—I just won't quit! Every time I think "you've had your lot, now just shut up," a larger part of me says, "no, there are things you can say better than anyone, and you must say them." The other thing that carried me through that period was the fact that I had a lot of responsibilities—I'd managed to have children, and both my parents died during those years.

Kristine McKenna: How were you affected by the death of your parents?

Joe Strummer: I wasn't close to them, because when I was eight years old I was sent to a boarding school, where I spent nine years. I saw my father once a year between the ages of nine and twelve, then twice a year from then on. As to whether I felt cheated by his absence, I didn't bother with that, because I was in a hard place. You know *Tom Brown's School Days?* Imagine being in a second-rate boarding school in South London in 1961. You had to punch or be punched, so I became hard and ceased being a mama's boy pretty quickly.

Kristine McKenna: You've been referred to in the press on several occasions as "the son of a diplomat who dropped out of art school to be a bohemian." Is that an accurate description?

Joe Strummer: No. In my first ever interview in *Melody Maker,* when I was suddenly regarded as "somebody," I said that my father was a diplomat simply because I wanted to give him his due for one time in his life. My father was an excellent eccentric who liked nothing better than dressing up for a party, and he was great fun, but he was basically a low-level worker in the hierarchy of the British embassy, and we actually had fuck all. A four-room bungalow in Croyton was all he managed to accrue during his life, and Croyton is not much of a salubrious suburb.

Kristine McKenna: When you were twenty-years old, your older brother, David, committed suicide. How did that mark you?

Joe Strummer: I was deeply affected by it, and I don't know if I've come to terms with it yet, because it's a mysterious thing to try and understand. We were only separated by eighteen months, but we were opposites: whereas I was the loudmouth ringleader who was always getting everybody into trouble, he was quiet and never said much. When we were teenagers in the '60s, there was a load of shouting about Rhodesia, and that led to his becoming a member of the National Front in 1968. At the time, I was too busy listening to Jimi Hendrix to really understand what was going on with him, but I don't think his politics had anything to do with his suicide. I think it had more to do with his shyness.

Kristine McKenna: What's the most valuable thing you could teach your children?

Joe Strummer: I don't think I've taught them anything, and don't feel like I've been a very good father. My first marriage split up after fourteen years when my two daughters were still relatively young, and you feel guilty about that forever. They get born, and suddenly the thing they were born into is pulled apart. It eats away at my mind, particularly since my parents stayed together.

Kristine McKenna: You married again in 1995; what's the secret of a successful marriage?

Joe Strummer: You have to love your partner more than you love yourself—and I do.

Kristine McKenna: What's the most widely held misconception about you?

Joe Strummer: That I'm some kind of political thinker. I definitely am not. I think about politics all the time, but it's become increasingly difficult to know what's going on in the world. I grew up hearing my parents go on about World War II, which was an episode of history that seemed very clear: Hitler equals bad, everyone else equals good. People are basically lazy and we want to see a good guy and a bad guy. Obviously, nothing is black or white, yet we yearn for that beautiful clarity, but I'm finding it more and more difficult to come to those kinds of conclusions—possibly because we're getting more information and we have to sift through it. I used to believe it was possible to learn what was going on in the world by reading the newspaper, but that began to change around the time that the Balkans thing kicked off. Either the newspapers aren't up to snuff or I'm losing my mind, but I found it very difficult to get a grasp on what was going on there.

Kristine McKenna: Do you believe music has a responsibility to address social and political issues?

Joe Strummer: I do, but I would add that the climate of the times dictates the way people write.

Kristine McKenna: How are you evolving as a songwriter?

Joe Strummer: Oh god, backwards man! I'm trying to be less idiotic. Every writer likes to feel that when he sits down to write he's gonna zoom off into a new field he didn't even know existed, but the truth is that writing is basically a process of blundering in the dark, and there's a lot of luck that comes into play.

Kristine McKenna: Are there specific issues that are particularly well suited to being addressed in music?

Joe Strummer: Love—because with music, you have the extra dimension of melody to communicate things that are beyond language.

Kristine McKenna: Name a song that never fails to make you cry.

Joe Strummer: Hoagy Carmichael's "Georgia." It has a quality of yearning and reminiscence that are incredibly moving to me.

Kristine McKenna: What was the last record you bought?

Joe Strummer: *The Call*, by Alan Skidmore, who was a bebop saxophone player who could probably be described as washed-up, not to be too rude. He went to South Africa and hooked up with a group called Amampondo, and they made this record together that's basically a bunch of crazed drumming with a bebop guy free-falling all over it. It's not bad, but when I put it on everyone else leaves.

Kristine McKenna: What's your favorite Clash song?

Joe Strummer: I really like the song, "If Music Could Talk," which is on side 21 of *Sandinista!* (*Laughing*). I like it because it's quite weird, and it shows we were willing to try stupid things all the time.

Kristine McKenna: What do you miss about being in the Clash?

Joe Strummer: That was so long ago that it's all faded, and I'm never on the nostalgia tit, but we did have a very good camaraderie and an extremely acute sense of humor. It was fun being in the Clash.

Kristine McKenna: Was there ever a time when you believed the myth of the Clash?

Joe Strummer: No, and that's why I managed to survive. They say you should never read your press, and that comes in handy when they're saying you suck.

Kristine McKenna: Does the adversarial nature of the music press help keep musicians honest, or does it simply undermine them?

Joe Strummer: On several occasions it's definitely knocked me for six, but then I'd grudgingly get up and dust my clothes off, and say better that than the other way. The press is harsher in England than it is other places, but I think it's a good thing because it keeps you on your toes and prevents you from getting too pretentious. Yes-men tend to collect around famous people, so the conditions are really conducive to becoming pretentious. So you might as well get the mean guys in to flay you alive.

Kristine McKenna: How has fame been of use to you?

Joe Strummer: It obviously has its uses, but it's really more of a liability than an asset to anyone interested in writing. If you want to write, the first thing is, you've got to experience life like everyone else experiences it. Secondly, you need room to think. If you're incredibly famous, all you can think about is, "oh my god, has that person over there recognized me, and did I bring enough bodyguards to the supermarket with me." By accident I managed this quite well, because the Clash never went on television in Britain. If you wanted to see the Clash you had to actually get up and go out to one of the shows. Consequently, I'm able to move about Britain without being recognized. for the most part.

Kristine McKenna: Are fame and money invariably corrupting?

Joe Strummer: Definitely. The Clash never had to struggle with the latter of those two things, however, because we never got any money. The music business is a bad racket, and the people on the first crest of a wave never get paid. I don't like to moan on about money, but you have to realize that although you might've heard of the Clash, we didn't sell any records. Nobody sends me five pounds every time somebody's heard of the group. We never had any real power, either, other than in an abstract, poetic way. What I wrote on a piece of paper might influence someone somewhere down the line, and that's something I still take great care with. Not writing things that are stupid, or easily misconstrued is something I keep onboard at all times. But it would've been nice to have the power to say, "50,000 people down to the Houses of Parliament now!" We might've been able to get 1,500 people at the height of our power, but ultimately, it's the big money men who have the power. Then again, I suppose somebody must've seen us as some kind of threat back in the day, because we were constantly being arrested for petty shit. We'd go to play small towns in the north of England and you could almost hear them thinking, "here they come, those punk rockers from London—we're not having any of that!" So they'd pull over our cars, search us, shake down our motel rooms—it was all very petty.

Kristine McKenna: Does the legacy of the Clash continue to get in your way?

Joe Strummer: Not anymore, because enough time has passed, but certainly, for ten years after the group broke up, I found it difficult to deal with. But I managed to chill long enough that it's allowable for me to come back and knock in a few good albums. It's not pissing anybody off.

Kristine McKenna: You've traveled quite a bit as a touring musician; what's the scariest place you've ever been?

Joe Strummer: Mozambique. There was a war going on there, and I was only there for a day, but the entire time I was there I was nervous about who might be lurking in the bushes along the roadside. It was also a little unnerving playing Ireland with the Clash, but you have to laugh. You fly in there, you check into the Europa Hotel in Belfast, and the clerk cheerfully informs you that this is the most bombed hotel in Europe. Twenty-eight bombings so far! Then you go up to your room where you ask yourself; should I crawl under the bed? Do I dare stand at the window? We were quite pragmatic and decided to just get on with things, because we couldn't see how either side could gain anything politically by blowing up a rock 'n'roll show. It wasn't as if the whole world was saying, "oh wow, the Clash are in Belfast." The only people who cared that we were there were the other scrawny punk rockers walking around Belfast.

Kristine McKenna: In *A Riot of Our Own*, the 1999 book about the Clash written by Johnny Green and Garry Barker, everyone in the band comes off well, with the exception of Mick Jones, who's depicted as being ridiculously obsessed with his wardrobe. Is the book accurate?

Joe Strummer: Yes it is, but you need some of that in a rock'n'roll band! If Paul Simonon hadn't been in the Clash I doubt that we would've been as successful as we were, because you need to look stylish. People don't think of Bob Dylan as a glamorous guy, but he was actually pretty good-looking. When you think of his Cuban heel phase, with the curly head, the Carnaby Street clothes, the polka-dot tab collars, the tight jeans, the boots—he was pretty styling.

Kristine McKenna: Rumor has it that Bob's had a face-lift.

Joe Strummer: That's probably a good idea. You have to remember, this is show biz, and it's not as if Bob's a merchant banker or a film critic or something. If he wants to go out on the road for another twenty or thirty years, he's gonna want to tuck it up a bit. It's not as if we're novelists who can hide in our studies like J. D. Salinger and never have our photos taken. It's easy for those people to say what the heck. You don't know what it's like having photos taken of yourself all the time. It's appalling to regularly see the destruction of age marked out sharply on your face in photos, videos, and on television. This is a visual thing we do. Johnny Cash dyes his hair, and I think it's only right that we try and scruff up a shambling face.

Kristine McKenna: At what point did you become an adult?

Joe Strummer: Are you kidding?! I'm nowhere near becoming an adult.

Kristine McKenna: What do you think you represent to the people who admire you?

Joe Strummer: Maybe they see a good soul.

Kristine McKenna: Tell me about someone who inspires you.

Joe Strummer: Bo Diddley is inspiring. When he was a young musician starting out he needed some maracas, so he went to the local scrap yard, got some of those floating balls that sit in the tank of a toilet, filled them with black-eyed peas, then used them to invent a whole new kind of music. That's heroic and inspiring.

Kristine McKenna: What's the biggest obstacle you've overcome in your life?

Joe Strummer: I wouldn't say I've overcome it yet, but it's my sheer laziness. I'd rather sit and watch Popeye cartoons than do anything. Nowadays I'm into *The Simpsons, South Park,* and *SpongeBob Squarepants.*

Kristine McKenna: The second album by your current band, the Mescaleros, is dedicated to the late Joey Ramone. What was the nature of his genius?

Joe Strummer: A sharp intelligence. People think of spirit when they think of the Ramones, but the more I listen to those records the more I'm struck by how smart they are.

Kristine McKenna: Where do you think Joey is now?

Joe Strummer: He's in heaven.

Kristine McKenna: Do you believe in heaven?

Joe Strummer: Maybe not for me, but certainly for Joey Ramone.

Kristine McKenna: What's the most one can hope for in life?

Joe Strummer: The sense of having accomplished something— and I don't have that feeling yet. Being in the line of work I'm in, you hold yourself up against the real greats like Dylan, Ray Davies, Jagger & Richards, Paul Simon, Lennon & McCartney, and John Fogerty. I'm not in that pantheon yet, but I'm gonna get there.

ROCK WARRIOR

By Dan Grunebaum

Originally appeared in Metropolis, *November 2001*

Even though there are extremists in the world . . . we've got to hold on to our sanity and not allow ourselves to get crazed with vengeance.

—Joe Strummer

I am looking at this as possibly our final jaunt into Japan," says Joe Strummer in a telephone chat from his country refuge in Somerset, an area three hours' west of London that he notes is famous for alcoholic cider. We're an hour late for the interview due to a time zone mix up, but Strummer is friendly and unfazed.

It's mid September and Strummer is preparing to set out on tour with his latest band, the Mescaleros. Formed in 1999, the band has just released *Global A Go-Go* (Hellcat), the follow-up to their 1999 debut *Art and the X-Ray Style,* which helped resurrect the career of an almost forgotten punk legend.

Strummer's not trying to sound depressing, just realistic. "Sooner or later I think we'd have to be defeated," he says. "Not that we'll give up, but I doubt we'll be able to travel many places in the future—and we fly economy! You've got to fly ten guys into Japan and get the hotels and feed them, so I would think that pretty soon Japan will be out of our reach."

You'd think the fact that Strummer fronted one of punk's most important bands would guarantee him an audience, but the soft-spoken singer explains that the mechanics of the contemporary music business mean that nothing is guaranteed.

"We exist in a kind of nether world beyond MTV where only hipsters venture," says Strummer about the Mescaleros, whose eclectic mix of rock, R&B, reggae, Latin, and techno makes them difficult to "niche market." When pressed, Strummer—while careful to note that the band operates as a democracy—admits that, "Calling ourselves Joe Strummer and the Mescaleros has made it easier for us than if we were just called the Mescaleros." This, despite the fact that the Mescaleros also include other rock illuminati such as guitarist Anthony Glenn, formerly of Elastica, and multi-instrumentalist Martin Slattery of Black Grape. "It's a very competitive world in rock," concludes Strummer. "So if you've got any kind of name in the world it's advisable to use it."

And a name he has indeed. Not only did Strummer's the Clash change the course of rock 'n' roll, but his career since the group disbanded in 1985 has been varied and productive. He's acted in movies by Alex Cox and Jim Jarmusch, filled in as Pogues' frontman, and composed soundtracks for *Sid and Nancy* (1986), *When Pigs Fly* (1993), and *Grosse Pointe Blank* (1997), just to name a few of his accomplishments.

But Strummer's various attempts to launch a solo career and new bands were dogged by setbacks throughout the '90s, a period his biographer refers to as "Joe's Wilderness Years." After the flop of his 1990 solo debut *Earthquake Weather,* CBS/Sony blocked any further solo efforts, hoping in vain for the Clash reunion Strummer insists will never take place.

Unable to come up with the five million pounds necessary to

buy himself out of his contract, Strummer went on strike in 1997. Finally, CBS/Sony gave in, terminating his contract and paving the way for his signing to Hellcat, the indie label headed by SoCal punk band Rancid singer Tim Armstrong, a rabid Clash fan of long standing.

Recently, the Mescaleros have been touring with many of their Hellcat labelmates, who represent the new wave of West Coast punk. So how does a grand old man of punk feel about the young kids on the block? "We get to see how they play on stage as well as hang out with them. A lot of them are excellent musicians and also very witty people," he enthuses. On the other hand, he says that, "As far as the content, I think it's more for younger people than I; it's music for a different generation."

Strummer—forty-nine and a father of three children—is confident about his band's ability to rock out. "When we get up there and knock into it there aren't too many people complaining," he boasts. "We've done our homework, and we haven't made anything bad." Strummer says that, perhaps surprisingly, fans don't request Clash tunes, even though he does say "We play all kinds of music that I have been involved in, from all parts of my particular history."

Strummer—who says he makes music for "his own age group"—is scathing about the current state of rock and its domination by worldwide conglomerates. "MTV has constructed its own universe—many songs are being written specifically to be the soundtrack to a video which is specifically being made to be shown on MTV twelve times a day," he complains. "MTV, which started out as an observer, is now a decisive factor in which kind of music is being made." He adds that his band can't be found on radio, either. "All the radio stations are on a corporate diet so it's a corporate menu."

But despite Strummer's view that "We won't be able to survive for too much longer," the singer is philosophical. "MTV world has nothing to do with my world," he says. "So we just kind of get on with it."

And get on with it they do. The Mescaleros are spending the better part of the fall touring the U.S. and UK, with a brief detour to Japan. It's a busy life about which Strummer has mixed feelings. "I've been to Japan many times but I've never seen anything," he laments. "As soon as they get you into Japan they want to work you. My usual schedule is twenty interviews a day. You get half an hour to go buy some funny presents for your kids and that's it."

While realistic about the chances of getting his message of peace through, Strummer—who grew up all over the world as the son of a British Foreign Office employee—insists that, in a world horrified by the September 11 terror attacks, commitment is critical.

"The message is even more pertinent," he concludes. "Even though there are extremists in the world, if we represent the sane people of the world, then we've got to hold on to our sanity and not allow ourselves to get crazed with vengeance and make an inopportune movement."

WHEN THE TWO SEVENS CLASHED

by Carter Van Pelt

Originally appeared in Arthur, *Spring 2003*

When Bob Marley sang his 1977 reggae-stepper "Punky Reggae Party," he called out "The Damned, the Jam, the Clash . . ." Marley may have overlooked the Pistols' reggae-loving Johnny Rotten, but few in the London punk movement were drawn to the party with the passion of the Clash's Joe Strummer and Paul Simonon, and nobody did more to represent reggae to the punk rock scene.

Members of the Clash grew up in close proximity to the Jamaican community that relocated to England in the post-WWII period. Paul Simonon's "Guns of Brixton" is a direct reflection of this experience, as is Strummer's "White Man in Hammersmith Palais." The latter documents Strummer's night in a Jamaican dance hall in West London, as he explained in 1991: "All over the world people are oppressed and in London there were the dreads and there were the punks, and we had an alliance. England is a very repressive country. . . . Immigrants were treated badly. . . . So these people had a sense of pride and dignity, and when we went into their concerts, where we should have had the grace to have left them alone. . . . And they didn't jump us, they didn't stomp us, they didn't beat the seven shades of you-know-what out of us. . . . They understood that maybe we needed a drop of this roots culture. And 'White Man in Hammersmith Palais' is a song that was going through my mind while I was standing in the middle of the Hammersmith

Palais . . . in a sea of thousands of Rastas and dreads and natty rebels. That song was trying to say something realistic."

Evidence of the group's interest in reggae could be seen before it was heard. The picture sleeve of the first single, "1977," strongly resembles the cover of Joe Gibbs and the Professionals' *State of Emergency* album—men lined up with their backs to the camera, hands on a wall, on the verge of arrest. On the "1977" sleeve, the theme was augmented by the Jamaican political slogans on Strummer's clothes—"Heavy Manners" and "Heavy Duty Discipline." These ideas were likely gleaned from Prince Far I's *Under Heavy Manners* album, an often-cited Clash favorite. Later visual references to the group's cultural interests include the cover of *Black Market Clash,* which features a picture of a lone Rasta in defiance of riot police at the 1976 Notting Hill Carnival. Strummer's and Jones' experiences at Notting Hill in 1976 were the inspiration for the song "White Riot."

The Clash's first attempt to work with reggae musicians was a short alliance in 1977 with the "Rasputin of reggae," Lee Perry. The result, "Complete Control," was less than inspired, but the group kept at it, achieving intercultural consanguinity in 1980 when they brought Jamaican deejay/producer Mikey Dread to the controls. Their collaboration on "Bank Robber" and "Robber Dub" (from *Black Market Clash*) was followed by the "Train In Vain," B-side "Rockers Galore-UK Tour," and the tracks "Junco Partner," "Living In Fame," "One More Time," "One More Dub," "If Music Could Talk," and "Shepherd's Delight" on the massive *Sandinista!* album. (Mikey Dread's vocals can be heard on "Living In Fame," "One More Time," and "If Music Could Talk.")

While Mikey Dread is still in contention today with the Clash's management over alleged unpaid publishing and lack of recognition for the album sales garnered by *Sandinista!*, his respect for Strummer's and Simonon's "reggae mission" remains.

"I see Joe Strummer as a leader in the rock world who never got the recognition that he deserved for his upfrontness, addressing issues that other people were reluctant to address—'White Riot' and all dem tings deh. When I met them, I was surprised that these people were supporting reggae, buying reggae every week, and up-to-date with what's going on . . .

"One thing I can say about the Clash, they were no racists. There were a lot of times I been to places where skinheads and punks wanted to kick my butt, as a black man, and [the Clash] would warn me, 'Tomorrow don't go out alone, have one of us follow you.' They start to wear their Doctor Martens shoes, and they buy me a pair as well so they know we're on the war path. Anybody come, we just mess them up."

Mikey Dread's live performances with the Clash involved taking the stage alone to sing over recordings of his own "Dread at the Controls" rhythm productions and later joining the Clash for encores. This Jamaican dance hall-style performance was understood and received enthusiastically in Europe, but Mikey ran into problems at his first U.S. appearance. "I wasn't supposed to be on tour with them, but they asked me to come along. They wanted to introduce me to their crowd, but I got a bad reception in LA I'll never forget Los Angeles. We played all over the world and when we came to Los Angeles, all the punkers tried to boo me off stage. The punks got really mad, and I'm looking at like 20,000 people and wondering what the hell is gonna go on. I told the guys, 'I'm not playing tonight, cause they don't want to see a black man out there.' We had one black bouncer and me. That is it for blacks. And it was pure white man out there, some bad punks! They wanted to eat me alive! Joe Strummer is the one who was like 'Go get them Mikey, don't let them tell you what to do!' And me just go out there and get serious and say, 'You know, I'm coming to the United States, [and] I was thinking I was going to be meeting a lot of intelligent people, people who are open-minded, people who are cosmopolitan, people who are not prejudiced and racist, people who want the world to live in unity.' I give them a speech and chastise them for their rude behavior. And trust me mon, the crowd went quiet like you could hear a pin drop. Then I said, 'I know you're here to see the Clash, but I'm going to introduce you to some reggae music, from the roots! Are you ready?' And they say, 'yea!' And we just start lick some tune and that was it. We broke the ice."

Not only did the Clash cover reggae tracks like Willi Williams' "Armagideon Time," Junior Murvin's "Police and Thieves," and Tools and the Maytals' "Pressure Drop," they name-dropped and referenced their reggae heroes in their lyrics—Prince Far I in "Clash City Rockers," Dr. Alimantado in "Rudy Can't Fail," The Abyssinians' "Sattamassaganna" in "Jimmy Jazz," and Dillinger, Leroy Smart, Ken Boothe, and Delroy Wilson in "White Man in Hammersmith Palais." Strummer even documented his and Jones's chaotic jaunt to Kingston in "Safe European Home." (Curiously, Simonon—arguably the band's biggest reggae head—was left behind in England, a major slight that he talks about with obvious residual bitterness in Don Letts' Clash doc, *Westway to the World*).

Strummer's love of Jamaican music continued in his solo career. The lyrics on "Techno D-Day" from the Mescaleros' *Rock Art and the X-Ray Style* describe "using the headphones for a mike; for Tenor Saw's delight, I sang another new sound is dying," a reference to Tenor Saw's "Ring the Alarm." Strummer also recorded a cover of Jimmy Cliff's "The Harder They Come" with DJ Tippa Irie and The Long Beach Dub Allstars on the *Free The Memphis 3* benefit album, and co-wrote the disquieting title track for Horace Andy's *Living in the Flood* album, released on Massive Attack's Melankolic label.

Over the last twenty-five years, the Clash's embrace of Jamaican music has inspired like-minded efforts by musicians including Bad Brains, Massive Attack, 311, Rancid, Sublime, Long Beach Dub Allstars, and No Doubt. The punky reggae party that started so improbably way back in '77 has never really stopped.

Thanks to Jim Dooley and Stanley Whyte for the fact assists.

CO-OPTING COMBAT ROCK:
WHY JOE STRUMMER AND THE CLASH ARE STILL A DRIVING FORCE

By Luciano D'Orazio

Originally appeared on PopPoltics.com

> The way you get a better world is you don't put up with substandard anything.
>
> —Joe Strummer, 1999

In late December, when word spread that Joe Strummer, lead vocalist and guiding light of the seminal punk outfit the Clash, had died at age fifty, I was enraged.

It wasn't just because an integral symbol of my adolescence was gone, although the Clash was the first band for which I developed a real affinity. Nor was it because the Clash had learned just last November of their forthcoming induction to the Rock and Roll Hall of Fame as rumors spread of a reunion.

This was worse. The kings of punk had not only begun to crumble, but their influence, noticeable among scores of present-day pretenders, pseudo-punks, wannabes, and never-wills, seemed during this mourning period to still be living a private life of its own, gaining more steam everyday, bastardized, re-branded and attributed to others.

Of course, every band that has ever released more than a few albums wants to matter generations after their run. But in the end, few exemplify and transcend their musical genre they way the Clash did. Few transform their espoused sound into exciting new constructs; few offer prescient social commentary. And, most important of all, few remain true to their original ethos. My anger wasn't just a reaction to the loss of Joe Strummer, it was a protest against the pop-music industry for not paying homage to the Clash every day and not having enough guts to admit it.

In 1976, when Joe Strummer, guitarist Mick Jones, bassist Paul Simonon, and drummer Topper Headon broke out as one of the first bands to arrive in the wake of Malcolm MacLaren's nihilist quartet, the Sex Pistols, the Clash emerged as the Pistols's only serious rival. In those days, the Clash sound borrowed much from the Pistols and their American antecedents, the Ramones, with standard screaming three-chord progressions. In fact Strummer himself once famously said that when he saw the Sex Pistols perform he realized he was not alone in not being able to play very well.

Yet it wasn't long before the Clash developed a distinctive voice. Instead of the husky, blaring guitars of punk musicians past, Mick Jones rode high on the register, playing a clinical, almost-earsplitting treble above a steady, pounding bass by Simonon and a subtler, controlled drumline by Headon. The result was a radical departure from the Clash's predecessors. Blind fury had become controlled and harnessed in the service of creating true harmonic beauty, something that always eluded MacLaren. And before anyone had time to notice, punk had finally become musical.

But pop music without lyrics is only half a product, and the Clash's lyrics didn't follow the punk norm either. The Ramones were famous for considering themselves a manifestation of the Beach Boys who played their music as if on speed. The Sex Pistols reveled in their self-destruction, largely for its own sake. But Strummer and company had none of that. The Clash were angry, but not just for the sake of their anger or for serving as an "other."

Instead of just destroying the status quo, the Clash presented a vision of a new society rising from the ashes. Yes, the current world is doomed, they implied; but the current world has a lot of good in it, and its problems are solvable. The defining message of the Clash was overwhelmingly idealistic and positive: Anti-establishment angst can build a better world. The Ramones provided escape; the Sex Pistols, disillusionment and despair. But the Clash made their mark for a more important virtue: They signified hope.

This hope was presented in precise social commentary. In "London's Burning," they denounce their Labourite city's stagnant, sedentary and inflationary dead-end culture. Issuing a warning that "London's burning with boredom now," the song details the mischief of a lad tooling around deserted streets as the rest of the city sits passively in flats staring at television sets. It is not a call to arms as one would expect from a punk band; it is a warning of what a disillusioned, bored and especially unemployed London youth can do in a city that doesn't care about his welfare.

A similar statement is expressed in "Last Gang in Town," where the Clash satirically details the exploits of roving gangs looking for trouble: "The Crops hit the Stiffs, an' the Spikes whipped the Quiffs. They're all looking 'round for the last gang in town." The song cleverly denounces the gang violence that ravaged the working-class immigrant communities in London's East End. It is these messages that made the band matter to people, not just music wonks.

The Clash's sound developed even further with the implosion of the Sex Pistols in 1978, leaving Strummer's band as the only punk group of significance. The band utilized the dropouts and the dub-heavy bass of early Jamaican ska and reggae; it is not the only outside influence with which they experimented, but it is by far the most prominent as evidenced by the songs "Wrong 'Em Boyo" and "Police and Thieves."

Of course the Clash also dabbled in other idioms: funk ("White Man in Hammersmith Palais"), rockabilly ("Brand New Cadillac"), classical guitar ("Spanish Bombs"), dub, gospel, soul ("Stay Free"), and classic rock (their two greatest commercial hits, "Rock the Casbah" and "Should I Stay or Should I Go"), to name a few. But for all of their experimentation, they retained their message and controlled fury. The result? One of the richest, most grounded and brave repertoires in rock.

Since the Clash disbanded in 1985 many pretenders and Joe Strummer wannabes have attempted to raise the banner. In the early 1980s, the San Francisco outfit the Dead Kennedys made what was probably the best stab at the crown, becoming up until now the most overtly political of punk bands, even though their approach never transcended the arrested development of three-chord bleariness. Alas, their music never achieved the mainstream success of their predecessors, their politically driven freneticism dove into the depths of Hardcore, and the search continued.

Presently we are in the thick of not just what music critics are calling a "punk revival," but what they should be calling a Clash revival. The music is showing up in some unlikely places: Jaguar, the luxury car maker, recently unveiled an ad campaign using lyrics from "London Calling"; and *The Royal Tenenbaums* uses the band's music as a repeating leitmotif for Owen Wilson's drug-addicted character, Eli Cash. In the wake of Strummer's death, fans are finding the Clash influence in the songs of U2, No Doubt, the Beastie Boys and Rage Against the Machine. (U2 leader Bono even recently spoke to the legacy of Strummer: "The Clash was the greatest rock band," he said. "They wrote the rule book for U2.")

And, most obvious, a new breed of twenty-something neo-punksters—the Vines, the Hives, the White Stripes, and the

Strokes most notably among them—are taking cues not just from the Ramones and the Velvet Underground but from the Clash, stripping away studio gloss, forgetting a few chords, turning up the amp, and cranking out short, scrappy, lightning-fast anthems of angst in garages from California to Sweden.

It's now in vogue, in other words, to imitate the Clash's rhythms and textures, never mind the fact that establishing the kind of tonal control they flaunted is out of these youngsters' reach. Take, for instance, the Vines's "Ain't No Room." The setup is rather conventional: three main chords repeated incessantly below a husky, somewhat muffled main line that creates an almost continuous drone, occasionally broken up by a drum line. It is a rather straightforward punk riff, with the emphasis on speed and volume.

This observation is by no means universal, however: Specific tracks by the White Stripes, such as "Jimmy the Exploder," nuance the cookie-cutter punk line through different instruments (in the above instance, through use of tambourines.), or by the blending of genres (rockabilly and country, primarily). Clash-like experimentation, in other words, is obviously a goal.

When it comes to lyricism, today's neo-punksters are even further away from the mark. These new bands, for the most part, focus on hackneyed teen-dream pseudo-angst: toward the girlfriend, the so-called "loser" friends, and the established society that can't feel their pain. One example is the Strokes's song "Last Nite" wherein the discussion wanders between lost love and disillusionment from mainstream society:

> *And people they don't understand*
> *Your girlfriends they can't understand*
> *Your grandsons they won't understand*
> *On top of this I ain't ever gonna understand*

This difference in quality becomes even more apparent when comparing two songs that both deal with the role of the police. The Strokes's "New York City Cops" is personal and not incredibly insightful; the NYPD are simply ignorant thugs who hassle them on Saturday nights:

Yes I'm leavin'
'Cause it just won't work
They act like Romans
But they dress like Turks
Sometime, in your prime
See me, I like the summertime

In their remake of "Police and Thieves," the Clash, utilizing Junior Murvin, and Lee "Scratch" Perry's inspired words and adding their own distinctive arrangement (featuring a funkier, more up-tempo baseline and minimal guitar), go for something deeper. Instead of bobbies cramping the band's style at the palais, the police are a brutal tool of social oppression, almost indistinguishable from the very criminals they are sworn to apprehend. The police aren't fighting the criminals. They're fighting the people they protect, "the nation":

Police and thieves in the streets
Oh yeah!
Fighting the nation with their guns and ammunition
Police and thieves in the street
Oh yeah!
Scaring the nation with their guns and ammunition

In fact, despite its efforts towards Clash-like significance, the poetic ground of today's neo-punksters seems, for the most part, to just be a retread of the Ramones' more simplistic, repetitive lyrics: words without room for nuance and interpretation. Suppose, for example, that instead of repeating the phrase "Gimme Gimme Shock Treatment" in their song of the same name, the Ramones offered a half-assed explanation of why they sort of, maybe, could do better with some, just a little, shock treatment. That is what bands like the Strokes are doing.

And what's sad is that they're intending to do more. They're creating a lyrical style that only relates in part to life's problems (the Hives are a distinct culprit in this regard), and, in the process, they're falling flat on their faces. Lost girlfriends and boring suburbs may be the world these guys live in—most of these bands are drawn from upper- or upper-middle-class backgrounds—but their rebellion against these seemingly innocuous rites of passage seems even more trivial glorified in the way the Clash concentrated their anger.

Patchworks fall apart without seams; that is a universal truth. And while they may already be more famous in terms of worldwide notoriety and market share than the Clash ever was, today's neo-punksters are only managing to publicly emulate bits and pieces of the Clash's influence while revering the band in private. They've taken the safe route of tried-and-true three-chord pounding, an early Clash standby. They've written slipshod attempts at social commentary without relevant subject matter and adequate composition. And, worse, they've been trying to sell it in a way the Clash (or even the Ramones) never would have appreciated (unfortunately, we can't say the same thing for Lou Reed). In the end, I can't fault these musicians for trying, but their efforts don't come close to the real article.

One has to be critically cautious in crowning a successor to a king, especially when that king never made a big splash in widespread pop cultural ways because the nature of his message was that of the underground. They may only make the newspaper when a member of the band dies, but for now, as well as for the foreseeable future, the Clash continue to sit proud on their underground throne as the greatest punk band in history, even with Joe Strummer gone.

Their legacy and influence will, as they have since the 1980s, continue to keep them in the social unconscious as a band that matters. And any group of reverent musicians interested in writing another chapter to their story would do well not just to study their electric guitar riffs, but to also take serious note of the world that surrounds them.

THE WORLD IS WORTH FIGHTING FOR: TWO CREATIVE-ACTIVISTS, MICHAEL FRANTI AND TIM ROBBINS, CONTINUE JOE STRUMMER'S LEGACY

By Antonino D'Ambrosio

Action is the antidote to despair.

—Joan Baez

Your silence will not protect you.

—Audre Lorde

The purpose of art is to lay bare the questions, which have been hidden by the answers.

—James Baldwin

'Rise like Lions after slumber
In unvanquishable number,
Shake your chains to earth like dew

Which in sleep had fallen on you—
Ye are many—they are few.
—Percy Bysshe Shelley, *The Mask of Anarchy*

A s a kid growing up in early 1980s California, Michael Franti was beginning to experiment with the scores of musical styles that would find their way into his own music. "I came to the Clash in kind of a backwards way," he told me. "I was really into reggae and found out that Mikey Dread was working with them so I had to learn more about their music."[1] Mikey Dread is nothing short of a music legend in Jamaica and in the London music scene, where he was a prolific DJ, artist and producer. Dread's work with the Clash would come to be looked upon as some of the most creative and influential collaborative productions of the punk era. Clash songs including "One More Time," "Bankrobber" and "Police on My Back" became iconic recordings thanks in large part to Dread's brilliance as a "dub master."[2]

For aspiring young musicians like Michael Franti and Chuck D the Clash's experimentation with what is traditionally considered 'Black music' was inspiring. As Franti explains, the Clash's approach was not your ordinary Punk styling. "Their music was fun and exciting . . . it taught me to look at everything around me as an influence and that you could make good music with a decisive political message." He adds, "When you listen to the Clash and the new Strummer recordings you understand that the world is a terrible, scary place but the world is worth fighting for."

Franti is no stranger to fighting for the world and the people he believes in. Beginning with the Beatnigs, a San Francisco–based avant-garde group that fused industrial and punk music as a vehicle for social and political change, Franti began to make important strides in music and activism. Shortly after, Franti formed the Disposable Heroes of Hiphoprisy with former Beatnigs band mate Rono Tse. The duo's first and only album *Hypocrisy Is the Greatest Luxury* established them as among music's foremost proponents of multiculturalism and justice. Their lyrics challenged hip-hop tenets like homophobia and misogyny while producing music with a distinctly intelligent, forward-thinking global analysis of issues including U.S. imperialism. Their 1991 song about the Gulf War—"The Winter of Long Hot Summer"— remains remarkably prescient in today's political climate.

It all seemed so idiotic all the accusations of unpatriotic
The fall we'll always remember, capitulating silence
election November before the winter
of the long hot summer
Somewhere in the desert
we raised the oil pressure
and waited for the weather
to get much better
for the new wind to blow in the storm
We tried to remember the history in the region
the French foreign legion, Imperialism,
Peter O'Toole and hate the Ayatollah
were all we learned in school
Not that we gave Hussein five billion

The loss of life on both sides
pushed the limits of resilience
The scent of blood in our nostrils
fuel of the fossil land of apostle
The blackness that covered the sky was not the only thing
that brought a tear to the eye or

> *the taste of anger to the tongues*
> *of those too young to remember Vietnam*

Other provocative Franti compositions include "Everyday Life Has Become a Health Risk," "Television: the Drug of the Nation," "Socio-Genetic Experiment," and a brilliant reworking of the Dead Kennedys' classic "California Uber Alles." His clarity and depth was a radical counterpoint to Dr. Dre's *The Chronic,* which was dominating the music charts at the time taking hip-hop into a decidedly different direction, mainstreaming gangsta rap and fashioning it as the new pop cultural force.

Yet, it is his current work with the group Spearhead that has allowed Franti to develop and expand both his music and activism. Like Strummer's most recent work with the Mescaleros, Franti brings maturity, and skillful musicianship to the compositions. *Sandinista!,* the much maligned fourth record from the Clash, is Franti's musical model in many ways due to the expansive sounds, beats, styles, and musical compositions. "I realized that when you listen to the Clash, the music they create is the Clash," he tells me. "You can't point to any one style and the only way to describe the music when you hear it is 'oh yes, this is the Clash.'" And that's what he has been able to fashion with Spearhead. When you hear Spearhead it is unmistakably Michael Franti's unique sound and emotion coming through.

On Spearhead's most recent album, *Everybody Needs Music,* the track "Bomb the World" takes on the absurdity of creating peace through war:

> *we can chase down all our enemies*
> *bring them to their knees*
> *we can bomb the world to pieces*
> *but we can't bomb it into peace*

whoa we may even find a solution
to hunger and disease
we can bomb the world to pieces
but we can't bomb it into peace

Franti sees himself as a musical communicator with the singular goal of maintaining a critical approach to crafting humanist music. For Franti, Strummer also served as a model to continue fighting no matter the odds. "Strummer's music was always uplifting," he says, "albeit the issues he was singing about were startling and distressing." He continues, "my message is clear . . . even though things seem hopeless we must keep struggling . . . that is what is at the root of Strummer's music and at the root of my music."

Likewise, Strummer's music gave Franti the courage to explore: "It showed me, and all who listen, that we are not alone in this world," Franti declares, "and political songs are important because they can help us change ourselves and then hopefully things we don't like in this world." Franti acknowledges songs can't change the world, but music does give the listener a belief that change is possible. Thoughtful music also helps us cope with our day-to-day lives and discover a sense of community. Franti adds that it shows us "we are not crazy and that there are people like me out there." The Clash and Strummer gave him a sense of community and now Franti is helping to create community for countless others.

Franti shares many of the same political ideals Strummer held, including his concern about the increasing consolidation of the music industry and the demise of independent record labels. "In the '70s and '80s labels like Island Records," he explains, "put out the socially conscious music of artists like Bob Marley and U2. They did great work to really get them out there to a wider audience.

They worked hard for these artists. But then Island got taken over by a larger label, which got taken over by another label, which got taken over by another label."

Franti and Strummer also connect in their unyielding belief that music and rebellion react to the conservative state of the world, creating a "groundswell that will lead to another moment where our message will get out there and challenge the way people think." However, the challenge lies in conveying that message. Like Strummer, Franti encounters opposition to his work, and Spearhead faces an essential "blackout" on the radio. When Franti asks why, the answer given is that they are "too political." In another example Franti tells me about a recent situation involving one of his bandmates, which he asked to remain anonymous to prevent further troubles for the band, who has a sister now serving in Iraq. Before she was sent over to Iraq, two government agents visited her family and asked the family about having one child in the military and another in Spearhead, a music group with "radical political views." "They knew almost everything about what we did, where we went," Franti explains, " and questioned why we named our management company Guerrilla Management." Franti pauses and then tells me, "You have to realize they are watching even those involved in the smallest political activity—like going to protests—I call this total information awareness."

"Punk rock was everything I needed when I first heard it because it informed me on all levels—socially, politically," Tim Robbins tells me as we sit in his production office in Chelsea.[3] "We would smash disco and smash the system," he adds with a smirk. Robbins is a creative-activist who has achieved enormous success while maintaining a vocal, committed progressive social consciousness in the face of political and media scorn. In 2004 he won a Best Supporting Actor Oscar for his role as man dogged by unbearable childhood trauma in *Mystic River* while at the same time producing, writing, directing, and starring in the sharply critical theatrical satire *Embedded.*

Embedded takes on the Bush administration's war in Iraq, neoconservative influence, and the corporate media's complicity in supporting a war seemingly built on intimidation, misrepresentations, and outright lies. Robbins crafts the play in the spirit of Bertolt Brecht, breaking down the boundary between artist and audience with the clever use of mixed media (music, video, film, etc). As Larry Bogad points out in *Radical Ridicule: Electoral Guerrilla Theatre,* it also stands as an allegory in activist aesthetics for that more intractable wall which separates art from reality under capitalism.[4] Robbins's insider-outsider status gives him a unique perspective as well as a significant opportunity to fashion a work that is socially, culturally, and politically rebellious. For me, viewing *Embedded* was a direct, intense experience that comes at the audience in a high-speed rush.

Embedded, which opened on March 14 at the Public Theater in New York City, is dedicated to Joe Strummer and is tied together by punk music (the play opens with the Clash's "Know Your Rights") that captures the play's anger and trepidation towards the government and media that seems to be the moving away from democracy. Like the Italian playwright Dario Fo, who took on Italy's Prime Minister Silvio Berlusconi this year with a biting satire *Two-Headed Anomaly,*[5] Robbin's attempt to take a serious political situation and frame it in a farcical light has not pleased the powerful. Several attempts were made to shut down the play, which had its first run in Los Angeles before finding a home in New York City's Public Theater. As Fo himself declared, laughter does not please the mighty.

Throughout a prolific career that includes acting, writing, directing, and music, Robbins maintains a sensibility that is every bit as punk as Strummer's ferocious performances and progressive politics. Robbins grew up in New York City and was introduced to art as a political tool at a young age, due to his musician father's influence.[6] The folk music of the 1960s combined with political art helped shape Robbin's early consciousness.

However, it was Bob Dylan's "The Lonesome Death of Hattie Carroll" that affected him in a way no other song had before. "The song pulls no punches," he says. "That's hard core song writing, that's poetry and he's not hiding behind anything." Robbins became inspired by the song's "take no prisoners message" and vehement anger about a society that condones the murder of a black woman at the hands of her wealthy white employer. "I'm going to knock you down and I'm going to watch you fall," he says. "I'm going to stand over your body to make sure you're down . . . that's the kind of writing that was nowhere to be found after the mid '60s."

Robbins's search ended in the mid-1970s when he heard punk for the first time. Robbins explains that his ear was open to punk, it's spirit and message. "They had no qualms about going after people, after their gut and going for a knockout." He continues, "It's not just that I disagree with your politics . . . it's that I want to destroy your politics. I want to destroy your hatred, bigotry, your insensitivity, and your mistreatment of the weak. I am going to take you and throw you down into the gutter and watch you suffer . . . that's what was missing." At this point in his life Robbins was on his way to becoming one of the premiere actor's of his generation, first in theater with the Los Angeles Theater Group The Actors' Gang, and then of course in television and film.

The music and activism of the Clash in particular gave Robbins an indefatigable confidence that he could, and should, imbue his own creativity with that same radical consciousness. "Telling the truth in a very direct way that was not half-ass, not touchy-feely," he tells me. "That wasn't equivocating, it wasn't apologizing for itself, it was fuck you . . . and ultimately that was what was so amazing about the Clash." At this point Robbins recounts his first big acting gig. It was on the hit television show *St. Elsewhere* and Robbins played a terrorist. He had already completed one day of shooting and that night the Clash were in town performing on the early part of their Combat Rock tour. Robbins decided to go and participate fully in what he described "the caring, comfortable community" Clash shows provided. The next day of shooting he was three hours late.

Robbins wryly tells me that he showed up for work the next day and said nothing about being late. "I was going to pull this part off using all the punk rock energy Strummer and the boys gave me the night before," he says laughing. It worked. He did not get fired, although he later learned that both the producer and his agent wanted to fire him. The *St. Elsewhere* performance opened Hollywood's eyes to Robbins's immense talent. "Punk made me what I am today," he adds, "and the only reason I am any good in acting is because I took this attitude from punk rock . . . I had nothing to fear."

"Take the song 'Spanish Bombs' for example," Robbins explains while singing a few lines of the song. "At first I listen to it and hear the amazing music, it draws me in, then I start to hear what they are singing about." Strummer wrote the song in the style of a punk Andalusian poem in tribute to the freedom fighters who fought for democracy against the fascists in Spain in 1939. It alludes to the brutal death of poet/antifascist Federico Garcia Lorca and the role of the United States in aiding the military dictatorship's terrible rise to power.[7] The song opens powerfully:

> *Spanish songs in Andalucia*
> *The shooting sites in the days of '39*
> *Oh, please, leave the vendanna open*

Federico Lorca is dead and gone
Bullet holes in the cemetery walls
The black cars of the Guardia Civil
Spanish bombs on the Costa Rica
I'm flying in a DC 10 tonight

"It made me want to learn more about Andalucia, Lorca, and what really took place at that time in Spain," Robbins adds, "this is what good music does—it teaches you."

As we discuss Robbins's more clearly political work including *Dead Man Walking, Bob Roberts, Cradle Will Rock,* and *Embedded,* he stops to point out something that is a constant source of frustration for him.[8] "Be careful about using the word 'political' because it will turn people off," he ardently declares. "'Political' is a way to marginalize." Robbins believes that he and Strummer among other creative-activists are really humanists or rebels not "political people." Returning to Strummer he continues, "You know there was no one that was less political than Joe Strummer." He adds, "If you look up the word in the dictionary—it's someone whose behavior is affected by calculation—Strummer's was affected by justice, a sense of fairness."

I mention to him that Franti and others always return to the fact that Strummer's work is first and foremost fun and entertaining. Robbins absolutely agrees. "We don't want to lecture to anybody. I want to feel. I want to be able to laugh . . . to be able to achieve that in the entertainment you are doing, that's the high art for me." Robbins, much like Strummer when I met him, rankles hard against contrived and pretentious intellectualizing in political art. Both also seemed to share the simple goal of crafting work that reaches as wide an audience as possible. "Creating something that touches people and still has substance is the real achievement." Robbins explains.

Still, for all his success, Robbins continues to face what Franti and other creative-activists encounter on a daily basis, what he calls "cultural assassination." Strummer faced this type of intense media scrutiny with his time with the Clash and more specifically after the release of *Sandinista!* I relay my conversation with Strummer to Robbins regarding the weariness Strummer and the band felt during the *Sandinista!* period. Everywhere they went they would face hordes of reporters that would focus on the naming of the album after the revolutionary group.[9] Were the Clash communists? Did they believe in violence as a means to political change? Where they providing support to the Sandinistas? In effect, Strummer's music was secondary and the politics became the focal point.

Robbins has faced this a number of times in his career. First in 1993 when he and Susan Sarandon spoke out at the Oscars about the detention of several hundred Haitians with AIDS in "working camps" at the U.S. Naval Base at Guantanamo Bay.[10] Then with his vocal and very public criticism of the Bush administration's build-up to the war in Iraq and the subsequent occupation. Still, the intense media scrutiny and subsequent backlash was nothing compared to what has engulfed the production of *Embedded*. "The media went after me with a vengeance," he says. "It was an attempt to shut down the play."

Looking at the reviews of most American theater critics, it is hard to deny that there seems to be a deliberate attempt to destroy the play.[11] As Robbins points out, nearly all the reviews don't even tell the play's story or look at what is unique about the play. Instead, the focus is on the playwright's politics. The foreign press has been much more fair and balanced and this is not a coincidence in Robbins's opinion. "If I look at this through the prism of my own ego and try not to be paranoid," he tells me, " and I do feel that I am a well-established artist, I have to ask 'Why is my new work ignored?' Is this an active decision, a personal thing?"

Robbins draws a parallel between the critical reception of *Embedded* and Strummer's dark time following the Clash's breakup. "What happens when you step out in front—and when the shit starts and there is nobody there?" he sharply asks me. "There is no sense of loneliness deeper than that," he continues. "You feel betrayed, bewilderment, you wonder how did this happen? I know what I am doing is right, is good. How did I get to be the one who is ostracized? How did I get the blame and am held responsible?"

Like Strummer, Robbins had to endure this attack when he tried to put out to the world his more personal and humanistic centered projects. Robbin's third directorial effort, *Cradle Will Rock,* was a painful lesson in how the media can agitate politically in an effort to destroy one's work. The film's account of the 1930s staging of the progressive play *The Cradle Will Rock* for the WPA-funded Federal Theater Project did not sit well with some major American film critics.[12] One in particular, at a lunch meeting of American film critics in Cannes, encouraged his colleagues to write reviews that undermine the film. He described Robbins as a "subversive" and the film as "being dangerous." The result was that *Cradle* was ignored and vanished from screens swiftly, denying the public the opportunity to see it. "It was a painful death," Robbins says.

Still, Robbins was far from defeated and took this as an important lesson making him stronger to endure some unsettling battles ahead. First, Robbins and his longtime partner, Susan Sarandon, were banned from the fifteenth-anniversary celebration of Bull Durham at the National Baseball Hall of Fame because of their public antiwar stance. Second was the right-wing furor that dogged the production of *Embedded*. In his April 2003 National Press Club address, Robbins described the situation. "Susan and I have been listed as traitors, as supporters of Saddam, and various other epithets by the Aussie gossip rags masquerading as newspapers, and by their fair and balanced electronic media cousins, Nineteenth Century Fox." Robbins continued, "And both of us last week were told that both we and the First Amendment were not welcome at the Baseball Hall of Fame."[13]

Robbins's kinship with Strummer runs deep after these experiences. "When they throw all these labels at you," he argues, "radical, revolutionary, I am trying to say 'no'; at the core I am humanist and what I believe comes from a simple place . . . I am just asking questions, that's all." Both Franti and Robbins are doing much more than asking questions. Their work serves as a beacon continuing a tradition of committed creative-activism, fighting for a world free of tyranny.

GET BEHIND THE STRUGGLE,
RIGHT NOW!

By Anthony Roman

Radio 4 is one of the most exciting and politically active groups to hit the New York City, or for that matter, the U.S. music scene in a long, long time. More like a collective than a band, they fuse punk, new wave, postpunk, Afro-beat, funk, electro among loads of other eclectic styles packed in between to create music that is frenetic and compelling. Still, Radio 4 goes further with socially conscious music that makes you dance and at the same time fight back. Like the Clash, Radio 4's music is fun, offering songwriting that is serious yet always optimistic. Named after a P.I.L. song, Radio 4— Anthony Roman, Tommy Williams, Greg Collins, Gerard Garone, P. J. O'Connor—builds upon the foundation boldly set by the Clash nearly three decades ago. The group's second full-length album, *Gotham!*, is without question the standard bearer for rebel rock in the new century. (Notice the exclamation point in homage to *Sandinista!*)

From start to finish, the record fiercely tackles many pressing issues of the day using early twenty-first-century New York City, like the Clash used '70s and '80s London, as a allegory for a society going backward rather than forward. In "Calling All Enthusiasts," the band echoes one of Strummer's underlying beliefs, the need "to kick things over" as they sing "I'm really sorry but we gotta start resisting/It's no request, we are really insisting on this now." Later in the same song they address our diminishing civil liberties with "can you believe arresting for protesting [in the U.S.A.]." *Gotham!* is a record produced by a band sharply criticizing the systemic reactionary political attack being waged in America today. Thematically, they infuse their work with an insightful class analysis advancing liberty and freedom with songs including "Our Town," "Save Our City," and "Red Lights." Other bold compositions address issues of police brutality ("Certain Tragedy"), class struggle ("Struggle"), and the need to build a unified movement against injustice ("Start a Fire").

Radio 4's anthemic songs come at you full blast, unleashing a creative political force much lacking in the over stylized, clichéd music of the retro-chic garage bands receiving much of the accolades in today's media. And that's just fine by Radio 4. Like Strummer, they press on, not compromising but promising something more, something better.

—Antonino D'Ambrosio

Back in the day: Anyone who knows me at all is aware of the profound impact that Joe Strummer and the Clash have had on my life. The first time I heard the Clash was when I was twelve years old. An older cousin played me "Clampdown" and I was immediately hooked. Every week I would go to Slipped Disc Records in Valley Stream, Long Island, and buy a new album by them. *London Calling* was the first record of theirs I got and to this day it remains my favorite. *London Calling* exposed me to a scores of music styles—punk rock, R&B, reggae, rockabilly, ska—just about everything. I never had heard anything like it in my life before. I was hooked on the Clash and the music. I used to stare at the album covers, and the liner notes and dust sleeves, as if they were in a window into the salvation that the Clash seemed to be promising. I bought all their videos from *Rude Boy* to *This Is Video Clash* and just watched them over and over again. I was mesmerized by their energy, their clothes, their hair. Everything about them was thrilling. They were and remain, the coolest.

A few years after my introduction to the Clash, I was flipping through the *Village Voice* and saw that Joe Strummer was playing a solo show at the Palladium, where ten years before, the Clash performed one of the greatest shows of all time, capped by Paul Simonon destroying his bass in frustration. The picture, chosen by Strummer, would grace the cover of *London Calling,* forever immortalizing that record, that Palladium performance, and the Clash as an incomparable force in music history. Two buddies and me took the Long Island Rail Road into New York City for the show. The performance was fantastic. Strummer did tons of Clash stuff, a lot of the *Earthquake Weather* album, the *Permanent Record* stuff, and even "Keys to Your Heart" by the 101ers. Afterwards, we walked to the back of the Palladium (now, like the rest of downtown New York City, a dorm or some other offshoot of New York University) and we decided we were going to try and meet Joe. After a little while of us standing around drinking beer and smoking (remember when you could drink and smoke in New York City?) he came out through the back door. He had a leather jacket on, the Strummer quiff was in full effect, and he was carrying the infamous Telecaster guitar carried in his hand with no case. Joe spotted us and suddenly approached us. We were completely stunned. We nervously managed to remark how that the Telecaster in his hand was the same one from the "Rock the Casbah" video with the Ignore Alien Order sticker placed among scores of other decals, scratches, and divots.

He asked us if we wanted to play the guitar. Now we're playing Joe Strummer's Telecaster as he begins teaching us the intro chords to "Clampdown" while he tried to remember the mumbled spoken word part that kicks off the song. He told us that the spoken word part was about a dream that Mick Jones had regarding a helicopter crashing into the studio where the Clash were recording *London Calling*. After this we discussed reggae, Latin music, the Replacements (he wasn't a fan), and he even grabbed my friend and pulled him closer when a New York City cab zoomed a little to close to him. Then he asked us if we wanted to go to the Cat Club with him, but we were so freaked out that we decided that we should just go to Penn Station and get quickly back to Long Island and not ruin this perfect night. Not surprisingly, in the years since that dreamlike night I have never come close to meeting any celebrity who freely gave of his time and showed such genuine interest in his fans. How one of the biggest names in rock 'n' roll history would find it interesting to talk to three teenagers from Long Island is still unfathomable to me. Yet, other people who have met him have offered similar stories. It is a true testament of how great this man really was, and what a role model he still is.

Fast-forward to the late 1990s: I'm putting a band together called Radio 4 that is taking heavy influence from the Clash and other bands from the late '70s early '80s. We wanted to match the Clash's fusion of dance music and reggae music with punk and politics. With *Sandinista!* in heavy rotation on everybody's stereos and right after the band was pulled together, Strummer announces another comeback tour. I find my way to the New York City show and am deeply inspired yet again by this guy's matchless energy and passion. He's nearing fifty and he's got the energy of a twenty-five-year-old, which is the median age of the his new band, the Mescaleros. Most important is how much you believe every word of what he's saying. He's got more conviction than anyone I've ever seen on stage. After this we go on to make *Gotham!*, a record that is really inspired by the later period Clash. We take all the chances we can absorb all kinds of music—disco, house, reggae, Afro-beat—and try and throw it into the mix. The end result is that *Gotham!* is an intensely political record as we really did our best to capture New York City circa 2001, a city reeling in the midst of troubling political and social change.

A lot of that influence was from how the Clash would talk about London of the late '70s and early '80s—"the Prisoner lives in Camden town," "On the route of the nineteen bus"—and make me daydream about what London was like. Supposedly, Bernie Rhodes (the Clash's first manager and a tremendous influence on the band) said that there should always be a reference to time and place in a song. I tried to stick to that in our music, particularly with our second record, *Gotham!* Consequently, when we set out touring behind the record people from all over the world asked us about New York City and what we were singing about. It proved to me that people still listen to lyrics. As a result, the record, with its music with a message, introduced us to a much bigger audience. Suddenly not only are we traveling the world we are making a "sort of" living as musicians.

Late March 2002: We're driving from Houston to Austin about to enter and perform at the venerable South by Southwest music festival. We get a phone call telling us we've been asked to open for Strummer at St. Ann's Warehouse in Brooklyn on one of the seven nights he's doing it there (this guy loves residencies!). At the gig, we were all nervous and excited and we sound-checked with "Magnificent Seven," a bold attempt to cover a Clash classic.

The piece went over fairly well to a crowd that had no idea who we were and what we were about. After our set Strummer came over and introduced himself(!) and asked us if we wanted to come upstairs to his dressing room. After some drinking and potent spliffs, we were then invited to the after party at Three of Cups. There, on Manhattan's Lower East Side, all my friends were given the opportunity to meet the man who graciously had time for everyone. All his New York City buddies were there, each talented, interesting artists in their own right—Jim Jarmusch, Matt Dillon, Steve Buscemi, Bob Gruen. The party went until about 5 A.M. and true to legend Joe was the last man standing. Then I saw him stroll off into the morning sun with a local rockabilly kid named Brian Luxe, off to another party somewhere. It was the last time I ever saw him.

December 22, 2002: I've been winding down at home from an exhausting European tour for about three days when I get the same morning phone call that a lot of people got that day. Strummer was gone. It doesn't seem real to me and I spend most of the day walking around New York City trying to Christmas shop but getting nowhere. The same thoughts of disbelief ran through my head as I am sure they did for many people the world over: He was so healthy; he was at the top of his game, etc. I couldn't bring myself to listen to the Clash for months. A year later we're invited to play a Strummer tribute show at Irving Plaza in New York City; this time we tackle "White Man in Hammersmith Palais." Everyone tells us not to touch that song but we figure that a lot of people probably told the Clash not to touch "Police and Thieves" among countless other songs. Later on, Barry "Scratchy" Myers , the Clash's DJ tells us it was gutsy move.

When thinking about why Strummer is so important it lies in the fact that like many other heroes of mine, like John Cassavetes and Jack Kerouac, he wasn't an intellectual. Sure, he was smart and well-read and knew his politics, but you didn't need a poli-sci degree to relate to what he was saying. He spoke directly to the "every man" connecting with all kinds of people from all walks of life. For me, this is the reason why he always had time for everyone, because he was truly interested in where they were coming from. Strummer taught me that you have to believe in what you're singing, what you're saying, and most importantly you have to be accountable for your actions. The Clash walked it like they talked it, positively affecting more young people than any other punk rock band. They broke into the system and used it to their advantage—instead of preaching to the converted they actually did the converting.

Recently they painted a large mural of Strummer on the wall of Niagara in the East Village. The day it was completed me and my wife drove in from Brooklyn and took a look. As we stared at it we watched as a young man passed by and upon noticing the mural, nodded his head, made the sign of the cross, and moved on.

FROM BRIXTON TO EL BARRIO NYC

By Not4Prophet

You have the right not to be killed.

Murder is a crime!

Unless it was done by a police man or aristocrat"

—"Know Your Rights," by the Clash

Growing up in the B-boy barrio slum sidewalks of *nueva york,* with junkies under the stairs, pig police patrolling the avenues, guards at the gates and guns on the roof, I was a young (Poor-to Rican) punk lookin' for the perfect beat with nothin to eat but the sounds that emanated from the street. Survivin' on shit and sonics and growing bored with the USA, I grew up groovin' to Public Enemy, BDP, Poor Righteous Teachers and storefront preachers, and music was the sustenance for the soul (food) that the gutters and gods couldn't provide, the (musical) meals that were never enough in my mecca bodega of the mind. Music was my (counter) culture, the notes between the notes between the cracks in the pavement

When they kick at your front door/How you gonna come?/With your hands on your head/Or on the trigger of your gun?/When the law break in/How you gonna go?/Shot down on the pavement/Or waiting in death row?

—"The Guns of Brixton"

291

I was sprouting up faster than the weed I was smoking, and rea-soning Malcolm, Marcus, Martin, Marcos, the Macheteros, Mumia, Move, the Young Lords, Latin Kings, the Panthers, ghetto gangsters with ghettoblasters, but I was always ciphering the sound, digging deeper than the beats, noise and politics, sonic and sedition, I wanted soundtracks that screamed survival, records that roared revolution, albums that were armed, and PE was the only one bringing the necessary noise. So I would dissect every lyric out of Chuck Ds mouth, turn every turn of a phrase into a 10 point program, dust the dust covers for ancient hieroglyphics that would indicate new (un)civilizations that were older than me and music itself.

> I'm all lost in the supermarket/I can no longer shop happily/I came in here for a special offer/A guaranteed personality
>
> —"Lost in the Supermarket"

Eventually my search for truth (and soul) caused me to venture into enemy territory, a backdoor boricua entering through the exit of racist rock clubs, and sneaking into segregated squats for hard-core punk shows, because I knew that though PE was in an (after school) class by themselves, they couldn't possibly be trotting this school of hard knocks by they lonesome Or could they? But I guess I was fooled by the allure of loud guitars and rebel yells, because in my soul sojourns all I ever found was louder mouths that were talkin' loud and sayin' nothin', and didn't even have a jungle groove to move to. No funk in their punk, no soul in their rock 'n' roll. So I continued to scratch at the signs of the surface, searching for sabotage and the sounds of survival and what Jean Michel Basquiat called "royalty and the streets."

Then one day, after many a trod through Babylon, I walked into a used (and slightly abused) record store in some anonymous avenue in money making Manhattan, where the clerks were unfriendly poser punx who were trained in special tactics on how to make a browsing Puerto Rican feel unwanted, uncomfortable, unwelcome, but still, I dived (hip hop) head first into turbulent waters, deep beneath the polluted seas and stale sounds, and came up with fishbone, Bad brains, Suicidal Tendencies, Black Flag, and deep at the bottom of the crates and craters was some old worn white boy(?) wax called SANDANISTA! I carefully took it out of the crate, checked for (one too many) scratches, dusted it off, and took it home for the title alone. And, shit, in my interest and excitement, I even forgot to pay for it. I'd heard of the Clash, even read about how these British blokes invited Kurtis Blow to open for them when they played in New York shitty because they dug hip hop, only to see him pelted with rotten vegetables by a less than appreciative "punk" audience. And I had no illusions about american (and European) history and the reality of Elvis, the Rolling Stones, and a slew of other white boy bands that specialized in cultural theft. Yeah, black folks had created all kinds of amazing sounds, from jazz to rock 'n' roll, to funk to reggae, to salsa to hip-hop, and been ripped off by ofays wit attitude every time. But I figured if the Clash were cool enough back in 1980, to name an album after a Latino armed rebel organization that the U.S. hated and tried to destroy, then, hey, they couldn't be all bad, now could they?

> I gotta shed this skin I been living in/Gotta shed this skin I been living in
>
> —"Shed This Skin"

Sandinista!, a sprawling three vinyl release that, back in 1980, was sold for the low low price of one record(due to the bands acceptance to take the monetary loss for the major labels refusal to go along with the Clash's idea that a three record set could/should be sold at a one record price as a gift to the consumer/fan), was a revelation wrapped loosely in revolution. I liberated (uh, bought) it mostly for the title, but I got so much more, and I would go on to free their entire anthology from the confines of record stores that insisted on placing them in the cheapie bin, close to the trash bin, or (conveniently for me) close to the exit door. *The Clash, Black Market Clash, Give 'Em Enough Rope, London Calling, Combat Rock,* shit, even *Cut the Crap* provided the punk politics I was looking for and even gave me some hope that maybe, just maybe, not all anglos were white supremacist red necked conquistador colonizing crackas who turned off ya mom's apartments heat in the dead of winter, and tossed your dad in a cold jail cell in the heat of summer. Yeah, the Clash knew they were white, and the legacy that entailed, and they knew that the days were racial tension and the nights were racial fear, and that London was burning and Brixton was already ashes. But precisely because (or in spite) of this, they also knew that something had to give, and so they tried to give something in the hopes that perhaps they could play a part. And all they really had to give that was worth a god damn in these troubled days was punk, so they put their punk sensibilities and abilities where it counted. Yeah, the black (market) planet was in revolt, so these white boys asked for a riot of their own.

> Kick over the wall, 'cause governments to fall/How can you refuse it?/Let fury have the hour, anger can be power/If you know that you can use it
> —"Clampdown"

The Clash were far from the best band on the planet, (though one mainstream rag called them "the only band that mattered"), and they were even further from being the best band for the job that they chose to accept. Their musicianship was par for the punk course, really, and their lead singer, Joe Strummer, sang like he had one too many marbles in his mouth after a bout of two too many ales. But I actually enjoyed (and respected) hearing Joe Strummer yelp what was supposed to be a rap, and claw his way through what was supposed to be funk, and all with an ear towards punk as politics. If anyone was "Overpowered by Funk," it was Strummer. He had to know that he wasn't gonna be givin' Melle Mel or George Clinton a run for their money anytime soon, nor was Strummer writing groovilicious hit songs that the record labels and radio stations would greedily latch onto, when he ventured into shallow funk punk polluted waters and uncharted rap rock territory. Most of the Clash hits were the fast, pure poppy punk of songs like "Should I Stay or Should I Go," "London Calling," all "Lost in the Supermarket," and, the somewhat funky in spite of itself, "Rock the Casbah." So why record the Latin(o) tinged "Washington Bullets," which beckoned folks to "please remember Victor Hara, *es verdad*," or for that matter toss badly mangled spanish into their tunes, as they did in "Should I Stay or Should I Go." And what in the world could explain the cornball grooves of "Overpowered by Funk," which (complete with a bad rap by Graffiti writer Futura 2000) actually copped to the question of cultural thievery when it placed Benny Goodman on a list and sentenced him to a trial by jury. And then knowingly asked whether perhaps the Clash's name might be on that same list? So hits was never quite the point in spite of the fact that the masters of DIY punk themselves, Crass, stated (very eloquently, I might add) that Epic "signed the Clash, not for revolution, just for cash." No, the Clash were never "sell outs." They tried way too hard to be against the grain and the mainstream brain to sell their soul, and knew, maybe better than anybody, that punk meant counter culture, and if it wasn't counter culture it wasn't punk.

Spanish bombs, yo te cuero infinito/Yo te cuero, oh my corazon

—"Spanish Bombs"

The Clash's significance musically, culturally, and politically is as important and relevant today as it was back in '77 (when it really seemed like Punk might/could actually "kick over the walls and cause governments to fall") because we are still dealing with the same "isms" and skisms that they tried to tackle with their proletariat prose and punk politics. And the fact that they never got back together for the big money reunion (like old Johnny Rotten's Sex Pistols did), or that Joe Strummer kept right on makin' socially conscious music until his very last breath, serves as yet another reminder that punk is not dead(!), just maybe on a revolutionary respirator. Yeah, the Clash is a reminder of the battle between "police and thieves," the clash between capitalism and culture. They weren't really around that long, but along the way, they got ripped off and taken advantage of by the corporate vampires (just like so many others who chose to swim in that putrid ocean by they lonesome), but they were among the very few bands that were what Bad Brains called "Fearless Vampire Killers" and their stake (and garlic) was in their words, and they really did rage against the machine as best they knew how. That's what moved and inspired one raging rican would be rockero who knew that brixton was right next door to brooklyn. These cats were trying (real hard) to make music that was honest and honestly political, and that blurred the lines of genre, and trampled down borders (and any border patrol who might be standing in the way) all through a punk principle of raw reality and rebellion and revolution rock, and what they came up with was pure culture clash.

THE JOE I KNEW

By Billy Bragg

Originally published for BBC News

T he Clash were the greatest rebel rock band of all time. Their commitment to making political pop culture was the defining mark of the British punk movement.

They were also a self-mythologising, style-obsessed mass of contradictions.

That's why they were called the Clash.

They wanted desperately to be rock stars but they also wanted to make a difference.

While Paul Simonon flashed his glorious cheekbones and Mick Jones threw guitar hero shapes, no one struggled more manfully with the gap between the myth and the reality of being a spokesman for your generation than Joe Strummer.

All musicians start out with ideals but hanging onto them in the face of media scrutiny takes real integrity.

Tougher still is to live up to the ideals of your dedicated fans.

Joe opened the back door of the theatre and let us in, he sneaked us back to the hotel for a beer; he too believed in the righteous power of rock 'n' roll.

And if he didn't change the world he changed our perception of it. He crossed the dynamism of punk with Johnny Too Bad and started that punky-reggae party.

RADICAL BAND

He drew us, thousands strong, onto the streets of London in support of Rock Against Racism.

He sent us into the garage to crank up our electric guitars. He made me cut my hair.

The ideals that still motivate me as an artist come not from punk, not even from the Clash, but from Joe Strummer.

The first wave of punk bands had a rather ambivalent attitude to the politics of late '70s Britain. The Sex Pistols, the Damned, the Stranglers, none of them, not even the Jam, came close to the radicalism that informed everything the Clash did and said.

The U.S. punk scene was even less committed. The Ramones, Talking Heads, Heartbreakers and Blondie all were devoid of politics.

Were it not for the Clash, punk would have been just a sneer, a safety pin, and a pair of bondage trousers.

Instead, the incendiary lyrics of the Clash inspired 1,000 more bands on both sides of the Atlantic to spring up and challenge their elders and the man that we all looked to was Joe Strummer.

INSPIRING FORM

He was the White Man in Hammersmith Palais who influenced the Two Tone Movement. He kept it real and inspired the Manic Street Preachers.

And he never lost our respect. His recent albums with the Mescaleros found him on inspiring form once again, mixing and matching styles and rhythms in celebration of multiculturalism.

At his final gig, in November in London, Mick Jones got up with him and together they played a few old Clash tunes.

It was a benefit concert for the firefighters' union.

One of the hardest things to do in rock 'n' roll is walk it like you talk it.

Joe Strummer epitomised that ideal and I will miss him greatly.

GETTIN' BACK TO THE BAD SEEDS:
THE LEGEND OF THE LONG SHADOW

By Antonino D'Ambrosio

All'estremità, tutta una persona ha è il loro honor e dignità—nessuno possono eliminare quella.
At the end, all a person has is their honor and dignity—no one can take that away.

> —Lorenzo D'Ambrosio, 1941–1988

Ever insurgent let me be
make me more daring than devout.

> —Louis Untermeyer

One's truth must add its push to the evolution of public justice and mercy, must transform the spirit of the city whose brainless roar went on and on at both ends of the bridge.

> —Arthur Miller

I t was sometime around Thanksgiving 2003. I was driving down I35 making my way through Texas from Austin to San Antonio and I had just picked up *Streetcore,* Joe Strummer's posthumous final recording. Unsure of what to expect and a bit a reluctant to listen, the music that poured out of the speakers was nothing short of a revelation. From the opening rift of "Coma Girl" to the closing bluesy ballad "Silver and Gold," the record is an achievement. Listening to Strummer's new music on a long, lonely stretch of highway in the middle of the state that boasts both Buddy and Willie as native sons, I could not help but think that this is just how Strummer would have wanted everyone to hear his new music. The record travels back and forth in time, emotionally capturing the essence of Strummer's music, his timeless optimism and political idealism. *Streetcore* is anchored spiritually and politically by two subtlety recorded and performed songs: "Redemption Song" and "Long Shadow."

During the production of *Streetcore,* Strummer spent some time in record producer Rick Rubin's Los Angeles studio. It was there that Strummer met Johnny Cash for the first time. These two performers had much in common. Both were music pioneers and profoundly committed humanists who passed through life with humility and honor. Upon meeting Cash, Strummer had intended to record Bob Marley's timeless protest anthem "Redemption Song" for his new album. The duet does not appear on Strummer's album but on a Cash box set released after his death titled *Unearthed.* The version on *Streetcore* was recorded with Blue's great Smokey Hormel and long-time Tom Petty keyboardist/pianist Benmont Tench.

Johnny Cash, a poor sharecropper's son who sang to himself as he picked cotton in the fields, would die ten months after Strummer on September 12, 2003, in Nashville, Tennessee. "My roots are in the workingman," Cash told the *Music City News* in 1987. "I can remember very well how it is to pick cotton ten hours a day, or to plow, or how to cut wood. I remember it so well because I don't intend to ever try to do it again." Instead, Cash became a powerful voice of hope, a working-class hero who refused to dream someone else's dream, choosing instead to live his own.

Strummer told me simply that Cash "IS music." Cash was a tremendous cultural force in music, recording over 1,500 songs in a career that spanned more than four decades. Cash created his own sound that went beyond traditional genres—he was at once an emotional folk singer, a rock 'n' roll desperado, and a down-in-the-mouth country crooner. The now famous photo of Cash with Elvis, Jerry Lee Lewis, and Ray Perkins (dubbed the Million Dollar Quartet) at Sun Studios tells us that his career began with the birth of rock 'n' roll but his rebel posture and straightforward, plain-spoken musical approach told us emphatically that his music was something more, his life was something more.

Strummer admired Cash's ability to forge on throughout a life and career that had more than one dark period. First he recalls listening to Cash's album, *Bitter Tears: Ballads of the American Indian,* which challenged the United State's treatment of Native Americans with such songs "Apache Tears," "The Ballad of Ira Hayes," and "Custer." In the latter, Cash sings "With victories he was swimmin' he killed children, dogs and women . . . It's not called an Indian victory but a bloody massacre/and the General he don't ride well anymore /There might have been more enthusin' if us Indians had been losin'."

"That album was filled with the anger and fire that would inspire me from my Clash days onwards," Strummer said. In his autobiography, Cash wrote, "I dove into primary and secondary sources, immersing myself in the tragic stories of the Cherokee and the Apache, among others, until I was almost as raw as Peter.

By the time I actually recorded the album I carried a heavy load of sadness and outrage; I felt every word of those songs, particularly 'Apache Tears' and 'The Ballad of Ira Hayes.' I meant every word, too. I was long past pulling my punches."

Second, Strummer points to Cash's work as a member of the Highwaymen in 1980, a quartet that included fellow "music outlaws" Willie Nelson, Waylon Jennings, and Kris Kristofferson, as an example of Cash's ability to keep growing. Strummer explained that Cash seemed to teeter on the edge of a cliff "and risk everything, seemingly inviting the end" in an effort to find a new voice. The musician John Mellencamp echoed this sentiment describing Cash as "an American original, uncompromised in his craft and incomparable in its execution. He makes you feel that he is playing solely to reach the best part of your spirit."

When, in 1994, Rubin approached Cash about recording an album of songs composed by contemporary musicians including Nick Lowe, Leonard Cohen, and Tom Waits, Strummer was one of many who contributed an original composition. The album, *American Recordings*, brilliantly captured Cash's crossover appeal and introduced him to an entirely new audience. Rubin explained his reason for working with Cash because "he was an outsider who was never part of a trend . . . a rock star is a musical outlaw and that's Johnny Cash." The song Strummer wrote and Cash recorded, "The Road to Rock 'n' Roll," remains unreleased, although Strummer did record it for *Rock Art and the X-Ray Style*. Strummer remained determined that Cash would record one of his songs. In the early 1990s he recorded a demo of "Long Shadow" and submitted it to Rubin and Cash for their consideration. Cash never had a chance to record the song for any of the four albums he recorded with Rubin.

It now stands as both a tribute to Cash, the rebel mentor and hero outlaw, and as a desperate, poignant epitaph for Strummer.

Strummer scrawled the lyrics to "Long Shadow" on a pizza box writing whatever did not fit on a paper towel and roll of insulation tape. And this is how Strummer presented it to Cash. Rubin describes Strummer as very thoughtful during the duration of recording, slipping away into his car to listen to his *cumbia* tape again and again. Rubin explained that for Strummer this served as a source of inspiration and chance for meditation in helping him gain energy and strength in their recording sessions together.

"Redemption Song" and "Long Shadow," the heart and soul of *Streetcore*, were the only two songs Rubin produced for the album. Strummer preferred to record the music in a garage on a small tape recorder rather than Rubin's state-of-the-art studio. While listening to "Long Shadow" along with the other nine songs that appear on this album, Strummer's pure emotion and joy comes shining through. You can almost see the glint in his eye, the flash in his smile, and the quiver in that famous guitar leg when he sings the anthem-like refrain of the revolution-themed "Arms Aloft" and the Telecaster-soaked jam "All in a Day." "Burning Streets" is a moving follow-up to the Clash classic "London's Burning" with Strummer quietly declaring that the new century has brought us little relief from the hostilities that divide and ultimately destroy cities and nations. Closing the album is "Silver and Gold" a heartbreaking cover of the Bobby Charles penned and Fats Domino recorded "Before I Grow Too Old."

Strummer was humbly writing the next chapter in his life without realizing that the journey was coming to an end. Yet as Dick Rude explained to me in describing Strummer's new work, this is far from an ending but more truthfully a life and work that will continue to manifest itself for generations to come. Strummer once said that "we must go back to sortin' things out" and that "getting back to the bad seeds" and "going underground" is where music needed to return. Johnny Cash and Strummer were both those "bad seeds." The quintessential rock outlaw, Cash supported the Civil Rights movement and opposed the Vietnam War; just a few of the unpopular political stances he would take throughout his life. For Strummer, Cash was someone who lived comfortably outside the lines because standing within them meant complicity in the injustice and hypocrisy that stains our society. Cash seemed to be always fighting the law with little regard to winning, walking the line only for love, and never compromising his integrity.

"Are you taking orders," Strummer once sang "or are you taking over." Cash famously responded to those who asked why he wore black: "I wear the black for the poor and the beaten down/Livin' in the hopeless, hungry side of town . . . But 'til we start to make a move to make a few things right/You'll never see me wear a suit of white." Authority for both was only a system of control that had no inherent wisdom. "Just look around," Strummer asked when I met him, "does the march to war now represent the interests of the world's people?" Music, whether it is punk, rock 'n' roll, country, blues, Tropicalismo is all just a pure expression of what must be said and what must be done.

Ultimately, Cash and Strummer forged a bond between two people coming from entirely different places but meeting with the same purpose in mind. Both were storytellers motivated by innate instincts rather than the ideological trappings of celebrity. Just as he was poised to offer the world his best music to date, Strummer would leave us. Cash resisted nagging health problems that dogged him for many years, recording up until the end. "Joe was a nice man, a good man," Cash said following Strummer's death, " and a good musician." No one could say it better. And for Strummer, I could only imagine that it would be the ultimate compliment. I can just hear him saying with that innocent enthusiasm of his, "Can you believe it? Johnny Cash thinks I'm a good musician."

"LONG SHADOW"

Written by Joe Strummer for Johnny Cash
Performed by Joe Strummer, appears on *Streetcore*

Well, I'll tell you one thing that I know
You don' face your demons down
You grab 'em jack
And pin 'em to the ground

The devil may care
And maybe God he won't
Better make sure you check on
The do's and the don'ts

Crawl up the mountain
To reach where the Eagle flys
Sure you can glimpse from the mountaintop
Where the soul of the muse might rise

And if you put it altogether
You won't have to look around
You know you cast
A long shadow on the ground

Then one day I can tell my tracks
By the holes in the souls of my shoes
And that's the day I said
I'm gonna make the news
And
Falling back in the garden
Of days so long ago

Somewhere in the memory
The sun shines on you boy

Playing in the Arroyos
Where the American river flows
From the Appalachians
Down to the Delta Roads

A man could think so long
His brain could well explode
There's trains running through junctions
And King's cotton down the road

And if you put it altogether
You won't have to look around
You know you cast
A long shadow on the ground

Listen to the country, to nightjar and the bell
Listen to the night streamliner
Sounding like all the wolves of hell
Head for the water-the waters of the cleansing spell
It was always our destination
On the express of the ne'er do wells

And we rock through Madison city
And we didn't even know she was there
And when we hit the buffers in Memphis
And Beale Street didn't have no prayer

And I hear punks talk of anarchy—
I hear Hobo's on the railroad

I hear mutterings on the change gang
'cause those who men built the roads

And if you put it altogether
You didn't even once relent
You cast a long shadow
And that is your testament

Somewhere in my soul
There is always rock 'n' roll
Yeah!

NOTES

Introduction

1. Crass offered the only valid criticism of the Clash that is with merit. The Clash inspired their political sensibility. Crass launched their own efforts to realize the non-compromise music-based militancy envisioned in the early days of punk. It is important to note the American punk band Bad Brains also expanded greatly the political activism of music during this time.
2. Strummer performed at the FBU benefit at Acton Town Hall, London, in November 2002, helping raise money and awareness for the Fire Brigade's fair pay campaign.
3. Many critics hold that *Sandinista!*, the album following the monumental *London Calling*, was a missed opportunity for the Clash to expand upon their ground-breaking prior recordings. *Sandinista!* is an important achievement in that in many ways it defined the Clash's sound for the sheer breadth of influences, styles, and genres. Standout tracks include "Police on My Back," "The Call Up," "The Leader," and "Washington Bullets."
4. The Bobby Fuller Four was influenced in its music quite a bit by another rock 'n' roll star who had also come from West Texas, Buddy Holly. Sonny Curtis, Holly's lead guitarist, wrote "I Fought the Law." In later years the influence of the Bobby Fuller Four was seen in music recorded by such groups as the Clash, the Blasters, and Los Lobos.
5. Future Forests is a UK-based company with a global vision: to protect the earth's climate. Their mission states: "We recognise

that to some degree we all contribute to global warming—but also that we can all do something to slow it down. That's why we make it quick and easy for people and companies to find out how much carbon dioxide they produce; to provide them with straightforward ways of reducing those emissions, and interesting options for 'neutralising' what can't be reduced. Those options include tree planting, and investments into climate friendly technology."

6. The program was recorded every Saturday afternoon at the BBC Studios at Bush House, London, and was broadcast around the world. The first program consisted of American folk, reggae, African rock, and techno from Germany. *Global Boom Box*, the pilot, was filmed and directed by Dick Rude, and was going to be a series on MTV2.

7. From Joe Strummer's press release for his second album with the Mescaleros, *Global A Go-Go*.

The Rebel Way: Alex Cox, Jim Jarmusch and Dick Rude on the Film Work of Joe Strummer

1. *Earthquake Weather* was released in 1989. The album hints at the work that Strummer would produce in the mid-1990s and early twenty-first century with the Mescaleros. A strong and interesting record, *Earthquake* benefits greatly from Joe Strummer's impassioned charisma, his trademark musical experimentation and exploration, and his unique voice. The album is highlighted by the conviction of a musician, who always gives a passionate and engaging performance.

2. Interview of Dick Rude, April 20, 2004. Go to www.dickrude.biz/letsrockagain.html to find out where you can see *Let's Rock Again*.

3. Strummer made this T-shirt for an Anti-Nazi League performance and then proceeded to wear it often for many years after. Brigade Rosse refers to the radical Italian political group Red Brigade. In 1978, they kidnapped and killed ex-Italian Prime Minister Aldo Moro. They are still very much politically active in Italy today.

4. The Clash would be part of the "MTV revolution" as well. The video for "Rock the Casbah" was a big hit for MTV, as it was played in heavy rotation in the early days of the network's rise to video dominance.

5. See my chapter in this book, "White Riot vs. Right Riot: A Look Back at Punk Rock and Anti-Racism."

6. Thompson, Stacy. *Punk Productions: Unfinished Business*. State University of New York Press, 2004. Pages 164–168.

7. Biskind, Peter. *Easy Riders, Raging Bulls*. Page 392.

8. It would take Scorsese another two decades to bring *Gangs of New York* to the screen. *The King of Comedy* is a stark examination of the American obsession with celebrity and fame. It stars Robert De Niro as the obsessed fan of Jerry Lewis's TV show host character.

9. *Clash on Broadway* is an enjoyable historical record of the Clash's Bond residency. The film captures the emerging hip-hop scene from break dancing to rap to grafitti. Even more interesting are the scenes filmed outside of Bonds, where the Clash had to contend with a fire marshal who ordered the shutdown of the venue, intimidating police presence, and a constant crush of fans.

10. Strummer produced the film along with his wife, Lucinda Strummer.

11. *Repo Man* was the directorial debut of Alex Cox. The film is an innovative mix of science fiction, punk rock, and postmodern satire, *Repo Man* takes on a 1980s Reagan American with sharp and humorous dialogue as few films had done before or since. Cox elicits great performances from Stanton as a hardscrabble repo man, Estevez as an antagonistic southern California punk, and Rude as a maniacal nihilistic hooligan. The score includes Latino punk band the Slugz with music by Black Flag, Suicidal Tendencies, and Fear appearing throughout the film.

12. Interview of Alex Cox. April 2004. For more information on Alex Cox, please go to www.alexcox.com.

13. As Cox explains: "William Walker was an American soldier of fortune who in 1853 tried to annex part of Mexico to the United States. He failed, though his invasion contributed to the climate of paranoia and violence which led to Mexico surrendering large areas of territory shortly thereafter. Two years later he invaded Nicaragua, ostensibly in support of one of the factions in a civil war. But his real intention was to take over the country and annex it to the U.S. He betrayed his allies and succeeded in making himself president. He ran Nicaragua, or attempted to run it, for two years. In the U.S. he had been an antislavery liberal, but in

Nicaragua he abandoned all his liberal pretensions and attempted to institute slavery. He was kicked out of Central America by the combined armies of Nicaragua, Costa Rica, and Honduras. Walker tried to go back twice and was eventually caught by the Hondurans and executed. He is relatively unknown today, but in his day he was fantastically popular in the United States. The newspapers wrote more about Walker than they did about Presidents Pierce or Buchanan."

14. Released by Virgin/EMI, the soundtrack has been deleted from the catalogue.

15. Flanagan, Bill. "The Exile of Joe Strummer." *Musician*, March 1988.

16. Grey, Marcus. *The Last Gang in Town*. Page 467.

17. Ibid.

18. Directed by Marisa Silver, *Permanent Record* (1988) deals with teen suicide and stars Keanu Reeves. Strummer recorded several songs for the soundtrack under the name Joe Strummer and the Latino Rockabilly War. Some of these songs appear on *Earthquake Weather.*

19. Of course, there were some missteps along the way like the inclusion of Strummer's cover of the Celtic ballad "Minstrel Boy" on the *Black Hawk Down* soundtrack. The film is based on the October 3, 1993, U.S. raid on Somalia, where eighteen soldiers were lost and Black Hawk helicopters were shot down. Directed by Riddley Scott, the film does not seem like something Strummer would support, particularly in light of his political activism around globalization, imperialism, and racism. Many leading American movie critics took umbrage at the film's obvious manipulation of the truth by failing to tell the Somalian side of the story while whitewashing the U.S.'s role in the military operation. As an example of one of the more troubling elements of the film, the character played by Ewan McGregor as a war hero is currently serving a prison sentence for raping a twelve-year-old girl. Not to mention that there is much evidence that the U.S. troops shot and killed women and children during the mission.

20. The video was released October 21, 2003. "Redemption Song" was the second single following "Coma Girl" off the album *Streetcore*. The mural appears outside of Jesse Malin's Niagara bar in

New York City. Malin, a close friend of Strummer's, is the lead singer of D-Generation, the true group spearheading the revival of garage rock.

21. In the 1990s, Strummer performed with the Pogues for a time, contributed songs to soundtracks including *When Pigs Fly* and *Grosse Point Blank,* and appeared in the films *I Hired a Contract Killer and Docteur Chance.*

Clash and Burn

1. Kouvelakis, Stathis, *Philosophy and Revolution: From Kant to Marx.* London: Verso, 2003, 3.
2. Ibid., 4.
3. Mack, Maynard, ed. *The Norton Anthology World Masterpieces: Sixth Edition, Volume 2.* New York: W. W. Norton & Company, 1992, 340.
4. Ibid., 642–3.
5. Kouvelakis, Stathis, *Philosophy and Revolution: From Kant to Marx.* London: Verso, 2003, 281.
6. Ibid.
7. Quantick, David and John Aizlewood, *The Clash (Kill Your Idols Series).* New York: Thunders Mouth Press, 2000, 14.
8. The illusion of the entire country bowing before the Queen, celebrating the monarchy, is to be echoed early in the Reagan Administration when "the Great Communicator" proposes putting up decals of a thriving South Bronx visible from the highways which traverse the area, in order to conceal the systematic looting and burning of the area by landlords and developers.
9. The album is on the verge of recognizing that in the post-Fordist regime the concept of the weekend itself is soon be obsolete. The new "flexible pattern of accumulation"—originally presented as flexible hours—is simply that we all work all the time.
10. Quantick, David and John Aizlewood, *The Clash (Kill Your Idols Series).* New York: Thunders Mouth Press, 2000, 4.
11. This is a far cry from the post-gentrification image of Notting Hill as a pristine playground for the rich that Hugh Grant and Julia Roberts frolick in, in the Hollywood film of the same title.

12. Hebdige, Dick, *Subculture: The Meaning of Style*. London: Routledge, 1979, 64.

13. Ibid., 65.

14. Quantick, David and John Aizlewood, The Clash (Kill Your Idols Series). New York: Thunders Mouth Press, 2000, 25.

15. Harris, John, "The Bland Play On" in *The Guardian*, Saturday, May 8, 2004, 16–17.

16. Hebdige, Dick, *Subculture: The Meaning of Style*. London: Routledge, 1979, 67.

17. D'Ambrosio, Antonino, "Let Fury Have the Hour: The Passionate Politics of Joe Strummer" in *Monthly Review*, June 2003, 43.

18. Mitchell, Tony, *Global Noise: Rap and Hip-Hop Outside the USA*. Middletown, CT: Wesleyan University Press, 2001, 9.

Always Paying Attention: Joe Strummer's Life and Legacy

1. Jason Gross, "Interview With Joe Strummer," *Perfect Sound Forever* (http://www.furious.com/perfect/joestrummer.html).

2. Shawna Kenney, "Joe Strummer: Still Punk After All These Years?—Interview," *Unpop* (http://www.unpop.com/features/int/strummer.html).

3. Greil Marcus, *Ranters & Crowd Pleasers: Punk in Pop Music, 1977–1982* (New York: Doubleday, 1993), 29.

4. Lester Bangs, *Psychotic Reactions and Carburetor Dung* (New York: Vintage, 1988), 239.

5. Ibid., 233.

6. Judy McGuire, "Interview with Joe Strummer," *Punk* magazine (http://www.punkmagazine.com/morestuff/joe_strummer.html).

7. (Uncredited), "Interview with Joe Strummer," (http://www.strummersite.com/Joe%20Strummer%20interview.html).

White Riot or Right Riot: A Look Back at Punk Rock and Anti-Racism

1. Interview of Joe Strummer, April 2002. Note: All Strummer quotes are from this interview unless otherwise noted.

2. On December 1, 1976, the Sex Pistols appeared on *Thames Today*

where Bill Grundy interviewed them a week after the release of the single "Anarchy in the UK." The interview was "designed to investigate the blossoming moral abyss, which was punk." The show featured an allegedly drunk Grundy goading the Pistols into what became a profanity-laden conversation.

3. The most memorable Rock Against Racism event was Carnival against the Nazis in April 1978. A huge rally of 100,000 people marched the six miles from Trafalgar Square through London's East End—the heart of National Front territory—to a Rock Against Racism concert in Victoria Park. Up to that point, this would be the largest crowd the Clash would perform in front of. Also on the bill were X-Ray Spex, Steel Pulse, and Tom Robinson. Today the Anti-Nazi League is campaigning again in the name of Love Music Hate Racism—a demonstration of the positive energy of the music scene against the hate-fuelled beliefs of the British National Party, National Front, and Combat 18.

4. Strummer was a diplomat's son and spent time in countries like Turkey, were he was born. Simonon grew up in Brixton, a poor section of inner city London largely populated by Afro-Caribbean's, and witnessed terrible instances of police and state instigated violence against Afro-Caribbeans.

5. Gray, Marcus, *The Last Gang in Town*. New York: Henry Holt and Company, 1995, 319.

6. "I Won't Let That Dago By: Rethinking Punk and Racism," page 213 in *Punk Rock So What? The Cultural Legacy of Punk*. Roger Sabin, ed.

7. The National Front was formed in Westminster, England, in 1967. Among their basic principles is that multi-racialism and immigration are wrong and must be stopped. All current racial and ethnic minorities must be removed by any means necessary. It continues to be a social and political force not only in England but also in other countries including France and East Germany. Presently, the National Front in England has morphed into the British National Party.

8. Skrewdriver was one of the first and the most successful white supremacist groups in not only the Punk scene but also the music scene in general. Violent and vicious, they believed in "racial

purity" and the "need for a race war." Ian Stuart, the leader singer/songwriter, is considered the founder of the Racialist movement. *Bulldog* magazine, September 1993.

9. "I Won't Let that Dago By: Rethinking Punk and Racism," page 210 in *Punk Rock So What? The Cultural Legacy of Punk*. Roger Sabin, ed.

10. Music history, not just punk, is rife with the use of fascist and racist ideology and the like to strike a dangerous, sinister pose. Here are a few examples. When Joy Division reformed after Ian Curtis's suicide, they then again used a Hitler-influenced name, "new order" for Hitler's plan for controlling the world. Other instances outside of punk but in English rock include: David Bowie's "Thin White Duke" phase, which was his self-proclaimed "fascist period"; Eric Clapton addressing a crowd which came to hear him play blues in a concert hall, asking them to stop Britain from becoming a "black colony" and added, "he'd like to get the foreigners out." In Columbus, Ohio, March 1979, Elvis Costello told an interviewer that James Brown was "a jive ass nigger" and Ray Charles "a blind, ignorant nigger."

11. There were notable exceptions. For example, the epic strike by Asian workers at Grunwick in North London was a huge catalyst for solidarity from left groups and white and black trade unionists.

12. "I Won't Let that Dago By: Rethinking Punk and Racism," page 216 in *Punk Rock So What? The Cultural Legacy of Punk*. Roger Sabin, ed.

13. Ibid.

14. Mailer's fascination with Black masculinity throughout *The White Negro* is indicative of his fixation on "machismo." For another example, see his novel *The American Dream*.

15. Baldwin, James, *Nobody Knows My Name*, 182.

16. Mailer, Norman, "The White Negro: Superficial Reflections on the Hipster" in *Advertisements for Myself*, 348.

17. Ibid.

18. Baldwin, James, "The Black Boy Looks at the White Boy" in *Nobody Knows My Name*, 182.

19. Ibid., 181.

20. Hibbs, Thomas S., "Angst, American Style: A Review of Existential

America, by George Cotkin." The Claremont Institute, September 22, 2003.

21. Bangs, Lester, *Psychotic Reactions and Carburetor Dung.* "The White Noise Supremascists," 275. Ivan Julian was the guitarist for Richard Hell and Voidoids.

22. Ibid., 279.

23. Ibid., 282.

24. Also, there are a few political punk organizations including Punk Voter, who are involved in political organizing in an number of areas including voting, the arts, and free speech.

25. Interview of Joe Strummer, April 2002.

26. Paul Johnson of *Time* magazine glowingly described Thatcher as a "Champion of free minds and markets, she helped topple the welfare state and make the world safer for capitalism." *Time,* Monday, April 13, 1998.

27. Linton Kwesi Johnson is a towering figure in reggae music. Born in Kingston, Jamaica and raised in the Brixton section of London, Johnson invented dub poetry, a type of toasting descended from the DJ stylings of U-Roy and I-Roy. Johnson was also instrumental (with his friend Darcus Howe) in the publication of a socialist-oriented London-based newspaper, *Race Today*, that offered him and other like-minded Britons both black and white an outlet to discuss the racial issues that, under Margaret Thatcher's reign, were tearing the country apart.

28. Forbes, Bev, *Word Warrior.* Searchlight, January 2000.

29. Crass produced politically and musically radical records. They took on issues from the horrors of war, the injustice in the legal system, sexism, racism, media hegemony, and the flaws of the punk movement. In many ways, they embodied the hope and potential of music as agent of social and political change. They put out their own records and formed an anarchist commune that worked with other artists and labels, for and on the behalf of various political causes.

30. Christgau, Robert, "*Sense Outa Nonsense*" in *Village Voice*, April 23, 1991.

31. Ibid.

You Can't Have A Revolution Without Songs: The Legacy of Victor Jara and the Political Folk Music of Caetano Veloso, Silvio Rodriguez, and Joe Strummer

1. "You can't have a revolution without songs" was a banner suspended over Salvadore Allende after his election as president of Chile. It shows the influence that the new song movement [*nueva canción*] had over the political process in Chile.

2. Strummer met Tymon Dogg when the latter was busking in the London underground. The formed a strong friendship and musical relationship. Dogg taught Strummer to play the ukulele and compose folk music. They would sporadically collaborate while Strummer was with the Clash but worked closely together when Dogg joined the Mescaleros on *Global A-Go-Go*.

3. *Rock Art and the X-Ray Style*, released in 1997, was the first full-length solo album from Strummer in ten years. Prior to that he had released *Earthquake Weather*, not his finest effort, and had done some fine work composing music for films. Notable soundtracks include *Walker and Permanent Record*. Strummer told me that no one should listen to his new work, which includes two albums proceeding *Rock Art*. "If people were expecting to hear the Clash," he told me, "do me a favor and don't buy it unless you are willing to really listen to something new from me."

4. Holstrom, John, "An Interview with Joey and Johnny Ramone" in *Punk* magazine, number 11, October/November 1977.

5. Wishnia, Steve, "Gabba Gabba Hey" in *In These Times*, May 28, 2001. It is important to note that the Ramones eventually shifted their political leanings to a more progressive stance. While never overtly political, Joey Ramone penned the song "Bonzo Goes to Bitburg" as a response to Ronald Reagan's 1985 visit to an SS Cemetery and his ceremonial placing of a wreath at the grave of an SS soldier.

6. The most obvious example of this was the Sex Pistols refrain "no future" on the track "God Save the Queen" from *Never Mind the Bullocks*. The Clash and Strummer on the other hand, were employing slogans like "positive change," "passion is a fashion," etc.

7. There are notable exceptions to this including Bad Religion,

NOFX, Anti-Flag, RICANSTRUCTION, Renegades of Punk, the 512 Collective, etc.

8. While they enjoyed a great deal of success for a short period of time, it is unclear how financially successful the Clash really were. They signed a record contract that heavily favored their record company, Epic: ten years, ten albums, $100,000. In addition, in a dispute with their label over the pricing of the three-record album *Sandinista!*, the Clash forfeited their royalties in exchange to price the album accordingly as one record not three to make it affordable for their listeners.

9. Strummer at one time described Mano Negra's music as having the same force as that of the Clash. Interview by Mark Vennard, BBC Online, winter 2002.

10. Standout Mano Negra records include *Puta's Fever, Patchanka,* and *Casa Bablyon.* Manu Chao solo albums include *Clandestino* and *Proxima Estacion: Esperanza.*

11. Interview of Joe Strummer, conducted by Antonino D'Ambrosio, April 2002.

12. D'Ambrosio, Antonino. "Soundtrack to Struggle" in *ColorLines* Winter 2003-2004. Leo Ferre was a precursor to the spoken word artists of today. The events of May 1968 in France left a mark on Ferré. In early 1969, he released a new album inspired by the agitation of May '68 with such songs as "Comme une fille," "L'été 68," and "Les Anarchistes."

13. The history of New Song coincides with political events occurring in Latin America and the United States's influence on Central and South American countries. Many times, the United States has sought to manipulate events in these countries for their own benefit. The artists of New Song use this as a basis for the themes of their songs.

14. The creation of Casa de las Américas was a way of guaranteeing that revolutionary artists who were persecuted and condemned in their own countries by official repression would always have a podium to speak from.

15. *Victor: An Unfinished Song* by Joan Jara. Reviewed by Tony Saunois. *Socialism Today.* Issue 46, April 2000.

16. The Popular Unity Party had plans to increase education, and to

supply increased housing, free socialized medical care, state control of oil refineries, mines, etc, and returning land to the people, among other social programs.

17. *Victor: An Unfinished Song* by Joan Jara. Reviewed by Tony Saunois. *Socialism Today*. Issue 46, April 2000.

18. There are many fine books and other media accounts of the coup d'état but none have the power and force like filmmaker Patricio Guzman's exceptional documentary *Battle of Chile*. Guzman was forced into exile to France following the coup. In addition, the plan to overthrow Allende was devised by then secretary of state Henry Kissinger and received additional financial support from the Ford Foundation and various U.S. conglomerates.

19. Thousands of people to this day remain missing and their families still are searching for them.

20. Many stories indicate that Victor Jara's hands and testicles were cut off and his tongue cut out so that he could not perform for his fellow prisoners. But in *The Unfinished Song* by Jara's wife Joan, she indicates that when she saw him after his death his hands were broken, not cut-off.

21. From the companion booklet found with the cd, Victor Jara: *El Creador.*

22. Quote from "The Uncompromising Song" chapter in *The Rough Guide to World Music*, Vol.2. For more on Gaughan check out his records including *No More Forever, Handful of Earth*, and *Redwood Cathedral.*

23. "Bard of Freedom: Dick Gaughan speaks with Bill Nevins." *Rootsworld*. Summer 1998.

24. Beres, Derek, "Caetano Veloso and the Meaning of Exile" in *Rattaplax*. Issue 9.

25. Much has been made about this perceived rivalry. In his autobiography, *Tropical Truth*, Veloso dedicates much time to stating that any rivalry was overblown and really did not exist at all.

26. Veloso, Caetano, *Tropical Truth: A Story of Music and Revolution in Brazil*, 31.

27. Rogerio Duarte was a Bahian intellectual, activist, and teacher who formed a lasting and profound friendship with Veloso beginning in 1964.

28. Veloso, Caetano, *Tropical Truth: A Story of Music and Revolution in Brazil*, 61.

29. Veloso modeled this on a similar festival created by Italian artists who found it affective in organizing creative political activity in Italy.

30. Mercedes Sosa is truly a giant in contemporary music. Strummer described her music as "heroic, possessing the essence of beauty." Sosa was viewed as a serious threat by the Argentine government and in 1975 she was arrested during a live performance. Forced to leave Argentina, she remained in exile for three years. Her brilliant works include *La Negra, Sino,* and *Miss Criolla,* for which she won a Grammy for in 2000.

31. From liner notes of *Cuba Classic Vol 1: The Greatest Hits of Silvio Rodríguez: Canciones Urgentes.*

32. Ibid.

33. Veloso, Caetano, *Tropical Truth: A Story of Music and Revolution in Brazil*, 61.

The World Is Worth Fighting For: Two Creative-Activists, Michael Franti and Tim Robbins, Continue Joe Strummer's Legacy

1. Interview of Michael Franti, April 15, 2004.

2. Mikey Dread's influence on the Clash and Strummer was extensive and far-reaching. It can be heard on Clash recordings including the antiwar song "The Call Up." In addition, "Police on My Back" continues the Clash's impressive reinterpretation of song first recorded by East London's the Equals led by West Indian Eddy Grant. See Carter Van Pelt's essay, "When the Two Sevens Clashed," in this book for more on Mikey Dread and the Clash.

3. Interview of Tim Robbins, May 5, 2004.

4. Bogad, L. M., *Radical Ridicule: Electoral Guerrilla Theater.* Routledge, 2004

5. See my article, "The Playwright vs. The Prime Minister," in the April 2004 issue of *The Progressive.*

6. One of Robbins's earliest performances was with his father when they performed the folk song "The Ink Is Black, the Page Is White" together in Greenwich Village.

7. Lorca's murder at the hand of Nationalists took away one of the world's most gifted dramatists and poets. He was thirty-eight. His work includes *Romancero Gitano, The Gypsy Ballads of García Lorca, Poema del Cante Jondo* (Madrid, 1921), and *Lament for the Death of a Bullfighter, and Other Poems.* Francisco Franco, who had ordered the death of Lorca, was head of state of Spain from 1939 until his death in 1975. Known as "el Caudillo" ("the leader"), he presided over the authoritarian dictatorial government of the Spanish State, which had overthrown the Second Spanish Republic.

8. *Bob Roberts* is a political satire shot as a mockumenatry, following a right-wing senatorial candidate played by Robbins who campaigns by singing folk songs that attack his liberal opponent played by Gore Vidal. Robbins wrote both the script and the songs, directed, starred in, and produced *Bob Roberts. Dead Man Walking* is based on a true story dealing with the debate surrounding capital punishment. Robbins's long-time partner Susan Sarandon won an Oscar for her performance in the film, which includes an excellent performance by Sean Penn.

9. The Sandinist National Liberation Front (FSLN) was named for Augusto Cesar Sandino, a former insurgent leader, was formed in 1962 to oppose the regime of Anastasio Somoza Debayle in Nicaragua. In 1979 the Sandinistas launched an offensive from Costa Rica and Honduras that toppled Somoza. They nationalized such industries as banking and mining. The U.S. organized and supported guerrillas known as contras to overthrow the Sandinista-dominated government.

10. In 1994, Human Rights Watch issued a report on U.S. Human Rights Violations stating: "The indefinite detention of HIV-positive Haitian asylum-seekers at Guantanamo Bay Naval Base, a practice discontinued in the summer of 1993 by court order, violated Article 7, which forbids cruel inhuman or degrading treatment, and Article 9, which requires a statutory basis for detention. It also violated Article 10, which forbids inhumane conditions of confinement, and Article 26, which forbids discrimination on the basis of national origin (only Haitians were subject to medical screening and detention based on HIV status; intercepted Cubans, for example, were not medically screened and were transported

directly to the United States). The practice of indefinitely detaining all undocumented people, including children, violates Article 9's prohibition of arbitrary detention."

11. Fox News, the Rupert Murdoch–owned right-wing media outlet, in particular, viciously attacked the play. Some of the things written include that the play is "anti-American," "not realistic, devoid of facts." Lawrence Kaplan of the *New Republic* wrote in a review titled "Devious Plot," "*Embedded,* moreover, is not only dumb. It is poisonous, a production-length conspiracy theory guilty of the very sins it attributes to the 'cabal' that it claims to expose."

12. In 1935, eight million Americans were out of work and three million youths between the ages of sixteen and twenty-four were on relief. On May 6 of that year the government created the Works Progress Administration (WPA) through Executive Order No. 7034. The Federal Theater Project (FTP) was one of four (later five) arts projects within the WPA; the arts projects were known collectively as federal Project Number One. The FTP was the largest and most ambitious effort made by the Federal government to organize and produce theater events.

13. Please see transcript of the speech given by actor Tim Robbins to the National Press Club in Washington, D.C., on April 15, 2003.

SELECTED DISCOGRAPHY

With the 101ers
Elgin Avenue Breakdown
Five Star rock 'n' roll

With the Clash
The Clash [UK version]
Give 'Em Enough Rope [U.S. version]
London Calling
Black Market Clash
Sandinista!
Combat Rock
The Story of the Clash, Vol. 1
Clash on Broadway
The Singles
Super Black Market Clash
Live: From Here to Eternity
The Essential Clash

Solo
Earthquake Weather

With the Mescaleros
Rock Art and the X-Ray Style

Global A Go-Go
Streetcore

Soundtracks
Sid and Nancy
Walker
Permanent Record
When Pigs Fly
Grosse Point Blank

SELECTED FILMOGRAPHY

The Punk Rock Movie (documentary)
Rude Boy (documentary)
Clash on Broadway (documentary)
King of Comedy (extra)
Straight to Hell (actor)
Walker (actor/composer)
Mystery Train (actor)
I Hired a Contract Killer (actor)
Docteur Chance (actor)
The Clash: Westway to the World (documentary)
Super-8 Stories (documentary)
Nelson Mandela: Aids Day Concert (documentary)
End of the Century: The Story of the Ramones (documentary)
Let's Rock Again (documentary)

SELECTED DISCOGRAPHY

With the Beatnigs
Television (EP)
Beatnigs

With Disposable Heroes of Hiphoprisy
TV: The Drug of the Nation (EP)
The Language of Violence (EP)
Hypocrisy is the Greatest Luxury

With Spearhead
Home
Chocolate Supa Highway
Stay Human
Everyone Deserves Music

TIM ROBBINS
SELECTED FILMOGRAPHY

Mystic River
The Education of Gore Vidal (documentary)
The Day My God Died (documentary)
Code 46
The Party's Over (documentary)
Cradle Will Rock (director)
The Typewriter, the Rifle and the Movie Camera (documentary on Sam Fuller)
Dead Man Walking (screenwriter/director/producer)
The Shawshank Redemption
Short Cuts
The Player
Bob Roberts (songwriter/screenwriter/director/producer/actor)
Jungle Fever
Tapeheads
Five Corners

SELECTED BIBLIOGRAPHY AND WORKS CITED

Aronowitz, Stanley, et al, eds. *The '60s Without Apology*. Minneapolis: University of Minnesota Press, 1988.

Baldwin, James. "The Black Boy Looks at the White Boy," in *Nobody Knows My Name: More Notes of a Native Son*. New York: Dell Publishing, 1961.

——"The Discovery of What it Means to Be an America," in *Nobody Knows My Name: More Notes of a Native Son*. New York: Dell Publishing, 1961.

Bangs, Lester. *Psychotic Reactions and Carburetor Dung*. New York: Anchor Books, 2003.

——"The Clash," in *Psychotic Reactions and Carburetor Dung*. New York: Anchor Books, 2003.

——"The White Noise Supremacists," *Psychotic Reactions and Carburetor Dung*. New York: Anchor Books, 2003.

Barrett, L. E. *The Rastafarians*. Boston: Beacon Press, 1997.

Belhadded, Souad. *Manu Chao et la Mano Negra*. Paris: J'ai lu, 2003.

Biskind, Peter. *Easy Riders to Raging Bulls: How the Sex and Drugs Generation Saved Hollywood*. New York: Simon & Schuster, 1998.

Bogad, L. M. *Radical Ridicule: Electoral Guerrilla Theater*. London: Routledge, 2004

Brecht, Bertolt (translated by J. Willet). *Brecht on Theater: The Development of an Aesthetic*. New York: Hill and Wang, 1964.

Buarque, Chico. "A Banda," on *Chico Total,* Motor Music, 1966.

Burchill, Julie and T. Parker. *The Boy Looked At Johnny: The Obituary of Rock and Roll.* London: Faber and Faber, 1987.

Camus, Albert (Ellen Conroy Kennedy, trans). "Essay on Music," in *Youthful Writings.* New York: Vintage Books, 1977.

Cash, Johnny. *Cash: An Autobiography.* San Francisco: Harper, 1998.

——"Man in Black," on *A Man in Black.* Sony, 1971.

——*Bitter Tears.* Columbia/Legacy, 1964.

——*At Folsom [Live].* Columbia/Legacy, 1968.

——*Hello, I'm Johnny Cash.* Columbia, 1969.

——*Junkie and the Juicehead Minus Me.* Columbia, 1974.

——*American Recordings.* American/Sony, 1994.

——*Unchained.* Warner Brothers, 1996.

——*American Recordings III: Solitary Man.* American, 2000.

——*American Recordings IV: The Man Comes Around.* Universal, 2002.

——*Unearthed.* Lost Highway, 2003.

Christgau, Robert. "Sense Outa Nonsense." *Village Voice,* April 23, 1991.

Clash (London). *The Clash* (EPIC, 1979, U.S.). *Give 'Em Enough Rope* (EPIC, 1978, UK). *London Calling* (EPIC, 1979, UK). *Sandinista!* (EPIC, 1981, UK). *Combat Rock* (EPIC, 1983, UK).

Cocteau, Jean. *The Difficulty of Being.* Trans. Elizabeth Sprigge. New York: De Capo Press, 1995.

Cochran, David. *American Noir: Underground Writers and Filmmakers of the Postwar Era.* Washington and London: Smithsonian Institution Press, 2000.

Cockcroft, James, ed. *Chile's Voice of Democracy: The Salvador Allende Reader.* Melbourne and New York: Ocean Press, 2000.

Consolidated. *Friendly Fascism.* Capital, 1991.

Coon, Caroline, 1988: *The New Wave Punk Rock Explosion.* London: Omnibus Press, 1983.

Cradle Will Rock Written, and directed by Tim Robbins. Havoc/Touchstone Pictures, 1999.

——*Bob Roberts*. Miramax, 1992.

——*Dead Man Walking*. Gramercy Pictures, 1995.

——*Embedded*. The Actors Gang, 2004.

Crass. *Love Songs*. West Yorkshire, UK: Pomona Books, 2004.

——"White Punks on Hope" on *Station of the Crass*. Crass, 1979.

D'Ambrosio, Antonino. "Passion Is a Fashion." *Clamor,* July/August 2002.

——"The Playwright vs. the Prime Minister." *The Progressive,* April 2004.

——"Soundtrack to Struggle." *Colorlines,* winter 2003-4.

Debord, Guy *The Society of the Spectacle*. Trans. Donald Nicholson-Smith. New York: Zone Books, 1995.

——"Why Lettrism?" *Potlatch,* 1955.

Deleuze, Gilles. *Cinema 2: The Time Images*. Trans. Hugh Tomilson and Robert Galeta. Minneapolis: University of Minnesota Press, 1989.

Disposable Heroes of Hiphoprisy. "The Winter of the Long Hot Summer" (4th and Broadway, 1992).

Dunn, Christopher. *Brutality Garden: Tropicalia and the Emergence of a Brazilian Counterculture*. North Carolina: University of North Carolina Press, 2001.

Fink, Michael. *Inside the Music Industry: Creativity, Process, and Business*. New York: Simon & Schuster, 1996.

Frith, Simon. *The Sociology of Rock*. London: Constable, 1978.

Frobes, Bev. Word Warrior. *Searchlight,* January 2000.

Garbarini, Vic. RUDE BOYS. *Musician Magazine,* June 1981.

Gilbert, Pat. "Cast a Long Shadow." *Mojo,* November 2003.

Gray, Marcus. *Last Gang in Town: The Story and Myth of the Clash*. New York: Henry Holt and Company, 1995.

Harvey, S. *May '68 and Film Culture*. British Film Institute. 1978.

Hebdige, Dick. *Subculture: The Meaning of Style.* London and New York: Methuen & Co., Ltd., 1991.

Herny, Patricia. *Break All the Rules! Punk Rock and the Making of Style.* Ann Arbor: UMI Research, 1989.

Hiro, Dilip. *Black British, White British.* New York: Penguin, 1972.

Holstrom, John. "An Interview with Johnny and Joey Ramone." *Punk!.* October/November 1977.

Hoskyns, Barney, ed. *The Sound and the Fury: A Rock's Backpages Reader.* London: Bloomsbury, 2003.

Joe Strummer and the Mescaleros. *Rock Art and the X-Ray Style* (Epitaph Records, 1999). *Global A Go-Go* (Epitaph Records, 2001). *Streetcore* (Hellcat Records, 2003).

Jolly. "Don't Give 'Em Enough Rope." *Punk!,.* May/June 1979.

Jara, Joan. *Victor: An Unfinished Song.* London: Bloomsbury, 1998.

Jeffords, Susan. *The Remasculinization of America.* Bloomington, IN: Indiana University Press, 1987.

Kaye, Lenny. Sound Clash. *Fader.* March/April 2003.

Kerouac, Jack. *On the Road.* 1957. New York: Viking Penguin, 1991.

Kwesi Johnson, Linton. *Dread, Beat and Blood.* Paris: Bogle L'Ouverture Press, 1996.

LeBlanc, Lauraine. *Pretty in Punk: Girls' Gender Resistance in a Boys' Subculture.* Piscataway, NJ: Rutgers University Press, 2000.

Lhamon, W.T., Jr. *Deliberate Speed: The Origins of a Cultural Style in the American 1950s.* Washington D.C.: Smithsonian Institution Press, 1990.

Let's Rock Again. Directed by Dick Rude Productions. 2004.

Mailer, Norman. *An American Dream.* New York. Dial, 1964.

——"Hipster and Beatnik," in *Advertisements for Myself.* New York: Putnam, 1959.

——"The White Negro: Superficial Reflections on the Hipster," in *Advertisements for Myself.* New York: Putnam, 1959.

Marcus, Greil. *In the Fascist Bathroom: Punk in Pop Music,*

1977–1992. Cambridge, Massachusetts: Harvard University Press, 1999.

—— *Lipstick Traces: A Secret History of the Twentieth Century.* Cambridge, Massachusetts: Harvard University Press, 1989.

Marshall, Peter. "Guy Debord and the Situationists," in *Demanding the Impossible.* New York: HarperCollins, 1991.

Miles, Barry. "The Clash Eighteen Flight Rock . . . AND THE SOUND OF THE WESTWAY." *NME,* December 11, 1976.

Miller, Arthur. *Timebends: A Life.* Penguin Group 1995.

Mystery Train. Directed by Jim Jarmusch. JVC/Mystery Train Inc./ Orion, 1989.

"Nueva Canción." *World Music: The Rough Guide,* Ed. Broughton, S., Ellingham, M., Muddyman, D., and Trillo, R., London: Penguin Books, 1994.

"Nueva Canción: 'El lazo,' by Víctor Jara." *Worlds of Music: An Introduction to the Music of the World's Peoples.* Ed. J.T. Titon. New York: Schirmer Books, 1992.

Punk Rock Movie, The. Directed by Don Letts. Cinematic Arts/Notting Hill Pictures/Pink Rock Films, 1978.

Press, Hans Jurgen. *Aventuras de la Mano Negra.* Barcelona: Espasa-Calpe, 1984.

Quantick, David. *The Clash (Kill Your Idols Series).* New York: Thunder's Mouth Press, 2000.

Savage, Jon. *England's Dreaming: Anarchy, SexPistols, Punk Rock, and Beyond.* New York: St. Martin's Press, 1992.

Repo Man. Written and directed by Alex Cox. 1984.

Rodriguez, Silvio. "Unicorno," on *Unicornio/Al Final de Este Viaje.* FNC, 1993.

Rogin, Michael. *Blackface, White Noise: Jewish Immigrants in the Hollywood Melting Pot.* Berkeley: University of California Press, 1996.

Rose, Tricia and Andrew Ross, eds. *Microphone Fiends: Youth Music and Youth Culture*. New York: Routledge, 1994.

Ross, Andrew. *No Respect: Intellectuals and Popular Culture*. New York: Routledge, 1987.

Rude Boy. Directed by Jack Hazan and David Mingay. Atlantic Releasing Corporation/Buzzy Corporation, 1980.

Sabin, Roger, ed. *Punk Rock: So What? The Cultural Legacy of Punk*. London and New York: Routledge, 1999.

Seldes, George. *The Great Quotations*. New York: Lyle Stuart, 1960.

Sid and Nancy. Written and directed by Alex Cox. Embassy Home Entertainment/Initial Pictures/Samuel Goldwyn Company/Zenith, 1986.

Sheppard, David. *Elvis Costello (Kill Your Idols Series)*. New York: Thunders Mouth Press, 2000.

Spearhead. *Bomb the World* (Boo Boo, 2003).

Straight to Hell. Written and directed by Alex Cox. 1987.

Sutcliffe, Phil. Rude Boy. *Sounds,* 12 January 1980.

Thompson, Stacy. *Punk Productions: Unfinished Business*. Albany: State University of New York Press, 2004.

Time, "The Time 100: The Most Important People of the Century: Margaret Thatcher," http://www.time.com/time/time100/leaders/profile/thatcher.html.

Touraine, Alain (Leonard F. X. Mayhew, trans). *The May Movement: Revolt and Reform*. New York: Random House, 1971.

Turner, Cherie. *Everything You Need to Know About the Riot Grrrl Movement: The Feminism of a New Generation*. New York: Rosen Publishing Group, 2001.

Two-Headed Anomaly. Written and directed by Dario Fo. Produced by Franca Rome and Dario Fo. 2004.

Vaneigem, Raul. *The Revolution of Everyday Life*. Oakland: A. K. Press, 2001.

Veleso, Caetano (Isabel de Sena, trans). *Tropical Truth: A Story of*

Music and Revolution in Brazil. New York: Alfred A. Knopf, 2002.

——"Algeria, Algeria," on *Caetano Veleso.* Electra, 1968.

Walker. Directed by Alex Cox. Incne Compania/Industrial Cinematografica/Universal. 1987.

Weatherby, W. J. *Squaring Off: Mailer vs. Baldwin.* New York: Mason/Charter, 1977.

Westway to the World. Directed by Don Letts. Sony Music, 2000.

Widgery, David. *Beating Time.* London: Chatto and Windus, 1987.

Wishnia, Steve. "Gabba, Gabba, Hey." *In These Times,* May 28, 2001.

Woody Guthrie. "Buffalo Skinners," on *Struggle: Documentary No.1.* Folkways Label, 1941.

X, Malcolm. *The Autobiography of Malcolm X: As Told to Alex Haley.* 1964. New York: Ballantine, 1993.

CONTRIBUTORS

Lester Bangs (1949–1982) was an American music journalist, author, and musician. Bangs was an extremely influential voice in music writing from the end of the 1960s until his death. Bangs started out writing as a freelancer for *Rolling Stone* in 1969, and later worked for *Creem* magazine, *The Village Voice, Penthouse, Playboy, New Musical Express,* and many others. His ranting style, similar to Hunter S. Thompson's gonzo journalism, and his tendency to insult and become confrontational with his interview subjects made him distinctive.

Charlie Bertsch is assistant professor of English at the University of Arizona in Tucson, where he specializes in post-1945 American literature, critical theory, and popular culture. He is a regular contributor to *Punk Planet* magazine and is co-editor of its book review section. He is also one of the founders and present co-director of the long-running Internet publication *Bad Subjects: Political Education for Everyday Life.*

Billy Bragg is an important creative and political voice in contemporary music. With a mix of folk music reminiscent of Woody Guthrie and punk rock inspired by Joe Strummer and the Clash, Bragg's musical career is eclectic and uncompromising. In a career that spans over twenty years, Bragg has produced witty and clever music. Standout records include *Talking with the Taxman about*

Poetry, Don't Try This at Home, and *William Bloke.* Bragg is also a political activist in the UK where he has helped to organize events like the Red Wedge tour, a socialist musician collective that also featured Paul Weller. A fixture at political rallies, protests, strikes, and benefits, Bragg recently released *English, Half English.*

Dennis Broe's articles on film, music, and media have appeared in *Newsday, The Boston Phoenix, Social Justice, Framework, Cinema Journal,* and *Science and Society.* He is currently completing a manuscript on film noir titled *Outside the Law: Labor and the Crime Film 1941–55.* He is Graduate Coordinator in the Media Arts Department at Long Island University. His was one of a group of American journalists that interviewed the Clash on their U.S. tour in 1979. He was five years old at the time.

One of hip-hop's most commanding and instantly recognizable voices, **Chuck D** has influenced an entire generation of fans and artists alike. Hailing from Long Island, he found fame as the front man for Public Enemy, a group known for their revolutionary lyricism and groundbreaking production. PE's fiery rhymes and unique stage show won them millions of fans across the globe. They released four classic albums: *Yo! Bum Rush the Show, It Takes a Nation of Millions to Hold Us Back, Fear of a Black Planet,* and *Apocalypse '91 . . . The Enemy Strikes Back.* Chuck D has remained politically and musically active, working on a wide range of projects, including a solo album, *Autobiography of Mistachuck,* released in '96. He also fronts a hard rock band Confrontation Camp, helps run two Web sites/online labels (rapstation.com and SlamJamz.com), writes for various press outlets, and also hits the lecture circuit. He currently can be heard on Air America where he co-hosts the radio program *Bring the Noise* with Kyle Jason.

Antonino D'Ambrosio is a writer, documentary filmmaker, photographer, and musician. He is the founder/director of La Lutta New Media Collective (www.lalutta.org) a media activist/ documentary production group started in New York City in 1997. His writing has appeared in *The Nation, The Progressive, Monthly Review, Colorlines,* and *The New Labor Forum,* among other publications. He co-hosted a radio program on WBAI focusing on independent media, film, and politics. He has produced, directed, written, and photographed a number of documentaries including *Once There Was A Village, Back in the Days,* and *The Treatment Court Story.* In winter 2005, his documentary *Desaparecidos* will be released followed by *Freedom Demo. The Nation* magazine selected La Lutta NMC as one of the top independent media groups in the country.

Luciano D'Orazio is a writer whose work appears in *Flak,* where he co-published its inaugural print edition in September 2003. This article appeared on January 13, 2003, in *PopPolitics.*

Mikal Gilmore has covered and criticized rock 'n' roll, its culture, and related issues for many national publications. He was music editor for the *LA Weekly* and the *Los Angeles Herald Examiner,* and for twenty years has worked on the staff of *Rolling Stone,* where he has profiled many national figures. His first book, *Shot in the Heart,* won the *Los Angeles Times* Book Prize and the National Book Critics Circle Award. He lives and works in Los Angeles, California.

Dan Grunebaum is events editor at Japan's number one English language magazine, *Metropolis.*

Greil Marcus is the author of *In the Fascist Bathroom, Lipstick*

Traces, Mystery Train, and with Sean Wilentz co-editor of *The Rose and the Briar: Death, Love and Liberty in the American Ballad,* published in 2004 by Norton in the U.S. and Faber & Faber in the UK. He lives in Berkeley.

Kristine McKenna is a widely published critic and journalist who wrote for the *Los Angeles Times* from 1977 through 1998. Her profiles and criticism have appeared in *Artforum,* the *New York Times, Artnews, Vanity Fair,* the *Washington Post,* and *Rolling Stone* magazine, and she was the recipient of a National Endowment of the Arts administration grant in 1976. In 1991 she received a Critics Fellowship from the National Gallery of Art, and she co-curated the 1998 exhibition "Forming: the Early Days of L.A. Punk," for Track 16 Gallery. In 2001, a collection of her interviews, "Book of Changes," was published by Fantagraphics, who published a second volume of her interviews, *Talk to Her,* in 2004. She is an archivist for the Charles Brittin Collection of Photography, and is presently writing the first authorized biography of Wallace Berman. She is co-curator of "Semina Culture: Wallace Berman & His Circle," a group exhibition that opens at the Santa Monica Museum of Art in 2005, then travels to five U.S. museums. She is also the co-producer of *Ferus,* a documentary directed by Morgan Neville about LA's first avant-garde gallery.

Not4Prophet is the lead singer/songwriter for the Puerto Punx band RICANSTRUCTION. Based in El Barrio, New York, Not4Prophet has been a long-time collaborator of La Lutta NMC's, participating in *This Is a Movement, Speak the Words the Way You Breathe, In Defense of Humans,* among other political pop culture events. RICANSTRUCTION albums include *Liberation Day* and *Love+Revolution.* Along with Kid Lucky, he is part of the spoken noise (de)constructive duo known as the Renegades of Punk.

Amy Phillips is a freelance writer who lives in New York City. She has contributed to the *Village Voice, The Philadelphia Inquirer, Blender, CMJ New Music Monthly, Venus, Seventeen, Willamette Week, Kitty Magik,* and the Philadelphia *City Paper.*

Anthony Roman is the lead singer and bass player for the New York City–based group Radio 4. Radio 4's albums include *The New Song and Dance, Gotham!,* and the forthcoming *Stealing of a Nation.*

Ann Scanlon is the author of *The Pogues: The Lost Decade* and *Those Tourists Are Money: The rock 'n' roll Guide To Camden.* She has written for a number of music magazines and newspapers, including *Sounds, Mojo,* and *The London Times.*

Joel Schalit is the Associate Editor of *Punk Planet* magazine and is an editor of the world's longest-running online journal, *Bad Subjects: Political Education for Everyday Life.* He is the author of *Jerusalem Calling: A Homeless Conscience in a Post Everything World* and editor of *The Anti-Capitalism Reader,* both published in 2002 by Akashic Books. Along with Megan Prelinger, Schalit is co-editor of *Collective Action: A Bad Subjects Anthology,* published in 2004 by Pluto Press. Schalit's articles have appeared in the *SF Bay Guardian, Tikkun,* and *XLR8R.* He lives and works in San Francisco.

Peter Silverton: Writer and features editor for *Sounds* in its punk years—Joe Strummer got him the job. Contributor to *Smash Hits.* Co-author, with Glen Matlock, of *I Was A Teenage Sex Pistol.* Author of *Essential Elvis.* Writer for *The Observer.* Episodic contributor to *Mojo.* Compiler and annotator of *If Loving You Is Wrong, I Don't Want To Be Right (Ace),* an acclaimed collection of the 1970s soul songs that put the adult in adultery.

Sylvie Simmons has been writing about rock since 1977, when she left London for L.A to correspond for the then-leading UK music paper *Sounds*. Long since back in London, her articles have appeared regularly in countless publications, including *Creem* magazine and *The Guardian* and *Sunday Times* newspapers. She is currently a contributing editor at *Mojo* magazine. Her books include *Serge Gainsbourg: A Fistful of Gitanes* (Da Capo), *Neil Young: Reflections in Broken Glass* (Canongate), and a new short story collection, *Too Weird For Ziggy* (Grove Atlantic).

Carter Van Pelt has a debilitating obsession with Jamaican music. He has written features for *The Beat, Arthur, Mean, Signal To Noise,* and other magazines. He was the last journalist to interview singer Dennis Brown before the singer's death and the first journalist outside Nigeria to examine in-depth the legacy of Fela Anikulapo-Kuti after the artist's death in 1997. Carter is pursuing an M.A. in Arts Administration from Columbia University.

Steve Walsh, music journalist, was a frequent contributor to the punk zine *Sniffin' Glue*.

PERMISSIONS

We gratefully acknowledge all those who gave permission for written material to appear in this book. We have made every effort to trace and contact copyright holders. If an error or omission is brought to our notice we will be pleased to remedy the situation in future editions of this book. For further information, please contact the publisher.